Thinking-Based Learning

*Promoting Quality Student
Achievement in the 21st Century*

Thinking-Based Learning

Promoting Quality Student Achievement in the 21st Century

ROBERT J. SWARTZ, ARTHUR L. COSTA,
BARRY K. BEYER, REBECCA REAGAN,
BENA KALLICK

Foreword by David Perkins

TEACHERS COLLEGE PRESS

Teachers College, Columbia University
New York and London

Published by Teachers College Press, 1234 Amsterdam Avenue, New York, NY 10027

Copyright page continues on p. viii

A previous version of this book was published by Christopher-Gordon Publishers under the title *Thinking-Based-Learning: Activating Students' Potential.*

Library of Congress Cataloging-in-Publication Data

Thinking-based learning : promoting quality student achievement in the 21st century / Robert J. Swartz ... [et al.] ; foreword by David Perkins.
   p. cm.
 Includes bibliographical references and index.
 ISBN 978-0-8077-5098-8 (peperback : alk. paper)
 1. Thought and thinking--Study and teaching (Elementary) 2. Critical thinking—Study and teaching (Elementary) 3. Cognition in children.
4. Learning. I. Swartz, Robert J.
 LB1134.T47 2010
 371.39—dc22
               201000

ISBN 978-0-8077-5098-8

Printed on acid-free paper

Manufactured in the United States of America

8 7 6 5 4 3 2 1   10 11 12 13 14 15 16 17

Contents

Acknowledgments

THE VOICES OF MANY EDUCATORS besides ourselves can be heard in these pages; so can the voices of many of the students of these educators. We have taken the liberty to change names and project details based on the experience we have all had working on teaching thinking these past 25 years. Nevertheless, all the details are authentic, and the voices that speak from these pages, teachers and students alike, are everywhere. We therefore graciously thank everyone with whom we have worked over these 25 years for contributing to this volume. It is through their efforts, their dedication, and their expertise that our inspiration has been derived, and for that, above all, we wish to thank them.

Copyright page continued from p. iv

Foreword
Knowledge Music

David Perkins

Is KNOWLEDGE MORE LIKE AN iPod or a saxophone? Okay, this is a fairly bizarre question, but there is a point to be made. Those iPods are pretty complicated on the inside but fairly simple to use. You turn them on and turn them up and they do their thing. Saxophones are also pretty complicated, but getting some music out of one is another complicated undertaking on top of that.

Back to knowledge: Knowledge is instrumental—having it is nice, but what you do with it is what really counts. So, instrumentally speaking, is knowledge more like an iPod or a saxophone?

Well, it depends on what kind of knowledge we're talking about. Certain kinds of knowledge are iPod-like—phone numbers, for instance. Let's see: What is Mary's number? Let me switch on my memory. Oh yes, got it, so now I can dial up Mary. However, much of the most important knowledge is not like this at all. Let's see: How do the basic principles of democracy or the complex history of the civil rights movement apply to the current election? How can the basic principles of electricity help me think about why one of the fuses in the fuse box keeps blowing? Let's say I remember the information; how do I use it to figure something out? Figuring something out goes well beyond switching on the knowledge. We are definitely in saxophone land.

Unfortunately, a good deal of schooling implicitly subscribes to the iPod model. The most important thing to do with the knowledge at hand is to get it into learners' heads so it stays there, like a catchy tune that is hard to forget, supposedly to do its job later once something switches it on. Too bad this doesn't work very well!

What do we need instead? The answer will hardly be a surprise to readers of five long-time colleagues' thoughtful book, *Thinking-Based Learning*: It's thinking, of course. Very broadly speaking, thinking is what we do to "play" the instrument of knowledge. Thinking is what brings knowledge to life, what puts it to work, what tests it against the standards of evidence, what mobilizes it to make connections and predictions, what shapes it toward creative products and outcomes. Without the playing, the knowledge just sits there and doesn't do much at all or gets blurted out in screeches and squalls, like sounds emanating from a beginner's saxophone.

Indeed, a range of findings in cognitive science assures us that the instrument of knowledge is best built through playing it, by thinking through and thinking with the knowledge on offer, rather than first committing the knowledge to memory and on some later occasion (middle school, high school, college, graduate studies, the school of life) attending to the thinking part. Knowledge learned through use is later both better remembered and better used. No more of "We'll learn it now and do something with it later." Instead, let's learn it now by thinking with it now. In such a spirit, *Thinking-Based Learning* offers an insightful contemporary research-based and experience-based vision of what learning could be like and should be like and, in a large number of wonderful classrooms around the world, is like.

The idea of teaching thinking is very old, but a fully developed art and craft of teaching thinking is actually quite new. Socrates demonstrated and encouraged patterns of thought for making better sense of a puzzling world, Aristotle formulated the notion of syllogisms as mechanisms for reliable inference, Francis Bacon articulated the scientific method toward enhancing the investigative precision of human thought, and it is not hard to point to other figures. However, all that acknowledged, the teaching of thinking in tandem with subject-matter understanding as a systematic and scalable enterprise hit its stride perhaps only during the latter half of the 20th century, when a number of philosophers and psychologists and teachers and others in diverse styles but with some degree of communication began to sort out what needed to be done and how to go about it. Today a rich history of laboratory studies, school-based studies, and concrete experience inform the practice.

The authors of the present volume have for many years been key contributors to the development of this art and craft, and strong advocates of the importance of bringing together the teaching of thinking with the teaching of content in and beyond the disciplines. Here they join together to offer an expansive vision. In these pages, we can learn about the character of skillful thinking, the role of mental habits, the way that skillful thinking involves not just skills but also dispositions—mindsets that foster thoughtful engagement. Here we can learn about metacognition, the craft of keeping an eye on one's own cognition and nudging it along in better ways. Here we can examine the direct teaching of thinking, how to cultivate various kinds of skillful thinking forthrightly and systematically.

We can become familiar with the roles of strategies, graphic organizers, transfer of learning, habits of mind, and much more.

All this could be quite forbidding if it took the form of a technical disquisition on the circuits and microchips of the thoughtful mind. Instead, readers will find a pleasant surprise: Every concept, every practice, every resource comes with a story—what happened in this classroom, what happened with those students, how one or another teacher approached the matter. We are never left stranded in the laboratory but always find ourselves well situated in the real world of pedagogical practice. The mission is sensible, commendable, and exciting. I'm confident that it will engage a range of educators. The music of knowledge is ready to be played.

Preface

THIS BOOK IS THE PRODUCT of five minds writing together as one. Collectively we represent 125 years of experience in the field, researching, promoting, training, conceptualizing, and translating into our own classroom practice the teaching of skillful thinking at all levels of education. Over those 25 years times 5, we have found that our thinking about teaching thinking has converged and that even though we might use different language, we are each promoting concepts and strategies that are consonant with what the others are promoting. What has emerged here is a whole that is far greater than the sum of its parts. Blending our ideas has yielded a new way to conceptualize our efforts, going beyond the use of the old terminology of *thinking skills*, *thinking dispositions*, and *habits of mind* to a new unified conception of what our goal is: the teaching of skillful thinking. This concept includes what, in our view, is right about thinking skill instruction and about what has been said about thinking dispositions, articulated in a way that makes crystal clear how it can be translated into educational practice in the classroom.

We feel very strongly about this new way to articulate what our goals are as teachers of thinking, and we believe that its place in any curriculum is to be infused into standard content instruction at all levels. In this book we show the power of this new conception as it plays itself out in numerous classroom situations that, for all of us, define what it is to teach students to be skillful thinkers effectively and well. What we mean by "effectively and well" is that the result of such instruction not only enhances students' thinking abilities and mental habits but also dramatically improves students' regular classroom performance. That is the main message we wish to convey in this book. No other approach to instruction can claim such overwhelmingly consistent improvement in what every educator strives to accomplish with his or her students.

We don't stop with instruction, however. We also show how clearly we can now define what effective assessment of thinking is, in terms of our model of teaching skillful thinking, and how easily, to the great benefit of our students, skillful thinking can be extended to skillful writing. Finally, we show how school leaders can draw on their skills and make thinking-based learning—the teaching of skillful thinking infused into standard content instruction—an educational practice that permeates the whole culture of a school, including its curriculum and all classroom practices.

Now, as 25 years ago, educators are lamenting the ineffectiveness of most traditional schooling, and today, more than ever, there is pressure on students to pass tests and on teachers to teach students so that they get the highest test scores. This has typically led to a return to a heavy content focus; to drill, rote, and superficial learning; and to a decrease of time and effort in classrooms developing our students' potential for thinking critically and creatively. This comes at a time when students should be prepared to deal with the demands of making sense of an enormous amount of fragmented information, a world with increasingly complex problems, and a nation facing crises in global economics, entrepreneurship, and creativity.

We believe—indeed, we have proof in our experience and in the examples we can draw from it—that thinking-based learning, as we will call this enterprise, can turn this around. It provides a way of teaching that will help students to develop more effective ways to use their minds and that will also enhance their deep content understanding of what we try to teach them day after day. Along with this, it will improve their self-images and their motivation to learn in ways that do not rely on scores from a single test. We believe, in fact, that what we describe in this book is education as it should be, not education as it is currently practiced, which is as it shouldn't be!

This book is intended for educators at any level, for ongoing staff development as well as for preservice educational training, and for administrators, curriculum designers, and those whose responsibility is assessment, to guide them in a new educational orientation that will upgrade their professional lives. Its message is also more universal, however. There are ideas in this book that can lead to improvement in the way anyone thinks, whether one is presently a student or not. Thus this book is, in a sense, written for the general community of parents past and present, not just to show them what education can be but to speak to their own self-education as well.

We are all very proud of this achievement. There were times when style and substance did not mesh and we struggled with this manuscript. Nevertheless, persistence, flexibility, listening to each other with understanding and empathy, thinking creatively, and striving to communicate with utter clarity and precision have resolved these struggles and produced the unified message of these pages. Above all, we have sustained the conviction that what we say in this book represents the best way we know of that the spirit of good education can be translated into the letter of what goes on in the classroom.

Although adults are our primary audience for this book, it is the children of today, the generation of tomorrow, who we hope will reap its benefits. These children of today are the children that the teachers of today teach, and those teachers who follow the guidance of this book ultimately will be transferring its insights to them. Our hope is that the number of these teachers of today and children of today will be huge and worldwide. For then we will feel confident that this book has done its work, that it has done the future inhabitants of this world a great service by making them more careful thinkers than we humans have been, collectively, so far. Thus we want to dedicate this book to this next generation—knowing that it is not us, now, but you, our readers, who will be making that happen.

Our purposes in writing this book are the following:

- To provide rich examples of instructional experiences that teach students how to become more skillful in their thinking, including opportunities for self-managing, self-monitoring, and self-modifying, so that they can become more self-directed in their thinking
- To demonstrate how you can do this in ways that infuse such instruction into standard content instruction with results that will help students to become more skillful thinkers and also dramatically enhance students' content learning
- To help you understand how and why this approach does a better job of educating our students than the dominant classroom practice today, and how accessible the techniques required to practice this type of instruction are

We believe that what we will show you in the rest of this book will provide you with strong motivation to try out this way of teaching. We also believe that when you do try it you will see, as we have again and again over the past 25 years, the potential for thinking and learning in our students that often lies dormant become actualized in ways that every educator hopes to achieve, but that few now do.

Robert Swartz
Art Costa
Barry Beyer
Rebecca Reagan
Bena Kallick

Thinking-Based Learning

Promoting Quality Student
Achievement in the 21st Century

CHAPTER 1

The Importance of Skillful Thinking

As the soil, however rich it may be, cannot be productive without cultivation, so the mind without culture can never produce good fruit.

—Seneca (3 B.C.E.–65 C.E.)

WE ALL THINK. In the course of our lives we engage in thinking in a variety of ways. Sometimes we engage in routine thinking—almost automatic, seemingly mindless thinking that carries us through the mundane tasks of everyday living and working. At other times we engage in rather impulsive thinking—almost reactive, knee-jerk thinking that on occasion may lead us to jump to unwarranted conclusions. Then there's intuitive thinking, when thoughts or solutions seem to just suddenly and effortlessly pop into our heads. There's even sloppy thinking, when—perhaps because of haste, inattentiveness, or ignorance of how to do what we're trying to do—we skip important mental moves, such as failing to check the accuracy of someone's claim before acting on it. Finally, there's skillful thinking. A great many of us don't do much skillful thinking. But we could—and should.

What is Skillful Thinking?

Skillful thinking is the proficient and strategic application of appropriate thinking skills and productive habits of mind, as needed, to develop thoughtful products, such as decisions, arguments, and other analytical, creative, or critical products. Individuals who are skillful thinkers can and do employ such thinking skills and habits of mind on their own initiative, and they monitor their use as needed.

Skillful thinking can help us to achieve the highest standards in our quest for knowing and understanding the world around us and for acting wisely based on this knowledge and understanding. Skillful thinking has three components:

1. *Thinking skills.* Using specific and appropriate mental procedures for the kind of thinking engaged in by the thinker.
2. *Habits of mind.* Driving the use of these procedures in ways that manifest broad and productive task-related mental behaviors.

3. *Metacognition*. Doing both of these based on the thinker's own assessment of what is called for by the thinking task and guided by the thinker's plan as to how to accomplish the task.

This book is not a book *just* about skillful thinking, however. It is primarily about how we can make use of effective educational practices to *infuse instruction in skillful thinking into standard content instruction* at any educational level and in any subject area to also achieve dramatic improvement in students' content learning, in their thinking, in their writing, in their motivation to learn, in their test performance, and in their self-image. These practices derive primarily from those involved in *direct instruction*. The result, we venture to say, is education as it should be—what we all strive to achieve as dedicated educators.

A real episode of skillful thinking involves the planned, proficient, purposeful application of appropriate thinking procedures in engaging in a thinking task, not skipping any key operations, supporting it with appropriate mental attitudes, and drawing on relevant knowledge. In skillful thinkers this process is habitual and automatic. Skillful thinkers think about how they are going to do the thinking they want to do before engaging in it as well as while doing it. They use a variety of thinking operations, often in combination, and in the context of various abiding mental attitudes, to accomplish their thinking goals. They stick to their thinking, troubleshooting and adjusting their approaches, until they are satisfied with the results.

For example, suppose I need to buy a new automobile. I might say the following to myself:

> I want to be careful here. I have made mistakes in the past mainly because I have been hasty and overlooked important things. This time I want to make sure I think this through as carefully as I can. So I will make a list of the important factors I need to take into account in considering a new car, make sure I look at as many possibilities as I think might serve my needs, and then gather information about them to see how close they come to meeting my criteria. Perhaps I can even get some firsthand information about the cars I am considering myself by test-driving them. Maybe I should keep a notebook and organize it by categories, based on the criteria I come up with, so I can record some of this information. And I certainly want to make sure that the information I get from others is coming from credible and reliable sources.

Then, when I think more about it, I might say this to myself:

> You know, I think I also should get the thoughts of my family. I am not the only one who will be using the car. Maybe they have some

> perspectives that I don't know about. That will be helpful. So I want
> to make sure that I bring them into this decision in a meaningful and
> respectful way.

I then run through the plan again in my head. Better yet, I might write down some notes so that when I start the process I won't forget anything.

Everyone reading this book is familiar with examples like this, either because you think like this yourself or because you wish you had once you realize that you have not thought very carefully about something important and have made a mistake. Former St. Louis Rams coach Rich Brooks gives us the same advice: "You don't make snap decisions on the rest of your life without giving it serious thought."[1]

Skillful thinking is clearly a big step above routine or even simple formulaic thinking. In the example above we can see that the thinking is self-initiated, and as it occurs it will be self-monitored and, if necessary, self-correcting. Thus, besides the sorts of things that go on during episodes of skillful thinking, how they come about is a crucial feature of this kind of thinking. We use the term *self-directed* to indicate this cluster of characteristics:[2] The individual alone determines how the sustained application of the thinking procedures and mental habits will be employed and so employs them.

Many of the thinking tasks we need to engage in skillfully are goal-directed. This is thinking that seeks the achievement of specific, clearly defined objectives, whether they be in reflective or active, creative or critical modes, like the well-thought-out decision about which car to purchase. In thinking through these tasks skillfully, one chooses and initiates the processes of thinking because one judges them to be the best way, or means, to achieve this goal.

Skillful thinking—as self-initiated, self-monitored, self-corrected (if necessary), and goal-directed thinking—is an absolute necessity for success in our lives, our professions, and our participation in a democratic society. It is also a clear route to successful achievement in school. No child should leave school without achieving this level of skillful thinking. Unfortunately, too many do. Skillful thinking is neither "caught" nor "discovered"; it must be learned. Sometimes our thinking becomes more skillful through experience—usually a long series of sometimes frustrating experiences in which we do nonskillful thinking and realize that we can do better. It can also be learned through less frustrating mediated and mentored reflection and instruction in the classroom, where it is much in demand to achieve the content learning goals established by our educational system. This leads to developed habits of using a wide repertoire of specific but varied thinking procedures, of mental styles and behaviors, of a good knowledge base on which to apply these, and of proficiency in taking charge of our thinking and carrying these out ourselves. For this to succeed requires flexibility as well as creativity and critical judgment. Most of all, it requires an "I can do it" confidence born of a record of successful experiences in a variety of increasingly complex tasks that call for skillful and careful thinking. It is therefore important to be clear about the ingredients of skillful thinking and what can be done in classrooms to foster it. This is the task that we have set ourselves in writing this book.

Nonskillful Thinking and What Can Be Done to Counter It

Unfortunately, people often don't exercise skillful thinking. Researchers have long identified and described dozens of examples of unskilled thinking, including jumping to conclusions, failing to explore alternatives, regarding the symptoms of a problem as the problem itself, ignoring cues for the application of a particular skill, failing to check one's work, skipping steps in a routine, and allowing one's feelings to influence one's conclusions.[3]

One way to get insight into skillful thinking is to focus on some specific and obvious examples of nonskillful thinking. Here's an example that is on the fringes of the experience of most who will read this book, but its point is a telling one. Not too long ago one of the authors of this book went into a drugstore to purchase a newspaper. There, just inside the door, the newspapers were stacked up. There was a large stack of *The Boston Globe* and a large stack of *The New York Times*, but there were other newspapers as well. One caught his eye. These had also been stacked, but there were only two papers left. The headline—"Space Probe Discovers Ancient Dinosaurs on Mars"—piqued his interest. Figure 1-1 shows the front page.

Many of us learn that such headlines are often sensationalistic and not very reliable, so we don't spend our money on these papers. The author had another thought, however. With a smile on his face, he bought one. "This will be a great way to start our new book on teaching thinking!" he thought.

Many people who purchased this newspaper might have had a different attitude. Perhaps they thought that they were purchasing a newspaper with some interesting news. We surmise that many of these purchasers, like many people in this country and in the world, didn't, and probably won't, think much about what they read in it. In fact, most will simply accept what they read because it is in print. That is true not only of this front page but also of most of what they read in newspapers and magazines, what they see on TV, what appears on the Internet, and what people tell them. To carry this idea to its extreme, we are reminded of what the British philosopher Bertrand Russell was supposed to have once said: "Most people would rather die than think. In fact, they do."[4] How much of an exaggeration is this?

Figure 1-1. Newspaper Headline

One way to think more skillfully about the claims that appear in the newspaper shown here is to ask, "What questions would we want answered if we are to make a well-informed judgment about such a claim?" Here are some that come immediately to mind:

- Who is reporting this and what is his or her expertise about either dinosaurs or Mars?
- Where did he or she get this information?
- Is this claim based on research and, if so, how was it conducted?
- What evidence is there of such things?

If we take the time, we can add other questions to this list. Admittedly, the fact that this headline appears in a newspaper that isn't known for serious journalism might make it seem that asking these questions is a waste of time. But we don't want to make a hasty judgment, either. Let's, for the moment, give the newspaper the benefit of the doubt. Maybe, in fact, it is a good idea in general not to reject or accept ideas even like these until we have answers to our questions and any others that we add (e.g., "What is the author's reputation for accuracy?") that give us a good, comprehensive, and accurate picture of the circumstances surrounding this headline. Then we will certainly be making a more well-informed judgment, and if challenged we will be able to explain why we accept or reject the ideas we are considering.

This example shows us how to start countering sloppy thinking and make it more skillful. As with the decision-making about the car, in which we described a person taking time to think carefully about this purchase before she made it, when this procedure is spelled out, we should see the characteristics of skillful thinking in the process.

Life is short. Is it worth the time required to try to answer such questions every time we hear or read something? If we learn the important questions to ask ahead of time, or use some analogous procedure, we will eventually learn to "size things up" fairly quickly, based on practice. Then asking and answering these questions will become natural and quick. Such internalization of skillful thinking is what we should aim for in instruction. It is what will counter Bertrand Russell's concern, and it is the natural goal of teaching students skillful thinking in our schools.

There is much increased public awareness of the importance of engaging in skillful thinking. Unfortunately, it comes from situations in which the failure to do so has led to serious problems. Some examples may remind us of these situations. The first is from the 2004 presidential election in the United States, which involved a seasoned news commentator who quoted from some documents that turned out to be spurious and from an unreliable source.[5] The second case relates to the war in Iraq: A presidential commission concluded that various U.S. intelligence agencies failed to validate the reliability of their sources in assessing prewar conditions and events in Iraq.[6] The reference, of course, is to those alleged "weapons of mass destruction" that served as the pretext for going to war with Iraq. Skillful thinking about the reliability of these sources could have avoided these problems, and yet some of the most important role models in the United States failed to exhibit such thinking.

It is our contention that skillful thinking can and should be taught to students in our classrooms at every level. Moreover, it can be taught without compromising the goals of the content instruction in which we engage by *infusing* it *into* such content instruction. In fact, far from not compromising these goals, such instruction dramatically *enhances* them. It is obvious that instruction, as it is typically practiced today, does not achieve these goals. What will?

Thinking Skills

There is a simple and straightforward answer to this question that has been offered by those who are sensitive to this issue, and that is to identify and teach important *thinking skills* that students need to develop in order to become more effective thinkers, learners, and citizens. Indeed, this is the approach that many educators have adopted.

The standard way that this approach has been interpreted is based on making explicit a chart (sometimes called a taxonomy) of thinking skills that provide a focal point for discrete lessons. Specialists in cognition, academic subject matter, and teaching have often produced lists of what they identify as thinking skills, sometimes organized into categories like "critical thinking skills," "creative thinking skills," "analysis," and so forth. These often include, to name just a few, comparing and contrasting, classifying, predicting, generating original ideas, cause and effect, decision making, uncovering assumptions, and determining the reliability of sources of information.

The emphasis on teaching thinking skills in the classroom has indeed led to change. The teaching geared to such lists has commonly consisted of asking students to engage in these types of thinking more and more in the classroom. Even textbook publishers have responded to this approach by including activities that call for comparing and contrasting, classifying, predicting, and problem solving, for example. One publisher has included a little box with the words Think Zone to indicate to students when these activities are being asked of them.[7]

This approach is too simplistic. A person, for example, might decide to buy a car (and hence engage in decision making) after comparing his choice with other possibilities, yet he might neither engage in very good thinking nor make a good choice. His comparisons might be very hasty and superficial, and he might not get very reliable information. He could be using some of the "skills" we have mentioned, like comparing and contrasting, but not using them very well. One way to describe the problem with this approach is that the activities on this list are not really thinking skills per se. Rather, they are kinds of thinking that we do, sometimes well but sometimes not. Asking students to engage in these thinking activities repeatedly does not guarantee that they will become proficient at them and hence become good thinkers.

Here is another example. This is a response given by a student who was asked to compare and contrast two major historical figures from the American Civil War, President Abraham Lincoln and Frederick Douglass. This was not the first time that this student had been asked to compare and contrast two things by the teacher. Yet here is Stephen's written response (Figure 1-2).

Figure 1-2. Stephen's Response

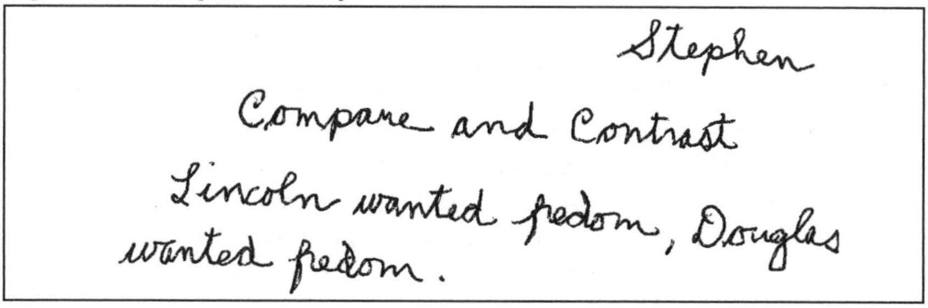

> Stephen
>
> Compare and Contrast
> Lincoln wanted fredom, Douglas
> wanted fredom.

Is this student comparing and contrasting? Yes. Is he doing this carefully and well? No. Much more is needed for this episode of comparing and contrasting to exhibit skill. He may be able to do it, but the kind of instruction offered was not sufficient to bring it out.

Here is yet another example. A student has been asked what he thinks could be done to solve the problem of the population explosion:

Student: I don't know.
Teacher: Well, think about it. It's a problem. We might not have enough food and space. It's a problem we will need to solve.
Student: We could send some people somewhere where they won't need food and space.
Teacher: Where?
Student: Into space.
Teacher: Why there?
Student: They won't need to eat our food or live here anymore.

The teacher has shown her eighth-grade class that projecting the size of Earth's population would lead to its doubling in the next 50 years. Has this student done some problem solving or decision making? Yes. Has he done this carefully and with skill? It seems not.

We are suggesting that it might be fruitful to consider comparing and contrasting, problem solving, and predicting—indeed, most of the items that are often called thinking skills—as types of thinking and not thinking skills. They are important types of thinking because doing them on appropriate occasions carefully, skillfully, and thoroughly can serve us well. However, merely engaging in these types of thinking does not mean that we are engaging in them carefully or skillfully. They can be done in quick, sloppy, and superficial ways without much thought. In these cases they will not serve us well. Thus, merely asking students to engage in these kinds of thinking, even with the sort of prompting used by the teacher in the example above, is not enough to teach students how to think skillfully.

When given the opportunity, some students do try to perform these thinking activities carefully. Most don't. If the way they solve problems is to do the first thing they think of as a solution, they will probably do the same thing when asked to solve another problem. If a student, out of habit, just lists a few similarities and differences when asked to compare and contrast two things, then in all likelihood this student will do the same thing when asked to compare and contrast two new things. Asking for more and more comparing and contrasting in the classroom won't help. Rather, when working with students on these types of thinking, teachers need to teach students how to compare and contrast skillfully and how to solve problems skillfully. That will improve the frequency with which students in their classrooms utilize these kinds of thinking skillfully. When they habitually use the appropriate steps, raising and answering relevant questions and engaging in appropriate information-gathering procedures, we can consider our efforts successful. That's what should define our objectives when we consider the kinds of thinking we will demand of students, if they are to meet the new educational standards of the 21st century.

What Makes Specific Types of Thinking Skillful

The student whose response to the request by his teacher to develop a solution to the problem of the human population explosion on Earth made a quick and hasty judgment without considering much about it. What would we want him to do to exhibit more skillful problem solving?

Certainly we would want him to explore pretty thoroughly the consequences of the solution he endorses before he endorses it—much as we would want someone to do in making a decision. Apparently he has considered only one consequence: the need by space travelers for food and space on Earth. Perhaps even that was not considered carefully. Where would they get their food to begin with, if not from Earth? Maybe they could grow it on a spaceship, but he seems not to have thought of the details of sending them into space. Being on a spaceship will in itself have some limiting consequences, to say the least. Will they ever return? How? What drain on earthly resources will this cause?

In addition, this student seems to have impulsively grabbed just one solution. Maybe he quickly thought of others, but did he explore them? Maybe one of them is better. Indeed, has he stopped to think of any other ways of dealing with overpopulation, such as laws restricting the number of children a couple may have? It seems not. Thus he certainly has not compared and contrasted these different possible solutions to try to determine which is best. We believe that we all would feel better about this student's problem-solving abilities if he, at the very least, put this kind of thought into developing a solution to this problem. Then his problem solving would have been done with much more skill.

It is easy to extract a list of questions that summarizes the key focal points in this picture of what would make an episode of problem solving more skillful. Figure 1-3 shows what we call a *thinking strategy map* for skillful problem solving.[8]

Similarly, we would be more willing to judge Stephen's thinking abilities differently if we found that he was taking the time to come up with more similarities, and some differences as well. Maybe he has come up with more similarities and differences and has rejected them as unimportant, but that appears unlikely. This suggests that a number of similarities

Figure 1-3. Thinking Strategy Map for Skillful Problem Solving

Skillful Problem Solving
1. What is the problem?
2. Why is there a problem?
3. What are some possible solutions?
4. What would result from these solutions?
5. What solution is best and why?

and differences in comparing and contrasting might not be enough to make the thinking very skillful. The similarities and differences might all be pretty superficial. However, if Stephen had pruned his list by thinking about which were important similarities and differences and why, and then thinking about what these similarities and differences revealed to him about Lincoln and Douglass by drawing some conclusions from them, we would certainly judge his comparing and contrasting to be more careful and skillful.

If Stephen had also interacted with other students and taken seriously what they had to say, and if he himself had initiated and guided his thinking as he did so, we would not hesitate to judge each episode of thinking as skillful. If, indeed, the context for this was our classroom, and we had been expending effort teaching students to utilize such organized thinking procedures, to do so in ways that manifested such important mental habits, and to take charge of their own thinking so that they determined its character and process, we would have every reason to be proud of this accomplishment. Figure 1-4 is a thinking strategy map for skillful comparing and contrasting.

A teacher who wants to help students develop skill at problem solving and at comparing and contrasting needs to teach students to slow down and carefully consider what we have been discussing prior to completing

Figure 1-4. Thinking Strategy Map for Skillful Comparing and Contrasting

Skillful Comparing and Contrasting
1. How are they alike?
2. How are they different?
3. Which similarities and differences are important?
4. What conclusion can be drawn about the two things based on their similarities and differences?

the task. These examples suggest that we can develop models for effective thinking strategies for skillful comparing and contrasting and for skillful problem solving; these models can be made explicit and then taught directly to students, as a way to start them on the process of becoming more skillful problem solvers and thinkers who engage in comparing and contrasting. Then, when students are taught to integrate appropriate habits of mind, such as thinking with others about tasks that call for problem solving and/or comparing and contrasting, and when they learn how to direct such thinking themselves, they are learning to become skillful thinkers.

We need to be cautious here and not overstate the case we are making for concentrating our efforts on teaching such strategies to students to help them make their thinking more skillful. This is a necessary condition, but it is by no means sufficient for the actual practice of skillful thinking. A person might, quite correctly, want to take the time to explore possible solutions to a problem—for example, the problem of the potential for overpopulation on this planet—but not have the foggiest idea of what kinds of things might mitigate it. For that, one must either have background knowledge about populations and what influences their size or know how to find out. Similarly, even such apparently simple activities like comparing and contrasting might be undertaken with a desire to uncover important similarities and differences between two people, but the person comparing the two may not be able to get very far if he doesn't know much about the differences in attitude between them, for example, or even what an attitude is. To be successful at thinking skillfully, access to and comprehension of relevant information is also a necessary, minimal condition.

Hence, the core processes of skillful thinking usually require one or more components to function well. These components are often embedded in the idea of following a thinking plan. So far we have discussed the following:

- The need for step-by-step procedures or routines, and occasionally some guiding rules or heuristics, by which a type of thinking (like problem solving) can be carried out with a high degree of efficiency and effectiveness

However, thinking does not happen in a vacuum. When we think, we always think about something. So for us to use these procedures, we also need the following to engage in skillful thinking:

- Knowledge of where, when, and why the use of a procedure is appropriate
- Knowledge of specific skill-related information, such as what an option is or what it means to seek a solution to a problem, as well as an understanding of the criteria to be applied to make a given kind of judgment (e.g., how we tell if someone is an expert on a topic

when we seek to judge skillfully the reliability of that person as a source of information on that topic)
- Information on what we are thinking about and/or where to find it, which can provide us with answers to the driving questions we pose in following the strategy

Developing proficiency in using a thinking procedure that makes a kind of thinking more skillful often brings with it proficiency in the three additional factors.

The active use of thinking skills is really being skillful with content itself. Helping students become knowledgeable in all this skill content and proficient in applying thinking skills to a variety of contents and contexts is what the effective teaching of skillful thinking is all about. Using appropriate instructional techniques of the sort that we describe in Chapters 2, 3, and 4 can help us to accomplish this goal.

Kinds of Thinking Important to
Teach Students to Engage in Skillfully

What kinds of thinking do we need to teach students to engage in skillfully? This is a question that is often asked and that a number of us have tried to answer in previous works.[9] Of course, we engage in many kinds of thinking. The kind of thinking may be conceptualized very generally, like analysis; more specifically, like predicting; or even more precisely, like critically evaluating the reliability of the sources of information available on the 1963 assassination of President John F. Kennedy. Even daydreaming is a kind of thinking. Figure 1-5 lists types of thinking that are important for us to teach students to engage in skillfully.

We need to raise four cautions about using what is in any list of thinking skills such as those shown in Figure 1-5, especially in education.

- The types of thinking listed in Figure 1-5 are abstractions from authentic situations in which these types of thinking play themselves out. Rarely, if ever, do we engage in thinking tasks that involve just one of the thinking skills we list.
- The way the types of thinking are listed does not imply anything about the sequence in which they might be taught. Such lists may also be abstractions from the curriculum frameworks into which they need to be embedded. The way they should appear in any given curriculum is fully integrated—for example, integrated into the standards in standards-based curriculum frameworks, as we illustrate elsewhere in this chapter, or "mapped" into specific content as we describe in Chapter 7. What is in Figure 1-5 or any other thinking skill list should be taken merely as an indication of what should be included in a curriculum related to thinking.

Figure 1-5. Important Types of Thinking to Teach Students to Engage in Skillfully

---

Important Types Of Thinking To Teach Students To Engage In Skillfully

Complex Thinking Tasks

Decision Making	**Problem Solving**	**Conceptualizing**
Goal: choosing the best course of action	Goal: finding the best solution to an identified problem	Goal: deep understanding

Each of these thinking tasks employs, in various combinations, some of the skills below.

Component Types of Thinking

I. PROCESSING AND EXTENDING INFORMATION

I-1. Generating Ideas	**I-2. Clarifying Ideas**
1. Coming Up With Ideas	1. Analyzing Ideas and Information
Brainstorming many and varied possibilities	Comparing and contrasting
2. Synthesis	Classifying and defining categories
Combining ideas and information into new ideas	Determining parts–whole relationships
	Establishing sequences / ranking
Composing metaphors based on analogies	Distinguishing factual and value claims
3. Extending Ideas	2. Analyzing Arguments
Inferring new ideas from other ideas and information	Finding reasons / conclusions
	Uncovering assumptions

II. CRITICALLY ASSESSING INFORMATION

II-1. Basic Information	**II-2. Inference**
Judging the factual accuracy of information	Judging the likelihood of causal explanations
Judging the credibility/reliability of sources	
Judging the credibility/reliability of observation reports	Judging the likelihood of predictions
	Judging the support of generalizations
Detecting and judging point of view/bias	Judging the strength of analogical reasoning
Judging the relevance of information to a topic or issue	

II-3. Arguments
Judging accuracy of assumptions
Judging the relevance and strength of reasons offered in support of conclusions
Judging the validity of conditional reasoning

- What is included on this list—whether it designates a complex type of thinking like decision making or a more circumscribed type of thinking like predicting—does not carry with it an indication of what we need to teach students for them to learn to employ these skillfully. The skillful practice of each type of thinking consists of procedures by which it is operationalized and by the use of information that informs the application of these procedures. These procedures, and not just what is on these lists, will provide guidance to the classroom teacher as to what to teach students to help them become skillful thinkers. These procedures are not very difficult to identify, as we have illustrated in this book and elsewhere,[10] but they cannot be inferred just by noting the kind of thinking mentioned.

- What is included on these lists does not imply anything about the classroom strategies that can be used to make teaching skillful thinking effective. For example, to supplement this list we might want to develop thinking strategy maps like those in Figures 1-3 and 1-4 for each type of thinking, and then introduce these into classrooms in which we are teaching students to follow the procedures on these thinking maps. In subsequent pages we will identify many such teaching strategies and materials, but they, too, cannot be inferred simply from the name of the types of thinking identified on this list.

These types of thinking cut across all subject areas. They can be taught and reinforced at every grade level, although their relative importance in some subject areas may be greater than in others. Why are these important to teach students? The primary reason is that when we engage with information in our lives and in our work, it has become natural to do so through the use of these types of thinking, and we do this frequently. Furthermore, we often have to do this ourselves without the prompting of anyone else.

We often need to make decisions and solve problems, for example. When we do, we usually try to draw upon what we know about the issues with which we are grappling. The more we know, the more likely we will solve these problems and make these decisions effectively—but only if our thinking is done skillfully. For example, the more we know about nutrition, the more likely we will make wise choices about our diet, but only if we take the time to think about this skillfully. And when we reflect with others whose ideas we read, listen to, and take seriously, the effectiveness of these processes is all the more enhanced. But the final decision has to rest with us, based on our own thinking. Even though doing all this may be natural, for most people it is not natural to do any of this very skillfully. That's why all the skills we have listed are important and need to be taught to our students.

There are four basic principles that we used to select the skills highlighted in Figure 1-5.

- They are clearly identifiable types of thinking.
- There are clear examples of occasions in which the type of thinking is engaged.

- They are types of thinking that require frequent use.
- They are instances of thinking that people, including our students, often don't do very skillfully.

As we show throughout this book, when the use of such forms of skillful thinking permeates the content learning experiences of our students, they quickly achieve a deeper and richer grasp and understanding of what we are trying to teach them than they do without engaging in these processes. Without infusing instruction in skillful thinking into content instruction, we usually see only one-dimensional learning—learning simply to pass tests but not learning for enhancing their life experiences.

Habits of Mind

We have noted that using specific strategies, such as trying to answer specific focus questions associated with a type of thinking like comparing and contrasting or decision making, is essential to make the practice of that type of thinking skillful. This is not enough, however. There are also certain mental habits that skillful thinkers display that apply to all the specific types of thinking we use to make their thinking more effective and hence even more skillful. For example, our earlier example of skillful problem solving involved asking and trying to answer in an organized way a number of important questions before determining what solution will be best. Have you ever tried to do something like this alone? It's difficult, and sometimes we get stuck. On the other hand, bouncing our ideas off others, and/or actively working with others on the same problem, usually has a better yield. In fact, this seems to be true of many of the forms of thinking we have been discussing. Thus, thinking interdependently and listening to others with understanding, empathy, and respect seem to be mental activities that are important to practice. They enhance the effectiveness of the specific kinds of thinking that we do when we try to be more skillful. Even better, if we develop these as habits we are enriching the engagement we have with skillful thinking whenever it is required.

There is a literature about thinking that dates back at least to the 1960s, in which the term *thinking disposition* is used to emphasize much the same thing. Other mental habits that have been identified include persisting in a thinking task, managing impulsivity, thinking flexibly, being open-minded, striving for accuracy and precision, and searching for all relevant information with as many senses as we can.

Indeed, exhibiting, as appropriate, the mental behaviors that such habits perpetuate is an integral part of what is involved in any exercise of skillful thinking. What have been called habits of mind in the literature on teaching thinking are dispositions or inclinations to behave automatically and consistently in certain broad and constructive ways while thinking.

There are, of course, nonproductive mental habits that people often develop, like impulsive judgment, jumping to a conclusion, or closed-mindedness. "Habits of Mind," as we use it, carries a positive connotation.

As with the habit to use the plans that define specific types of skillful thinking that we need to teach our students, we should not take for granted that these broader mental habits are either present, or will naturally develop, in our students. They do in some instances, of course, but they can in all our students. In many ways the pace of 21st century society fights these attitudes and habits. So along with instruction to help make such mental procedures habitual, instruction that leads to the very development of these broad mental habits is necessary. Just like the thinking strategies that make specific types of thinking skillful, these, too, have a dual character: There are the mental behaviors that manifest them, and there is the habituation of that behavior.

Here's an example of a teacher beginning this process. It is in the eighth grade classroom described earlier in which students have been asked what they think could be done to solve the problem of population explosion:

> *Student 1:* I don't know.
> *Teacher:* Well, think about it. It's a problem. We might not have enough food and space. It's a problem we will need to solve.
> *Student 1:* We could send some people somewhere where they won't need food and space.
> *Teacher:* Where?
> *Student 1:* Into space.
> *Teacher:* Why there?
> *Student 1:* They won't need to eat our food or live here anymore.
> *Student 2:* (giggles) That's stupid. Of course they'll need food in space.
> *Student 3:* I think that wars will keep the population in check.
> *Student 2:* That's a dumb answer, too. Wars don't solve problems.
> *Student 4:* Some people think so. That's why we have so many wars.
> *Student 5:* My uncle was killed in Iraq.
> *Teacher:* Let's hold on a moment. I can see that we're not listening to each other. Let's stop this conversation and learn how to listen to each other with more understanding and respect.

This teacher is aware that, for this group of students to conduct classroom dialogues well, they must learn to listen with understanding and empathy. This situation, she believes, offers the students a chance to practice this skill so that they can get better at it. Of course, this will take practice, and this teacher, along with other staff members, will offer many opportunities in social studies lessons and in other classroom situations for students to practice, apply, monitor, and evaluate their own growth in developing these listening skills. For example, as they further probe the population problem, she will introduce them to the basic strategy for skillful problem solving to help put more organized and careful thought into their responses, and she will ask them to practice their new listening skills as they do so.

The teacher starts this process with some direct instruction in skillful listening: "Over the next few days and in future discussions, I want us to practice three steps that can improve our listening skills. You will remember them by the three Ps of listening: pausing, paraphrasing and probing." She also tells them that she will use the term *listening with understanding and empathy*, taken from a book she read, to describe this way of listening to others.[11] She explains that empathy is an attitude that puts the listener in the place of the speaker, as if the listener had the speaker's point of view and feelings. This, she says, will enhance the understanding the listener has of the speaker's ideas. The teacher then writes these focal points on a piece of newsprint which she posts on the wall (see Figure 1-6).

This is what she wants the students to practice as they discuss the population issue further. In fact, it is what she wants to help them develop into a habit—a prime example of an important habit of mind that any skillful thinker needs to develop. For this, we have noted, more than just this introductory experience is needed. More details about the character of such instruction will be developed as we move along in this book.

This example reinforces the idea that habits of mind, like those discussed at the beginning of this section, consist of two major components. First, each mental habit is distinguished by certain purposeful behaviors by which it is operationalized. David Perkins, a long-standing researcher in this field, call them "mindful" behaviors, because they are actions thoughtfully adopted and deliberately intended to enact the habit but eventually employed so automatically as to be habitual.[12] Persistence in thinking, for instance, is operationalized by sticking to a task that requires thinking until it has been successfully concluded, by searching for and applying alternative thinking strategies when one encounters an unanticipated obstacle, by looking at a task from different perspectives, by maintaining a willingness to "go at it" another way, and by being alert to novel or alternative ways of applying one's thinking.

Figure 1-6. Strategy for Skillful Listening

Skillful Listening with Understanding and Empathy
1. Pause and give the person you are listening to a chance to finish what he or she is saying.
2. Paraphrase what the person is saying in your own words.
3. Probe what the person means by asking clarifying questions.

Second, these behaviors are also often informed and directed by heuristics, or self-made rules derived from experience or instruction. These heuristics are consciously invented or adopted and are used deliberately to activate the behaviors that enact the mental habit. Individuals who persist in a thinking task often respond to unexpected obstacles by stepping back to look at it from another perspective or by taking time out and then trying again from another angle. These details must enter classrooms in ways that inform the behaviors of students if they are to learn how to do such things as being persistent or listening to others with understanding and empathy. Instructional techniques that lead to the habituation of such behaviors in appropriate circumstances also must enter classroom practice if these are to really become habits of mind.

In this regard we see little qualitative difference between what has been called *thinking skills* and *thinking dispositions*.[13] The main difference is one of generality. Both must be habituated. To be a skillful thinker one must develop the ability to generate numerous options to consider in making decisions, as well as the ability to work collaboratively with others in thinking through what should be done. In addition, both of these must become habits as we move through our lives.

That is why we think it is unfortunate that *thinking skill* and *thinking disposition* continue to be used in the literature to describe these two aspects of skillful thinking. *Thinking skill* emphasizes one side of this duality (the ability side), whereas *thinking disposition* emphasizes the other (the habitual side—the value-based driving force that energizes and to a considerable extent directs the ability side to action). Without clarifying each of these terms as we have done in this chapter, the use of this terminology gives the impression that there are special skills that we need to teach students for them to become good thinkers, the way we teach any skill, and that there are other things, called *dispositions*, that we need to teach in some other way. If we aren't careful in appreciating the ability-skill component of habits of mind, for example, we will diminish our effectiveness in contributing to the improvement of the thinking of our students.

Important Habits of Mind to Teach

In some of our previous work we have discussed a number of important habits of mind.[14] Just as there are many different types of thinking, so there are many habits of mind. Some of them, as we have remarked, work against skillful thinking, like closed-mindedness. But some of them are essential for skillful thinking and ensure more responsibility in our thinking and the likelihood that it will represent our best efforts. Figure 1-7 is a list of important mental habits that we need to help students develop based on the ideas in this book. These enhance the conduct of our thinking, the depth of our thinking, the attitudes we have toward our thinking, and our social interaction when we engage in skillful thinking.

The particular mental habits that we endorse in this book aren't some mysterious group of habits that we should assume are important to develop just because they are on a list. Habits of mind, like those identified here, are grounded in values and a commitment to act consistently on those values. Among these baseline values are those that are sometimes referred to as *intellectual passions*, such as the passions for objective truth, accuracy, and intellectual honesty. These and other passions undergird such mental habits and explain not only why we should engage in the behaviors that operationalize these habits but also why doing so has a real sense of importance for us. For example, in most cases it is likely that if we persist in trying to solve a problem by systematically following a strategy for skillful problem solving, and don't just give up when this becomes a little difficult, we will arrive at a viable solution. If we avoid impulsivity and carefully accumulate evidence, we will more likely make well-founded inferences rather than jumping to unwarranted, and probably incorrect, conclusions. If we listen to and work with other people with respect and empathy, we are more likely to gain perspectives on issues that will make more objective judgments likely. Thus, we learn to increasingly value the habits of mind we have identified.

Without explicit and direct instruction in specific types of skillful thinking *and* these important mental behaviors, we will not succeed in teaching students to be skillful and effective thinkers. Thinking skills without the habits of mind will be practiced in minimally effective ways; mental habits without thinking skills will not compel the application of appropriate types of thinking skills that we need to use as we engage in important thinking tasks. Each is necessary if we are to meet the thinking demands of educational standards in the 21st century.

Figure 1-7. Important Habits of Mind

Habits of Mind That Contribute to Skillful Thinking	
• Persisting at a task that requires thinking	• Responding with wonderment and awe
• Managing impulsivity in thinking and acting	• Creating, imagining, and innovating
• Thinking flexibly	• Taking responsible risks in thinking
• Striving for accuracy and precision	• Finding humor
• Thinking interdependently	• Questioning and problem posing
• Listening with understanding and empathy	• Applying past knowledge to novel situations
• Communicating with clarity and precision	• Gathering data through all the senses
	• Remaining open to continuous learning

Directing Our Own Thinking

There is a third important ingredient in skillful thinking that we high-light in this book: the ability to *direct our own thinking*. This needs to be-come habitual as we practice skillful thinking. We have already touched upon this, but it requires more comment. What does this involve, and how can it be practiced to enhance the development of skillful thinking?

We have the ability to direct our own lives. Most of us do this at least to some degree, and often do it successfully, without thinking much about it. We get up in the morning, dress, have breakfast, and get ourselves to work. If the weather is bad we might leave a bit early. This adjustment might help us get to where we are going on time in circumstances that would otherwise delay us. We size things up and do what we have to do. Sometimes, of course, we may have to deliberately stop and take some time to plan what we will do more consciously. For example, I may have a lot to do on a particular day. When I think about where I need to be, what I need to do, and what I have available that will allow me to get there and/ or do these things, I will then set a deliberate schedule for what I will do that day and follow it: "I will see my dentist at 8:00 A.M., then go to look at and hopefully buy a new computer at the computer specialist across town, then I will go to my noon lunch appointment." Most of us have learned to manage these things based on practice and experience, although some-times—and maybe for some of us more often than we like to admit—we flounder and don't do these things very well.

Thinking is no different. How we engage in a thinking task can be similarly managed. Often, with many routines some of us manage our thinking well. I might want to go to the cinema this evening. But where and when? I know I need to find out what's playing, when the films start, and how far I will have to travel to get there. I have to do some calcula-tions to figure out—predict—whether I can make it in time. Many of us don't have to take time to think about how to engage in such tasks so that we can make good decisions. We size up the situations and act. But sometimes we do have to stop and think more consciously and deliber-ately. I might have to make a decision I don't face very often. My doctor might have diagnosed a bodily disorder that needs attention. It might be something that can be approached in different ways: medication, surgery, diet, and so forth. I can then stop and deliberately think about what in-formation I need to be able to decide the best course of action, how I can get it, and when to schedule such a quest so that I will have the informa-tion I need before I attempt to come to a decision. I might also want to make sure that I can bounce my ideas off a few other people as well and get their ideas—maybe even get a second opinion. And, of course, I will need to make sure to investigate each of the possible solutions, not just one. What guides us in the way we think things through in circumstances like these—whether deliberately or just based on sizing things up—is a special kind of sensitivity to how we can think things through effectively, given the circumstances—a sensitivity that is also learned. This, in fact, is an example of the way we put *metacognition* into practice in our lives.

Engaging in metacognition—thinking about our thinking—in ways that lead to results like those just discussed is one of the most important thinking activities that students need to master. It is not just any kind of thinking about our thinking that is important here. It is quite focused. We need to be able to figure out the best ways to conduct a thinking task that we face. Teaching students how to do this is the challenge of meta-cognitive instruction. Sometimes metacognition is clustered as one of the important thinking dispositions and habits of mind, but we think it is im-portant enough to stand out *as one of the essential ingredients of any act of skillful thinking* (unlike some of the other broad mental habits, which can have more limited application in our thinking).

We believe that we *can* teach students to learn how to think about thinking in those ways that enable them to determine for themselves how to engage in tasks *skillfully*, and to follow up and do them as skillful think-ers. In fact we believe that this is not difficult to do. We will devote Chapter 4 to metacognition and how it can be taught, but we want to be up front now in adding it to our conception of the important cognitive ingredients in skillful thinking. If we ourselves don't know how to size up situations, figure out what kinds of thinking they call for, develop a plan for engaging in those thinking tasks, and direct ourselves through the process (perhaps monitoring our thinking as we go along for self-correction), any thinking we do runs the risk of being routine or even missing the mark. We can muster a whole range of thinking skills and learn how to display a variety of important thinking demeanors or mental habits, but if we don't use these appropriately when needed, we will not become skillful thinkers, any more than a basketball player who knows all the moves, but doesn't make them on the court, becomes a skillful basketball player. Thus, as a guide to what needs to happen in classrooms in which skillful thinking is a goal, metacognition must be included.

Teaching to Standards for Content Understanding and Thinking

The pure content curriculum—at least at the district, state board, and ministry level—is a thing of the past. What we now see over and over worldwide is that thinking is written into curricular goals, objectives, and standards. This is done either separately and explicitly, but with the understanding that instruction to meet these objectives is to take place in standard subject-area contexts, or is blended into content objectives and standards directly. For example, the social studies and humanities objectives developed by the Hong Kong Ministry of Education[15] references "senior primary" students (grades 5 and 6 in the United States) as follows:

> Learners will learn to
> - Understand and make deductions/inferences from sources
> - Cross-reference other sources to determine the reliability of the source

The Michigan State Board of Education[16] sets as an objective for science education that middle school students should be able to *predict* the effects of changes in one population in a food web on other populations. In its high school objectives, it says that students should be able to *compare and contrast* ways in which selected cells are specialized to carry out particular life functions. The Board does, of course, expect its students to do these tasks skillfully.

The remake of curriculum objectives into learning standards, which has occurred in the United States and elsewhere, brings with it an analogous move into statements of standards that are not just standards of content learning but also standards that apply to the abilities students are expected to display in such learning. Specific types of thinking are often embedded in subject-matter standards through specific verbs that describe what students are to do to meet the content standard (e.g., "analyze the differences" between two kinds of government or "draw conclusions" from a certain kind of experiment). Here's an example from the Virginia Department of Public Instruction:[17]

> The student will develop skills for historical and geographical analysis, including the ability to
> - *Analyze* documents, records and data
> - *Evaluate* the authenticity, authority, and credibility
> - *Formulate* historical questions and defend findings based on inquiry and interpretation

Other standards appear in statements that specify what students must do to demonstrate that they have mastered a specific kind of content, such as this example from the National Center for History in the Schools:

> Students should be able to demonstrate how the "second industrial revolution" changed the nature and conditions of work by
> - (7–12) *Assessing* the effects of the rise of big business on labor
> - (7–12) *Analyzing* how working conditions changed
> - (5–12) *Analyzing* the causes and consequences of the employment of children[18]

Developing and articulating standards for effective learning is of great importance if we are to be able to judge our effectiveness as educators. It should be obvious from even just these few examples that to teach to subject-matter standards actually makes teaching thinking more important than ever. These standards not only present us with a pressing need to provide instruction in thinking, *they also legitimize taking the time to provide the kind of instruction necessary to accomplish this goal.* Furthermore, they suggest that successful instruction in skillful thinking should be done *while* teaching subject matter instead of *in addition to* teaching subject matter. Such standards are a mandate to infuse purposeful instruction in thinking into instruction in subject-matter knowledge. Thinking and subject-matter content are neither separate from nor in opposition to each other.

Articulation of these curricular mandates is one thing; their implementation in the classroom is quite another. Although we laud the inclusion of thinking-related standards in the curriculum objectives, we have two important concerns about how this is being done. The first relates to what is in these curriculum documents, the second to what is not in them.

To many teachers, at first, almost all standards documents emphasize seemingly enormous amounts of subject-matter information. Most of these standards, as they are stated, also specify or imply a wide range of types of thinking as well as subject-matter knowledge—types of thinking deemed by the authors of these standards to be essential for students to learn and/or apply to demonstrate their mastery of the subject matter. Many instructors, however, fail to teach these kinds of thinking, focusing instead only on the subject matter. Because the vast majority of our elementary and secondary school students are neither experienced in nor accustomed to applying these types of thinking with sufficient proficiency, they need instruction in how to apply them more skillfully if they are to learn and demonstrate the subject-matter knowledge required by these standards. We are concerned that the profound message of these new curricular designs is not being heard and that instruction in the standard classroom is going on much as it has in the past, with some tweaking, but not with the kinds of deeper changes that are necessary to really teach to these standards.

Our second concern is that the way in which references to thinking are typically included in such curriculum documents is very misleading and leaves out what their authors are really interested in promoting. Let us take one example involving a type of thinking we have already discussed: evaluating the authenticity and credibility of information. At first this sounds fine, but when we think about it we realize what we mentioned earlier: It must mean to *skillfully* evaluate the authenticity and credibility of information. Just asking students to evaluate something can lead to some pretty hasty and superficial judgments. We have, of course, made this point before. If such statements of standards for instruction are to have the necessary impact on instruction, they should be formulated in ways that make explicit the standards for skillful thinking.

The examples of standards quoted above are taken from documents produced by state departments of education. These are designed to guide both instruction and assessment. In standards like these we see a clear recognition that understanding concepts, retaining information (that applies to these concepts), and communicating such information—the three mainstays of our goals in content-focused education—are not all that we should be striving to achieve. In addition, it seems, these states want their students to do certain kinds of thinking. Table 1-1 shows an expanded list of thinking words that we have culled from educational standards articulated by a variety of states in the United States, provinces in Canada, and ministries of education in other countries.

The standards from which the above thinking words have been extracted represent a random sampling of standards included in present curricular objectives. The implication is that a student cannot demonstrate mastery of any of the required standards without performing one or more important thinking procedures and, presumably, performing these accurately and skillfully.

Infusing Instruction on Skillful Thinking Into Content Instruction

We have been speaking as if the classroom is the only place where we can help others become more skillful in their thinking. Actually, there is a tremendous variety of contexts in which one person can have an impact on others by helping them to avoid difficulties in the way they do their thinking and to become more skillful at it. These include both formal and informal contexts, organized and casual ones. For example, I might be shopping with a friend who, I notice, is having a hard time deciding on a purchase. I might suggest that he stop for a minute and make a list of his options, and then chart the three or four most important factors he needs to consider about each. Maybe that will help. That doesn't have to

Table 1-1. Types of Thinking Referenced in the Standards

Analyze	Contrast	Judge
Apply	Evaluate	Observe
Assess	Generalize	Organize
Classify	Hypothesize	Predict
Compare	Identify	Solve
Conclude	Inquire	Summarize
Connect	Interpret	Test

take more than a few minutes. A parent might do something similar in helping her child decide what sorts of games to play at a birthday party. A travel agent might caution a prospective traveler to think about a number of possibilities and make sure that he weighs the costs and benefits of each before deciding where to go on his next vacation. Such opportunities are countless.

Although we need to recognize the multitude of contexts for helping others to develop more skillful thinking habits, we are concerned in this book with what can be done in education, for there we have the most extensive opportunity to influence the thinking habits of more people than in any other social context. For example, a teacher might be concerned that her students are relying on word of mouth to select their electives for next year and are not assessing the credibility of their sources of information. She can suggest to her class that they try the same decision-making strategy about these electives after she discusses with them the need for more skillful decision-making and sketches out a strategy for engaging in this kind of thinking. This includes considering a variety of options and prioritizing them by gathering information about the consequences of each, after sorting out which kinds of consequences are most important. There are many opportunities for this in the day-to-day operation of a school, just as there are in the operation of any organization, but where in the curriculum do we fit it?

We endorse making the regular content curriculum the context for instruction in skillful thinking—a technique that has been called *infusion*. Others have tried such instruction in thinking skills, or critical thinking, in separate courses or units. The latter approach, however, is now well researched, and this research indicates that there are two major problems with it. First, from a practical point of view, it requires separate curricular time away from the regular content curriculum. Second, and more important, students in such courses rarely transfer the thinking skills and strategies they learn to their other academic work or to outside the classroom. Transfer of such learning usually does not happen on its own.[19]

The concept of infusion was introduced into the educational literature in the 1980s.[20] Since then it has been adopted to describe classroom instruction that blends the teaching of thinking skills with standard content instruction in some very specific ways.[21] According to McGuiness, when we infuse one thing into another we "introduce into one thing a second thing that gives it extra life, vigor, and a new significance."[22] This is a powerful image. In our experience it describes exactly what happens when infusion is practiced in K–12 education (and in college education, for that matter). This is because teaching thinking skills in subject-matter courses improves not only proficiency in thinking but also achievement in the content being studied.[23] Since the 1980s various research projects have been undertaken to assess the consequences of infusion. The results are unequivocal: In classes where students receive instruction in thinking skills infused into content instruction, the students get higher scores on subject-matter tests than do students who take the same subject-matter courses but don't receive thinking-skill instruction in those courses.[24] Moreover, qualitative assessment data reinforce the fact that classroom performance, interest in learning, and overall learning improve, sometimes dramatically, in infusion classrooms. Student motivation to learn a new or complex thinking skill is sharply enhanced when instruction in that skill is provided precisely at the point at which students feel a need for it.[25]

Every reader of this book should be familiar with the limitations of rote learning and the dissatisfaction that many educators have voiced about instruction that relies on this as a dominant practice. We all want what students learn about the history of this country to yield a deep understanding of politics that impacts the choices they make when they cast their votes in an election. We all want what students learn about nutrition to lead to a deep understanding of what constitutes good nutrition, and we want this to influence what students eat and don't eat. Rote learning doesn't accomplish this; infusion does.

One often-quoted example of infusion speaks specifically to this point. In American history, the American Revolution is a standard topic. One teacher, moving beyond the textbook, gave students conflicting accounts of who started the fighting on Lexington Green in Massachusetts in 1775—the British or the colonists.[26] One account is from a 20th-century American textbook, the other from Winston Churchill's *History of the English-Speaking Peoples*. Which should students accept? When some students responded by saying, "Let's see what people who were there say and compare it to what these authors say," this teacher was ready. He produced a number of eyewitness accounts of the battle. Many of them showed the same split between British and American sources. A few did not, however. One, by a British soldier, said that the British opened fire unprovoked. Nevertheless, this teacher did not say that this must be the correct account. Rather, he asked the students what they would need to find out about this person to be confident that he is a reliable source of information. From this, and from similar reflection on some of the other accounts, the students developed a checklist of factors to take into account in determining the credibility of any source. This procedural checklist (Figure 1-8) was made explicit so that it would guide the students in their thinking.[27]

They then applied this to the other accounts they were considering and tried to make considered judgments about the sources' credibility. As they did this, the teacher stressed how important it is to be thorough in applying the checklist—they should consider *all* the factors they could uncover rather than make a quick determination after reviewing just one or two. Then they could be sure that they did not overlook anything. He stressed that this is a good general habit of mind to adopt whenever students are working from a plan with many steps.

Figure 1-8. Procedural Checklist

Criteria for Evaluating Evidence

P   Is it a primary (more reliable) or secondary (less reliable) source?

R   Does the person giving the evidence have any reason to lie (less reliable)?

O   Is there other evidence that supports or verifies what this evidence says (more reliable), or is this the only evidence presented on the topic (less reliable)?

P   Is it a public (less reliable) or private (more reliable) statement? It is public if the person giving it knew other people would read or see it.

Many students found that "We can't tell whether this is a credible report" was sometimes a better answer to this question than "Yes, credible" or "No, not credible" as they considered the sources. Being noncommittal is sometimes the right answer.

This teacher then asked the students to discuss with each other, and make note of, other contexts in which they might be able to use the checklist that they had developed. Everything from "Who started the fight in the playground?" to "How can I make sure that my observation reports in my science work are credible enough to assure others that they are accurate?" to "Which presidential candidate is likely to be giving us accurate information?" appeared on their lists. The teacher suggested that they engage metacognitively by practicing their strategy in as many situations as they could, and if they found other important factors to consider that were not on the PROP list, they should consider adding these to the checklist to make it more complete.

Note how this teacher worked into his instructional practice a deliberate emphasis on each of the three ingredients of skillful thinking and how these revolve around the specific matter of judging the credibility of sources of information. Note, too, how the teacher has done this by making the infusion context of his instruction an important topic in his content curriculum, the start of the Revolutionary War in the British colonies in North America. We will elaborate the details of this kind of instructional practice in the next three chapters.

These students learned a tremendous amount about the circumstances of the start of the Revolutionary War, what was at stake, and who the players were, well beyond what they ever would have come away with had they relied solely on their textbooks for information. This took more time, but it was worth it. Infusion has been put into practice in many classrooms in many countries, and its application has expanded in K–12.[28] There is much research that shows that the content acquisition alone makes the extra time worth it. The depth of understanding that infusion can generate, along with the development of habits of skillful thinking, make it a technique that can deliver the level of education we all strive to achieve. We will demonstrate this throughout the book by looking in depth at many more lessons like this.

Thinking-Based Learning: A Priority for the 21st Century

Let us sum up the ideas we have advanced about skillful thinking as a goal of meeting the standards developed for education in this century. Skillful thinking is just that—thinking in which the thinker assesses what is required to accomplish a thinking task and deliberately applies with proficiency the task-appropriate tools of thinking skills and mental behaviors in strategic combination to produce thoughtful products of high quality. This should all become an abiding habitual practice for the skillful thinker.

Skillful thinking involves three basic ingredients:

1. *Thinking skills.* Using specific and appropriate mental procedures for the kind of thinking engaged in by the thinker.
2. *Habits of mind.* Driving the use of these procedures in ways that manifest broad and productive task-related mental behaviors.
3. *Metacognition.* Doing both of these based on the thinker's own assessment of what is called for by the thinking task and guided by the thinker's plan as to how to accomplish the task.

This is summarized in Figure 1-9.

To be sure, many students can achieve some proficiency in thinking simply by trial and error over the years, but at the same time many of the dysfunctional thinking habits that we have identified also develop. When locked in, these become very difficult to shake or rectify in later years. Systematic instruction in skillful thinking, when started early, can both accelerate the development of proficiency in thinking and prevent the early adoption of these dysfunctional application procedures. Such instruction can accomplish this at a time when types of skillful thinking are identified in many contemporary educational standards as requirements to accomplish important subject-matter learning objectives.[29]

However, even though skillful thinking can be developed through classroom instruction, not just any instruction will do. The development of skillful thinking is not a discovery activity, not a "think harder" activity, not something that is aimed simply at encouraging, stimulat-

Figure 1-9. The Dynamics of Skillful Thinking

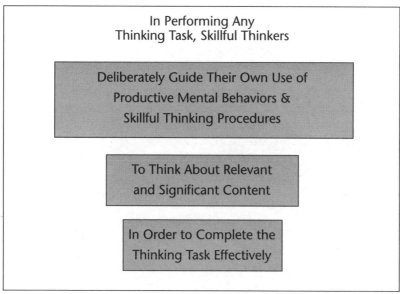

ing, or enhancing student thinking. Teaching skillful thinking means teaching—deliberately, explicitly, and directly—what these procedures, mental behaviors, and metacognitive moves are and how to apply them. It requires effort and skill by both learners and teachers, for although skillful thinking ideally is a self-actuated, almost intuitive, operation or behavior, it becomes so only through repeated, conscious, effortful, continual mediated application, instruction, and reflection.

We have argued that 21st-century educators should infuse instruction in skillful thinking into their content instruction. This means not only teaching students skillful thinking but also teaching them to use the appropriate forms of skillful thinking with the content material they are learning. When this is accomplished, our educational system will be transformed into a powerful vehicle for learning that meets all the standards that have been developed to guide instruction. The result will be an educational system second to none. It will yield skillful thinkers who have mastered the content material they have studied by employing skillful thinking to engage with it.

This book attempts to provide some new insights and directions in bridging that seemingly dichotomous tension between covering content and taking the time to teach students how to think better. It is not an either-or but rather a both-and resolution. Developing skillful thinking and important content understanding should be dual objectives of instruction that aims at engaging students in thinking skillfully about the content

Figure 1-10. Objectives of Thinking-Based Learning

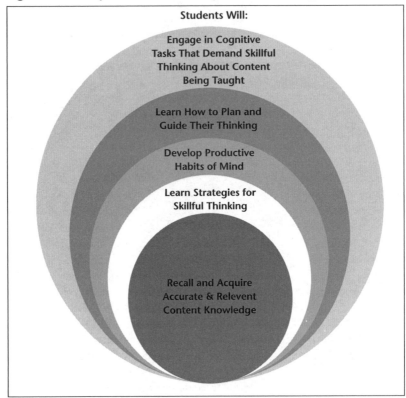

they need to learn. We call this *infusing instruction in thinking skills and habits of mind into content instruction*. This is what produces thinking-based learning—the most powerful type of learning in education. Figure 1-10 expresses the objectives—and the challenge—of thinking-based learning.

Notes

1. Former St. Louis Rams coach Richard Brooks, quoted by Bryan Burwell in *USA Today*, 12/06/95, p. 2C.
2. This reflects a favorite statement by philosopher/educator Matthew Lipman, who describes skillful thinking in much the same way to distinguish it from other ways of thinking. Lipman, M. (1988). Critical thinking—what can it be? *Educational Leadership, 46* (1), 33–43; Lipman, M. (1991). *Thinking in education.* Cambridge, UK: Cambridge University Press.
3. Bloom, B., & Broder, L. (1980). *Problem-solving skills of college students.* Chicago: University of Chicago Press. Clark, A. J., & Palm, H. (1990). Training in metacognition: An application to industry. In K. J. Kilhooy, M. T. G. Keane, R. H. Logies, & G. Erdos (Eds.), *Lines of thinking: Reflections on the psychology of*

thought (Vol. 2). Chichester, UK: John Wiley. Feuerstein, R. (1980). *Instrumental enrichment*. Baltimore: University Park Press.

4. Bertrand Russell, as quoted in Flew, A. (1995). *Thinking about social thinking*. New York: Prometheus Books.

5. CBS '60 Minutes Wednesday' cancelled; Sitcoms will fill in. *USA Today*, 5/19/05, p. 3D.

6. New safeguards to avoid intelligence errors. (2005, July 29). *New York Times Digest*, p. 3.

7. *Addison Wesley Science*, Vol. 5, p. 32. Menlo Park, CA: Addison Wesley Publishing.

8. These formalized question strategies have been called Thinking Maps in previous works (see Swartz & Perkins, 1990). However, shortly thereafter the term was trademarked by a publisher of prepackaged materials that were marketed to schools. What this publisher called a thinking map was not one of these question strategies, but one of a number of traditional graphics, like a web or Venn diagram, which can be used to record the results of certain types of thinking. These graphics do not serve the same purpose as the kinds of verbal thinking maps that we describe in this book. To avoid confusion, we will use the term *thinking strategy map*, not *thinking map*, to label organized question strategies for skillful thinking.

9. Beyer, B. (2001). Developing a scope and sequence for thinking skill instruction. In A. Costa (Ed.), *Developing minds* (3rd ed.), Alexandria, VA: Association for Supervision and Curriculum Development, pp. 248–252; see also Beyer, B. K. (1987), *Practical strategies for the teaching of thinking*. Boston: Allyn & Bacon, pp. 25–37; Swartz, R., Fischer, S., & Parks, S. (1999). *Infusing critical and creative thinking into content instruction: A lesson design handbook in secondary science*, Pacific Grove, CA: Critical Thinking, p. 8.

10. See Beyer, B. (1988). *Developing a thinking skills program*. Boston: Allyn & Bacon; Swartz, R., & Parks, S. (1994). *Infusing instruction in critical and creative thinking into content instruction: A lesson design handbook for the elementary grades*. Pacific Grove, CA: Critical Thinking.

11. Costa, A., & Kallick, B. (2000). *Activating and engaging habits of mind*. Alexandria, VA: Association for Supervision and Curriculum Development.

12. Perkins, D., Jay, E., & Tishman, S. (2000). Beyond abilities: A dispositional theory of thinking. *Merrill Palmer Quarterly, 39* (1), 1–21.

13. Ennis, R. (1984). A taxonomy of critical thinking skills and dispositions. In R. Sternberg & J. Baron (Eds.), *Teaching thinking: Theory and practice*. New York: Freeman.

14. Costa, A., & Kallick, B. (2000). *Habits of mind: A developmental series*. Alexandria, VA: Association for Supervision and Curriculum Development. The four volumes are: *Book I: Discovering and exploring habits of mind; Book II: Activating and engaging habits of mind; Book III: Assessing and reporting on habits of mind; Book IV: Integrating and sustaining habits of mind*.

15. Hong Kong Ministry of Education. (2002). *Personal, social, & humanities education*. Hong Kong: Curriculum Development Council, p. 53.

16. Michigan State Board of Education. (1991) *Michigan goals and objectives for science education (K–12)*. Lansing, MI, pp. 53 & 77.

17. Virginia Department of Public Instruction (2001). *History and social science standards of learning for Virginia schools*. Richmond, VA, p. 38.

18. National Center for History in the Schools. (1996). *National standards for United States history, grades 5–12*. Los Angeles: University of California Press, p. 152.

19. Perkins, D., & Salomon, G. (1987). Transfer and teaching thinking. In D. Perkins, J. Lochhead, & D. Bishop (Eds.), *Thinking: The second international conference*. Hillsdale, NJ: Erlbaum.

20. Swartz, R. (1987). Teaching for thinking: A developmental model for the infusion of thinking skills into mainstream instruction. In J. Baron & R. Sternberg (Eds.), *Teaching thinking skills: Theory and practice*. New York: Freeman.

21. Ong, A. C. (2006). The infusion approach to teaching thinking. In A. C. Ong & G. Borich, *Teaching strategies that promote thinking*. Singapore: McGraw Hill, pp. 241–261. Also, McGuinness, C. (2004). *Teaching thinking through infusion: ACTS in Northern Ireland*. Available online at c.mcguinness@qub.ac.uk.

22. *Webster's Dictionary*, quoted in McGuinness, C. (2005). Teaching thinking: Theory and practice. In *Pedagogy: Learning for teaching*. BJEP, Monograph Series II. 3, London: British Psychological Association, pp. 107–129.

23. Doyle, W. (1983). Academic work. *Review of Educational Research, 53*(2), 159–199; Edwards, J. (1988). Measuring the effects of the direct teaching of thinking skills. *Human Intelligence Newsletter, 9*(3) 9–10; Sternberg, R., & Davidson, J. (1989). A four-prong model for intellectual development. *Journal of Research and Development in Education, 22*(3) (Spring), 22–28.

24. Estes, T. H. (1972). Reading in the social studies: A review of research since 1950. In J. Laffery (Ed.), *Reading in the content areas*. Newark, DE: International Reading Association, pp. 178–183; Nickerson, R. (1988–1989). On improving thinking through instruction. In E. Z. Rothkopf (Ed.), *Review of research in education*. Washington: American Educational Research Association. Vol. 15, 3–57; Schoenfeld, A. (1979). Can heuristics be taught? In J. Lochhead & J. Clement (Eds.), *Cognitive process instruction*. Philadelphia: Franklin Institute Press.

25. One interesting result is that student motivation to learn a new or complex thinking skill is sharply enhanced when instruction in that skill is provided at the point where students perceive a need (have a felt need) to use the skill to accomplish an assigned (valued/desired) subject-matter learning objective. Bereiter, C. (1973). Elementary schools: Convenience or necessity? *Elementary School Journal, 73* (8), 435–446; Dempster, F. N. (1993). Exposing our students to less should help them learn more. *Phi Delta Kappan, 74* (6), 433–437; Pressley, M., & Harris, K. (1990). What we really know about strategy instruction. *Educational Leadership, 48* (1), 31–34.

26. O'Reilly, K. (1990). *Evaluating viewpoints: Critical thinking in American history series: Colonies to Constitution*. Pacific Grove, CA: Critical Thinking, pp. 101–103.

27. Ibid., p. 35.

28. McGuinness, C. (2005). Op. cit. See also Swartz, R., et al., *Infusion lesson books in language arts, Grades 1–2, 3–4, and 5–6*. Pacific Grove, CA: Critical Thinking.

29. Perkins, D. N. (1987). Myth and method in teaching thinking. *Teaching Thinking and Problem Solving, 9* (2) (March/April) pp. 1–2, 8–9.

CHAPTER 2

Teaching Skillful Thinking:
A Demonstration Lesson

It is not enough to have a good mind. The main thing is to use it well.
—René Descartes

THE STUDENTS IN Alice Fischer's eighth-grade classroom are involved in a science activity. They are explaining how a bird of prey is able to get enough food to survive. They are to write a description of what happens from the time this bird, the American kestrel, sights its prey to the time it eats its prey. These students have been working from the passage shown in Figure 2-1, a composite the teacher has put together based on information in various books on birds of America, and from their prior understanding of the way that certain abilities (e.g., sight) of living organisms work.

The students in this class have been asked to write as if they have been hired by the publisher of a bird book to write one more paragraph describing the dynamics of this bird in action. The teacher is stressing this essential question: How does the operation of key parts of this bird contribute to its success as a hunter and hence to its survival as an organism and a species? Figure 2-2 shows one of the pieces of student writing.

Figure 2-1. Teacher's Composite About the American Kestrel

The American Kestrel

American Kestrel. The American kestrel is one of the most common birds of prey in both North and South America. Its population has flourished. It is characterized by long, narrow, gray markings. It is known for its habit of hovering in one place while hunting its prey, generally consisting of snakes, lizards, large insects, and small rodents. This evolved hunting skill involves the ability to detect any small movement on the ground, the ability to hover while scanning the ground for prey, and the speed and strength to plunge onto the prey from heights of 50 feet or more. All these skills depend on the kestrel's good sense of depth perception.

Figure 2-2. Student Writing on the Kestrel[1]

As the kestrel hovers, it turns its head from side to side and scans the ground with its eyes for the movement of recognizable prey. When it spots prey, the kestrel uses its stereoscopic vision, which depends on the coordination of both eyes to gauge the location and distance of the prey. The kestrel then changes the motion of its wings, dives, and uses its tail to guide it to the prey. When the kestrel reaches the prey, it grasps it in its claws, using its talons to immobilize and even kill the prey. The kestrel then uses its wings to fly to a spot where it puts the prey down and pecks off morsels, which it puts into its mouth with its beak and tongue. If the prey is alive, the kestrel kills it with the sharp tip of its beak.

Although this writing is not perfect, it shows very clearly and precisely how this bird works as a predator. This student's mastery and use of technical scientific terms like *stereoscopic vision* and *talons* contributes to the piece's clarity. Overall, the depth of understanding it displays about predator–prey relationships and about the adaptation of the bird's parts to make it effective as a predator, and hence ensure its survival, is clear. The organization of the writing, giving an account of the way this bird gets food, is dramatic and powerful.

Not all the students in this classroom have written a similar account. Some students stress a few of these contributing occurrences more than others (e.g., the way the bird kills its prey). Most students, however, have also written careful, clear, and precise accounts of how this bird hunts for its food in a way that shows their deep understanding of this concept.

This piece of writing didn't appear "out of the blue." Nor was it typical of the writing that these students did prior to the lesson. Rather, it was the direct outcome of a carefully structured lesson whose goal was that students learn and use a basic analytic thinking skill, skillful parts–whole thinking, coupled with a manifestation of intellectual behavior that results in expressing their thoughts and understandings with clarity and precision. Instruction in such skillful thinking and this habit of mind was infused into a life-sciences activity in which the students were trying to master an important fundamental concept, predator–prey relationships, as a dynamic that contributes to the survival of a species. The writing activity built on this thinking-skill lesson. The careful and non-impulsive thinking in which the students were prompted to engage in this lesson, informed by a desire for clarity and precision in the understanding that resulted, was mainly responsible for this result. The instruction that led to this thinking was, in fact, a necessary precondition for the students to be able to compose writing like this.

This result is not atypical of the kinds of results that teachers have had across the curriculum and grade levels teaching similar lessons. These lessons all involve the implementation of three basic instructional ideas:

- Direct instruction of the students in skillful thinking procedures (in this case, thinking procedures for skillful parts–whole analysis)
- Reinforcement and further instruction in the habits of mind that must be called upon to produce high-quality work
- Infusion of this instruction into standard content instruction

Direct instruction is a powerful and well-researched instructional technique. When applied to infusing a thinking skill and its accompanying mental habits into content instruction, this technique involves the *explicit* introduction to the students of the qualities that make a specific kind of thinking skillful. Scaffolded and cued application of this kind of thinking by the students to important ideas in the content curriculum, with teacher-mediated repeated practice and application of these techniques, is carried out until such thinking and intellectual behaviors become internalized and habituated. Then the students no longer need the teacher to guide them in skillful parts–whole thinking; they guide themselves.

Because this instruction is infused into content learning, the students also reap the benefit of achieving a deeper, more reflective understanding and appreciation of the content. In this case the students will learn about the ways in which predators are especially adapted to hunt their prey efficiently so that not only they, as individuals, survive and flourish, but their species does as well. This will take the students well beyond what they would have learned if they had relied solely on their textbooks and had learned primarily to pass their tests.

This kind of instruction in thinking skills and mental behaviors is not unlike the techniques we use to teach students any number of other skills—in mathematics, science, athletics, and music, to name just a few. In this case, it is skillful *thinking* that the students are being introduced to as the first step in the process. In particular, the type of thinking that this teacher helps students learn to do—parts–whole analysis—is important to do skillfully, as is the mental habit of expressing its results clearly and precisely. When done skillfully, parts–whole analysis will typically yield a deep understanding. Here it is being analyzed for how it works and what it does. When we strive to express the results of such thinking with clarity and precision, it can bring out the best of our thinking.

In this chapter we will use the specific example of parts–whole instruction to develop a good clear understanding of what is meant by direct instruction in actual practice. In the next chapter, we will elaborate what is meant by direct instruction, explain some of its variations, and then provide a rationale for using direct instruction to teach skills like skillful parts–whole analysis.

Skillful Thinking in the Classroom: Infusing Skillful Parts–Whole Analysis Into Content Instruction

There are a number of key ingredients in the lesson we are about to examine. The teacher will do the following:

- Introduce students to the content material in the lesson
- Introduce students to the thinking skill and mental habits that the lesson will focus on and explicitly describe what makes the practice of these skillful
- Prompt the students to actively use this thinking skill and display these mental habits to think about the content in depth
- Engage the students in monitoring and evaluating their own thinking

Let's see how these actions play themselves out in Ms. Fischer's lesson on the kestrel.

Ms. Fischer starts her 50-minute class by announcing that the students are going to explore some of the basic concepts in the chapter they were assigned to read in their science textbook, "Predator–Prey Relationships as a Primary Mechanism for the Survival of Species." These concepts include food chains, as well as the ways that certain creatures are adapted to hunt for food. She asks her students to pair up and spend a minute explaining to each other what the chapter is about. When they have talked to each other awhile, she adds the following:

> In order to help you think carefully about this idea, we will also be working on a type of thinking in class, the thinking involved in how to analyze whole objects into their parts. We will be learning how to do this kind of thinking in a more careful and skillful way than we do now.

As she says this she writes "Parts–Whole Analysis" on the board and underlines it for emphasis. "Expert use of this kind of thinking is very important whenever you try to understand how something works and what it does," she says. Then she relates this to what they are learning in science:

> As we improve our ability to do parts–whole thinking we will use that kind of thinking to analyze how a specific predator works—a predator we are about to study called the American kestrel, a kind of hawk. Our goal is to find out whether there is anything special about its parts that make this bird an excellent hunter, and if so what.

Ms. Fischer reminds them that they will be developing a thinking strategy map for skillful parts–whole thinking and then using a special graphic organizer to guide them through this process and give them plenty of room to record their ideas about the way the parts of the American kestrel contribute to it as a good hunter. Their analysis will help them to understand how this bird operates as a bird of prey.

At this point in the lesson, and to anticipate what the students will be doing subsequently, Ms. Fischer has identified two key ingredients that should be present in any introductory lesson on a thinking skill that is infused into content instruction: explicitly introducing the students to a procedure for engaging in a kind of skillful thinking, then having the students actively apply this procedure to think about the content that they are working with in the regular curriculum. She is ready to embark on these ingredients of direct instruction. She indicates that as the students do this, they will also be attending to one of the mental habits with which they are already familiar: thinking, describing, and communicating the relationship between the parts and the whole in clear and precise detail.

Introducing the Students to Procedures for Skillful Parts–Whole Analysis

Ms. Fischer now starts by asking the students to think about what is involved when they analyze something into its parts, again pointing to the name of this kind of thinking on the board. She asks them, for example, to think about the way they have been asked to think about the parts of objects in previous learning activities. "For example," she says, "what is this?" as she holds up her hand. When the students identify it as her left hand she asks, "What are the parts of this hand?"

Immediately students respond with "fingers," "palm," "skin," "nails," "muscles," "a thumb," and so forth. After a few more responses Ms. Fischer stops them and asks what just happened that got them thinking, noting that 3 minutes earlier thumbs, skin, and muscles were probably the furthest things from their minds. Many of the students recognize that her question prompted their thinking.

She then asks them a reflective question about what just happened: "What went on in this thinking?" After some fumbling they recognize that the question prompted them to look at Ms. Fischer's hand; they became aware of certain parts, and that stimulated them to remember what these parts were called. That's what they then contributed to the class—words for the parts they could identify. When Ms. Fischer asks them if that's a fair way to characterize what parts–whole analysis means to them, many of them say that it is.

Ms. Fischer now reminds the students that when they give the names of the parts of something, that doesn't automatically represent or communicate much understanding of the parts. "So," she asks, "what else is important to think about besides the names of the parts? What are some other interesting questions that can be asked about the parts of any whole object so you can understand it more fully?" Three additional questions are mentioned, which Ms. Fischer puts into a certain order and lists on the board giving the sequence a title.

Notice that this teacher has made a shift from what is important to think about in parts–whole thinking to questions for which you might want answers. In fleshing out what else is important to think about if our parts–whole analysis is to become more skillful, such as what the functions of the parts are, she is operationalizing this basic component in skillful thinking in terms of asking and answering relevant prompting questions. She recognizes that this enriching process makes their thinking skillful. She has developed, with the students, a question strategy for skillful parts–whole thinking and has translated it into a written thinking procedure with a name that she then makes into an overhead transparency, which she projects onto the screen in her classroom. She tells the students that she will call such written thinking procedures "thinking strategy maps." She is just learning how to make PowerPoint slides and decides that the next time she teaches this lesson she could put this thinking strategy map on a slide. When the students get individual computers, she could then network it into them. Whatever technology is used, however, the same result is achieved: It makes the thinking strategy map explicit and puts it right before the eyes of the students so that they can use it to guide themselves through this procedure when thinking about the kestrel. She knows that this will make their thinking deeper and more skillful.

There are two important points to stress at this juncture in this lesson. The first is that the questions on this thinking strategy map, though prompted by questioning from the teacher, have been generated (and perhaps even formulated) by the students themselves. Whether it is the students or the teacher who generates the questions, however, the resulting thinking strategy map needs to be used as a proposal or hypothesis about procedures that will make the students' thinking more skillful. As they use such thinking strategy maps they may want to revise them, try them again, and do some further revision as they try to perfect a workable, efficient, expert procedure for engaging in skillful thinking.

The second point has to do with the form that the thinking strategy map takes. Thinking strategy maps such as these need not be phrased only in terms of questions. They can be a series of directions, like steps in procedures for taking apart a complicated piece of machinery, or they can be cast as a flow chart rather than as a step-by-step strategy. Instead of asking "What smaller things make up this whole object?" she could have written "List the smaller things that make up this whole object." What is important is the map's use and that it is kept open to revision.

The thinking strategy map in Figure 2-3 elaborates the procedural details of the thinking skill this teacher is attempting to introduce to her stu-

Figure 2-3. A Thinking Strategy Map for Parts–Whole Thinking[2]

Skillful Parts–Whole Thinking
1. What smaller things make up a given whole object?
2. What would happen if each of these parts were missing?
3. What is the function of each of these parts?
4. How do the parts work together to make this whole object be what it is or do what it does?

dents. In this sense, it *defines* the thinking skill. Her main objective is that the students begin to internalize the procedure described so that when, eventually, she is not around and they recognize a need for using skillful parts–whole analysis, they ask and answer all these questions spontaneously for themselves without having to be prompted. Then they are en route to becoming more skillful thinkers. This lesson is just the beginning of this process.

A note of caution: Thinking strategy maps should be treated as guides, not prescriptive models. There is a reciprocal interaction between applying a skill (i.e., following a given map) and learning about how, when, and where to apply that skill, which leads to new insights into how to apply the skill and thus to changing representations of it. Teachers should thus allow students to revise, alter, and modify the maps as they gain experience in applying any skill. As one develops increasing expertise in any skilled operation, one consolidates some steps into fewer steps while at other times adding new steps to fit certain different situations. A thinking strategy map ought to be continually revised by students as they apply a skill until it becomes descriptive of how they are doing it. Thus these maps should change over time as students elaborate a skill, clarify what they are doing, combine steps, and generate new heuristics. In addition to introducing the students to the thinking-skill focus in this lesson, Ms. Fischer takes a few minutes to help students recall the habits of mind that are important to practice in doing any kind of skillful thinking:

> There's more that I want you to think about in this lesson. Remember how we have, over the past weeks, identified a number of important habits of mind that good thinkers practice as they engage in thinking tasks? We've got posters on the wall of the classroom describing these. What are some of them?

Her students respond by mentioning such important habits as persisting, thinking flexibly, thinking interdependently, and listening to other points of view with understanding and empathy. She continues: "In this

lesson we want to emphasize particularly one of these—the one we became familiar with last week—thinking and communicating with clarity
and precision." She asks what this means and why it is important. She also
asks, "What might that look like and sound like?" The students respond
with a variety of answers:

> "I ask myself if I'm clear about what I want to say before I say it."
>
> "I pay attention to my words and try not to use words like *stuff* and
> *things* and *ya'know* and *nice*."
>
> "I ask myself if what I'm going to say will make sense to others."
>
> "When I write something, I ask others to read it to see if makes sense
> to them."

She goes on as follows:

> I want you to continue to try to identify, as we go along, when it is im-
> portant to think clearly and precisely, why it is important, and what went
> on in your mind as you monitored your clear and precise thinking and
> language. I will ask you to jot down your thoughts in your journals. We
> will come back to it after we've worked through the main part of the les-
> son and compare notes.

Ms. Fischer is now making explicit a second thinking-related objective
in this lesson, to practice communicating clearly and precisely. She will
want her students to develop a detailed description of what is involved in
the effective practice of thinking clearly and precisely—of *how* to do that—
based on its practice in the lesson. Later she will shift the attention of the
students to this matter so that it can be an open and direct object of reflection and discussion in her class, but for now she has chosen to concentrate on parts–whole analysis. Having completed the introductory part
of this lesson, Ms. Fischer is now prepared to move to its core, where the
students apply this thinking skill to analyze how the American kestrel
operates as a bird of prey and how its parts contribute to this operation.
Before turning to that part of her lesson, however, let's examine what she
was doing and why in her lesson introduction.

Why Take the Time to Explicitly Introduce
Students to What Makes Thinking Skillful?

In the part of the lesson about the kestrel described above, the teacher
introduces her students to a new thinking skill. In so doing she works with
the students to first make explicit a procedure to explicate how to engage
in parts–whole analysis with skill. She does this by expressing the procedure in the form of a question strategy, presented in a thinking strategy
map. She also takes the time to help the students recall and make explicit

a habit of mind to which they have been previously introduced and which she wants them to practice as they try to engage in parts–whole analysis skillfully. This part of the lesson takes about 15 minutes, and the students are not discussing anything about predator–prey relationships, birds of prey, or hunting as a survival mechanism in nature. The focus of attention is completely on the skill itself and, briefly, on a related mental habit. Let us reflect on why this is time well spent.

The short answer to this question is based not just on the learning reflected in the writing sample at the beginning of this chapter. Such writing is, indeed, based on the students' using the thinking strategy map as a plan for thinking more skillfully than they do when they simply give the names of the parts of a whole object in response to "What are the parts of this bird?" Rather, it is based more significantly on the fact that the thinking strategy map gives the students a tool that will enhance their understanding again and again, well after the lesson on the American kestrel has been completed, when they encounter other things that have significant components—ecosystems, the government of their country, the stories they read, and even procedures for solving equations in mathematics. Once this teacher has introduced a thinking strategy map like this one, she will not have to do it again.

Ms. Fischer uses a projector to introduce the thinking strategy map and to display it. She does this so that it is in front of their eyes and all the students can use it. She might also write it on a whiteboard. After the lesson is over, she will enlarge it, transfer it to a piece of newsprint, and put it on the wall of the classroom so that it is there for the next several weeks or so as a guide through the process of parts–whole analysis when the students do it again. She can also make it available to them on their classroom computers by networking it in under "Strategies for Skillful Thinking."

Making the thinking strategy for parts–whole analysis explicit, as Ms. Fischer does, seems relatively straightforward and not very difficult. Nevertheless, much instruction that educators assume involves teaching thinking skills will fail to do this. Sensitivity to the need for more thoughtful engagement by students often leads teachers to employ more thinking challenges for their students, or even to ask students to do certain kinds of thinking openly. This is laudable. For example, many teachers now ask more questions like "Why did the plague spread so rapidly in medieval Europe?" "Why do you think Huck Finn's father abducted him and kept him locked up in a cabin?" "What energy source do you predict the United States will use as its dominant source in the next 50 years?" and, in the primary grades, "What can Peter Rabbit do to avoid being caught by Mr. McGregor?" Students may respond to such questions, but this usually stops short of their developing an explicit understanding of what needs to be done procedurally to make their thinking skillful. For this reason, simply challenging students or discussing their thinking is not in itself very successful in teaching students to think skillfully.[3]

Usually, the students who are doing well, have some self-confidence, and know how to do skillful thinking will do the same thing again in these circumstances. Those students who don't know how to think skillfully, however, will usually do what they ordinarily do—remain silent or just guess. In fact, the desire by a teacher for quick answers in such circumstances actually encourages guessing. It is easy to see how a teacher could misinterpret student efforts as evidence that he or she is teaching students thinking skills. This is usually an illusory leap of faith. In such classrooms no significant instruction in skillful thinking is taking place, and, in fact, not much skillful thinking may be taking place at all, even given the challenging questions that are posed.

Contrast this with the power of the kind of instruction we have been describing when a teacher introduces a thinking skill explicitly to prepare students to answer such questions more skillfully. Making the skillfulness of thinking, such as parts–whole analysis, *explicit* is a kind of missing link that gives a procedural plan to students who don't know how to do such thinking well. Suitably prompted, these students can and will succeed in such classrooms. More important, besides increasing engagement with the content, this way of starting a lesson paves the way for the students to develop the *habit* of thinking skillfully about parts–whole relationships, and doing so in ways that manifest even more good intellectual habits. The power of this kind of instruction is inestimable.

Guiding Students Through the Active Application of Skillful Parts–Whole Analysis

In this part of the lesson, Ms. Fischer involves her students in actively applying the new thinking skill. Here she will have her students use a graphic organizer for parts–whole analysis that will help the students to "download" their thoughts in an organized way. The graphic organizer she uses looks like the one in Figure 2-4.[4]

She will then guide the students through a procedure in which they work in small collaborative thinking groups, where they will develop their ideas together, each group working on a different part of the bird. She will guide them to express their understanding of how this bird hunts based on their analysis of its parts. Finally, she will engage the students in reflecting on the thinking they engaged in to get this result and have them plan how they will do the same kind of thinking again when it is needed.

As she moves into this part of her lesson, Ms. Fischer doesn't just say, "Now use this thinking strategy map to think about the parts of the kestrel." Rather, she guides them through this process. She prompts the students with such statements as "Work on the first question on the thinking

Figure 2-4. Graphic Organizer for Determining Parts–Whole Relationships

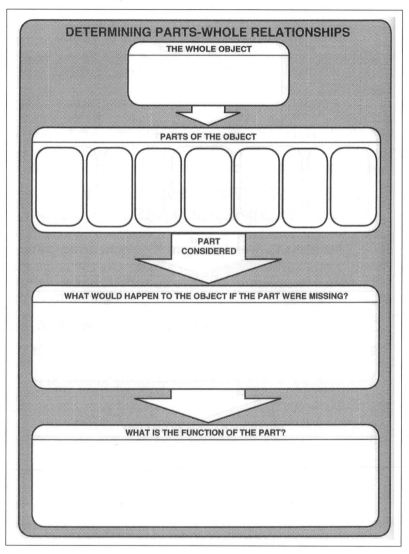

map and then let's hear some of your results" and "Now let's consider one part and ask: 'What would happen if that part was missing?' Write your thoughts in the appropriate box on the graphic organizer. You can include as many things in this box as you would like." After this process, she concludes with this direction:

> You are going to be culminating this activity by describing how the operation of the key parts of the kestrel make it a good hunter, as if you were writing something to go into the *Birds of America* book

that has the excerpt we looked at earlier. You will need to think this through carefully so that you can write something that is clear and precise that the book publisher would accept.

Ms. Fischer is planning to enter this graphic organizer on her networked classroom computers, but at this stage she gives each group a hard copy in order to encourage them to make their entries a collaborative group effort.

Let's examine this part of the lesson in some detail now. At first Ms. Fischer keeps the students together as a whole class. She asks them to discuss the first question with a partner and write their ideas in the appropriate place on the graphic organizer. "What are the smaller parts of the kestrel?" she asks.

> Let's get a good big starter list and then choose parts that are really important. What I'd like you to do is to identify some of the larger parts of the kestrel first and then write these at the top of the boxes on the graphic organizer. Then, under each, write a list of smaller parts of these larger parts. For example, what is one larger part?

Some students identify the head or the wings. She then says, "What are some of the smaller parts of the head, for example?" *Eyes, beak, brain* other students offer, and she writes these on an overhead transparency, noting, "That's what I'd like you to do in each parts box." She adds that when they think about this they should make sure that what they say is based on what they see in the picture, what's in the short passage they read earlier, and what they already know about birds and animals. She then asks for volunteers and, in order to spread this out, selects other students at random to share their ideas. The result is a good rich list, shown in Figure 2.5.[5]

She continues as follows:

> Now, let's think about the next important question on the thinking strategy map. I would like you each to consider one part and ask, "What will happen if this part is missing?" Actually, I want you to work together on this question and then use your results to develop

Figure 2-5. Parts of the Object

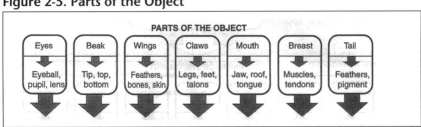

a response to the next question, "What is the function of this part? When you do this I would like you to write your response in the boxes for these questions on your graphic organizer. In order to do this in a careful way, I'd like you to work together in larger groups this time—let's call these "thinking groups."

She forms groups of three or four students chosen at random and when the students move into their groups she says the following:

First I want you to select a part that you think is an important one for this bird. I want you to make sure that when you work in your group you *think interdependently*—don't just come up with your own ideas as if you were alone. Remember how we developed ways of doing that?

So let me repeat: The first thing you should do is to select one part to work on that your group thinks is important and then try to answer in sequence the second and third questions on your thinking strategy map for skillful parts–whole thinking.

She then guides them in responding to the questions about what will happen if the part they choose is missing and what its function is:

Now write down some ideas of what might happen if the part you choose is missing. Then see if you can change some of the negatives to positives and move to the question about the function of the parts. Don't just write down one thing that might happen if the part was missing. Write as many things as you can think of. Do the same when you describe the function of the part. Remember, you will want to be as clear and precise as possible. Please make sure you are using the right words in your description, and if there is a scientific word for what you are describing and you know it, use it instead of an everyday word. When you have filled in what you think will happen if your part is missing, and have stated what its function is, I will look at your work. If there are scientific words that you don't know, I will tell you what they are.

After providing these guidelines, but before each group chooses a part and works on it, Ms. Fischer demonstrates this process by asking them to all work initially on one part that she chooses. She writes the results on an overhead transparency (or, when her school has the equipment, uses PowerPoint slides) of the graphic organizer, recording what the class is doing as it goes along. She tells the students that they should use this as a model for what they will be doing on their own in their groups. This takes her about 10 minutes. Figure 2-6 shows the results.[6]

Notice how the students have formulated their statements of what would happen if the part was missing and what its function might be. A

Figure 2-6. Determining Parts–Whole Relationships: The Kestrel

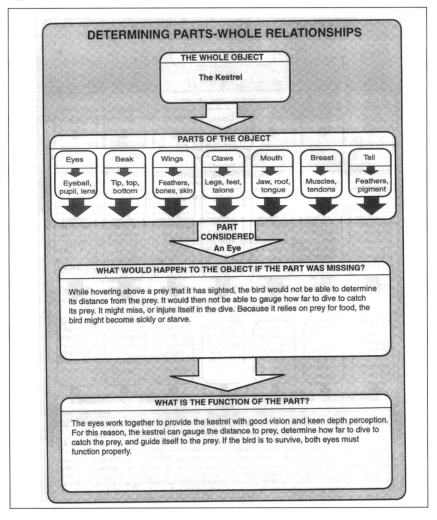

close examination shows how the students have followed the guidelines that the teacher has written.

When they are finished with the part she has chosen—the left eye— she asks them whether, based on what they came up with, they think this is an important part. Her students all agree that it is. She asks why. They base their answers on what they have written. She then says, "So let's see if there are any other reasons."

What Ms. Fischer has done so far is not a very complex process, but it is an exacting one, and it is at the heart of the thinking that the students have been doing. That Ms. Fischer's students do it with ease is a function of this kind of guidance.

After another 10 minutes of work in their small groups on a second part, Ms. Fischer asks a spokesperson from each group to report and summarize their results on a large chart that she has posted on the wall. Each group also has a version of this chart on their computers to record what is written on the larger chart. Figure 2-7 shows the summary chart that the teacher has the class develop after each group completes its work.[7]

Each student now has available the results of the work of all the groups, representing about seven or eight parts. Their homework is to respond to the fourth question on the thinking strategy map: How do the parts work together to make this object do what it does?

This activity gives the students an opportunity on their own to think carefully and skillfully about the various parts of the kestrel, what their functions are, and how the ones that they identify as important for the bird's survival contribute to it. It also is the background for the next

Figure 2-7. The Whole-Object Kestrel Organizer

DETERMINING PARTS–WHOLE RELATIONSHIPS

THE WHOLE OBJECT

The Kestrel

PARTS OF THE OBJECT

Eyes	Beak	Wings	Claws	Mouth	Breast	Tail
Eyeball, pupil, lens	Tip, top, bottom	Feathers, bones, skin	Legs, feet, talons	Jaw, roof, tongue	Muscles, tendons	Feathers, pigment

WHAT WOULD HAPPEN TO THE OBJECT IF THE PARTS WERE MISSING?

| If one eye were missing, depth perception would be hindered; the bird might starve | If the tip of the beak were broken, the kestrel would have a hard time killing its prey. | A missing wing feather would somewhat hamper the kestrel's flight | If a talon were broken, it would be hard, but not impossible, to capture prey. | If the tongue were injured the bird might not be able to swallow food. | Without properly functioning breast muscles the kestrel could not fly. | A missing tail feather could mean that the kestrel could not turn properly. |

WHAT IS THE FUNCTION OF THE PARTS?

| The eyes are essential for seeing prey and for judging how far away it is. | The tip of the beak is a tool for killing prey and for picking off morsels. | Wings give buoyancy and can flap rapidly enough to allow hovering. | The claws are used to grasp, hold, and sometimes kill prey. | The mouth is used to take in food that has been held by the beak. | The strength of the breast muscles allows for rapid wing flapping. | The tail stabilizes the bird in flight and steers it on course. |

writing assignment that Ms. Fischer gives to these students, which they will continue to work on in tomorrow's class. This writing assignment yielded the rich piece of writing that we used to launch this chapter. Now we can see where the ideas that these students put into their writing came from, and why they used precise language to express them. Most important, we can see how the thinking they do beforehand contributes to the depth and understanding they express in this writing. We will have more to say later about specific techniques that teachers can use to help students translate good thinking into good writing.

Prompting the Students to Reflect on the Elements of Skillful Parts–Whole Thinking

Ms. Fischer now involves her students in two final activities. They are important because they redirect student attention onto explicit consideration of the two thinking objectives of this lesson. Her intent is to bridge the thinking that the students do in this lesson to the continued application in other appropriate contexts and to the development of the mental habit of communicating with clarity and precision.

After the students have discussed how the important parts of the kestrel contribute to its ability to hunt effectively, Ms. Fischer says that she wants to take a few minutes to reflect on what they have done in the lesson. She wants them to stop thinking about the kestrel and now think about how they engaged in the thinking they did.

Ms. Fischer first asks the class to reflect on what they did as they thought about the parts of the kestrel and their relationship to the whole bird. This is a prime example of the teacher prompting the students to shift their focus and to start to reflect metacognitively on the thinking that they did. They identify this as skillful parts–whole thinking and tell, step by step, how they applied it, reporting especially on the questions that moved them through the process. They refer to, or repeat from memory, the questions on the thinking strategy map that the teacher has posted in the classroom or that is on their computers.

She then says, "As you reflect on this lesson, how might you apply parts–whole analysis in other situations? What other situations can you think of where using this kind of thinking again in this way would be useful?" Some of the students' suggestions include understanding the school building, seeing how a basketball team works, and understanding how their computers work. These are her concluding directions:

> Now that you've thought about your thinking a little, I'd like each
> of you to develop a plan for applying the skill of parts–whole analy-
> sis that you can use next time you engage in this type of thinking

> based on what you did in this lesson. Put these plans in your own words and enter them in your database for skillful thinking strategies. When we do parts–whole analysis again, I will ask you to refer back to these plans and use them.

Many students write their plans in the form of a checklist of steps they would take or a flow chart they would follow. Figure 2-8 is an example.

Ms. Fischer intends to follow up this lesson with more classroom activities that call for parts–whole analysis in order to better understand other subjects.

She has not quite finished engaging her students in thinking about their thinking. They have just reflected on the procedure that they used to think more skillfully about the parts of a whole, and what, based on this, they might want to do in the future to sustain this. Ms. Fischer has also stressed one of the habits of mind that she thinks is important to practice to make this specific engagement of parts–whole thinking effective. It is communicating with clarity and precision. This is especially important as the students craft their understanding of how the kestrel operates as a bird of prey based on their engagement with parts–whole thinking.

Ms. Fischer's students have previously been introduced to the practice of this habit of mind. This lesson has given them an opportunity to practice it again and to refine the way they do it. So Ms. Fischer now says the following:

> Let's now leave how we will do parts–whole analysis next time it is needed and focus on the specific habit of mind that I emphasized in this lesson that enhanced how we did parts–whole thinking. I observed that you all tried to display this in things that you did. So let me ask you: How did you make sure that your thoughts and your writing on the graphic organizers and on the chart were clear and precise? How did this help your understanding of this bird and how it works?

The students very quickly agreed that trying to be precise helped them to understand much more clearly how this bird worked, and it prevented confusion about what the parts did. Ms. Fischer reminds them

Figure 2-8. Checklist for Parts–Whole Analysis

_____	Identify the parts.
_____	For each part, determine what would happen if it were missing.
_____	For each part, state its function in the whole.
_____	Describe how the parts work together.

that communicating clearly and precisely is one of the important habits of mind that they have been practicing. She then says:

> OK. So what specific things did you do to give a clear and precise description of what the parts do and how this bird works? Pair up to write two important manifestations of this type of mental behavior in the lesson as you went through it.

When they have spent a few minutes discussing this and writing down some ideas, they then share these orally, and Ms. Fischer writes them under the heading "Thinking and Expressing Our Thoughts With Clarity and Precision When We Do Parts–Whole Analysis." They include the following items:

- We imagined what it would look like if a part were missing—we formed a picture inside our mind.
- We discussed what the best words were to describe what we thought would happen.
- We discussed whether what we were writing was a clear and exact way to describe what would happen.
- We asked whether we had described everything that happened when the part was missing.
- We tried to find scientific words for what we were describing.

When they have compiled a substantial list, Ms. Fischer says, "Stop for a minute. How would you describe what we are doing right now?" Most students catch on and contribute such comments as: "Thinking clearly and precisely about thinking clearly and precisely!" Finally, she asks them to discuss in what other situations, school subjects, and thinking skills would thinking and communicating with clarity and precision be valuable. She concludes by probing for examples.

Conclusion

We have described in detail one example of a lesson in which a teacher conducts direct instruction in skillful thinking infused into standard content instruction. The lesson demonstrated in this chapter is a eighth-grade science lesson. However, no type of skillful thinking is limited in applicability to certain subjects. Like most examples of skillful thinking, the skill of parts–whole analysis as well as related habits of mind can be introduced and taught in a variety of subjects and grade levels. Table 2-1 gives a sampling of other introductory lessons on parts–whole analysis and correlative habits of mind that can be taught using the techniques of direct instruction and infusion.

The thinking skill and habits of mind demonstrated in this lesson are, of course, just samples of many thinking skills and mental habits that we have identified as important to teach students. Similar lessons can be taught for each of the other thinking skills and habits of mind. Even though the lesson we have presented in skillful thinking is set in a specific

Table 2-1. Sample Lessons

Skillful Parts–Whole Analysis Lessons Infused Into Content Instruction

GRADE 1 SCIENCE

Lesson Focus: What are the parts of a wood screw and how do they help this screw to work? (Simple Machines)

Habit of Mind: Persistence at a thinking task

GRADE 4 LANGUAGE ARTS

Lesson Focus: What are the parts of a specific story and how do they function to give the story its drama and meaning? (Language Arts)

Habit of mind: Thinking interdependently

GRADE 5 HISTORY

Lesson Focus: What are the parts of the government of the United States and how do they function to make this country work as a democracy? (United States Government).

Habit of mind: Striving for accuracy and precision

GRADE 9 MATHEMATICS

Lesson Focus: What are the parts of a bar graph and how do they function to give the graph meaning? (Graphs)

Habit of mind: Striving for accuracy and precision, gathering data through all senses

GRADE 10 HISTORY

Lesson Focus: What are the parts of the U.S. Constitution, and how do they function to ensure majority rule as well as the rights of minorities? (U.S. Constitution)

Habit of mind: Thinking flexibly or listening with understanding and empathy

GRADE 12 BIOLOGY

Lesson Focus: What are the systems of the human organism and how do they function to support the life and survival of this organism? (Human Body)

Habit of mind: Thinking and communicating with clarity and precision or responding with wonderment and awe subject matter and grade level, we present it as typical in structure and methodology for any direct instruction lesson that introduces a new thinking skill and practices a related habit of mind. In subsequent chapters we will identify similar lessons that focus on other thinking skills and mental habits. In the next chapter, we will look at some of the research that underlies the principles of direct instruction. By so doing, we seek to clarify the reasons for the teaching decisions Ms. Fischer makes in this lesson and to show the solid research base that supports these decisions.

Notes

1. See Swartz, R., Fischer, S., & Parks, S. (1999). *Infusing critical and creative thinking into secondary science: A lesson design handbook.* Pacific Grove, CA: Critical Thinking, p. 176.
2. Ibid., p. 168.
3. Beyer, B. (2001). What research says about teaching thinking skills. In A. Costa (Ed.), *Developing minds: A resource book for teaching thinking.* Alexandria, VA: Association for Supervision and Curriculum Development, pp. 275–282.
4. Swartz, R., Fischer, S., & Parks, S. (1999). Op. cit., p. 169.
5. Ibid., p. 175.
6. Ibid., p. 175.
7. Ibid., p. 176.

CHAPTER 3

Direct Instruction and the Teaching of Skillful Thinking

More than to give information, a teacher needs to help guide a student's mind to think, and even beyond that to help him shape his character. Giving information is easy. Forming a thinking mind is hard. . . . Giving information is only the beginning of a teacher's responsibility; the end is to stimulate, excite, motivate, lift, challenge, inspire.

—Bruce R. Clark, educator

L ISA WILLIAMS, a seventh-grade social studies teacher in an urban school, has seen lessons in which other teachers have infused direct instruction in skillful thinking into content instruction. She has, for example, observed a science teacher in her school teaching the parts–whole lesson on the kestrel. She is impressed with the instructional power of infusing direct instruction in skillful thinking into content instruction. Watching the lesson on the kestrel has especially moved her. However, she is even more intrigued with the possibilities for rich lessons in which instruction in skillful comparing and contrasting is provided—instruction that extends traditional comparing and contrasting beyond just listing some similarities and differences, as we saw in Chapter 1. The compare-and-contrast lessons she has observed are in fourth- and fifth-grade language arts, one in which the students compared and contrasted two characters in a novel, and the other on two writing forms. She liked these lessons and their spirit of challenging the students to do deeper thinking than they usually do when they just list some similarities and differences to compare and contrast two things.

These teachers used many of the same techniques of direct instruction that Ms. Fischer used in her parts–whole lesson on the kestrel. For example, these teachers made explicit for the students a thinking strategy map for comparing and contrasting, which, they believed, represents a way to do this kind of thinking skillfully. This thinking strategy map, shown in Figure 3-1, incorporates a variant on the focus questions for skillful comparing and contrasting from Chapter 1 (Figure 1-4).

When students followed this map in each of the fourth-grade lessons, Ms. Williams was impressed with how that promoted the students to think about the similarities and differences they uncovered in a way that ultimately led them to draw significant and insightful conclusions. Ms. Williams wants to do the same thing in her seventh-grade social studies class.

Figure 3-1. Thinking Strategy Map for Open Compare and Contrast[1]

Open Compare and Contrast

1. How are the two things similar?
2. How are they different?
3. What similarities and differences seem significant?
4. What categories or pattern do you see in the significant differences?
5. What interpretation or conclusion is suggested by the significant similarities of differences?

She starts to think about what she will do in this lesson. Perhaps it should be organized a little differently from the ones that she has observed.

At the same time, Carol Chen, a first-grade teacher who has also participated in these observations, is grappling with a similar question. This thinking strategy map is too sophisticated for her students, but she doesn't want to fall back on simply asking them to list some similarities and differences. She is convinced that she, too, can challenge her students to think about the similarities and differences that they uncover and draw some insightful conclusions, and that she can make that happen in her classroom by using some of the techniques of direct instruction. How can she engage her students beyond just listing similarities and differences in a way that will not overwhelm them? Ms. Chen starts to think about what she will do in this lesson.

These teachers are grappling with the question of which techniques of direct instruction in thinking skills they can use to provide effective instruction in skillful thinking. Any teacher who sets out to design a lesson that infuses direct instruction in skillful thinking into content instruction will grapple with the same sorts of questions. It is important for teachers like Ms. Williams and Ms. Chen to know what their options are and what we know about the effectiveness of the techniques from which they can choose. We will start this chapter by looking at what each of these teachers decides, then discuss the basic techniques of direct instruction in skillful thinking from which they chose.

Planning Direct Instruction in Skillful Comparing and Contrasting

Seventh-Grade Social Studies—Ms. Williams

After some thought, Ms. Williams decides that she will ask her students to compare and contrast Europe and Asia in the 19th century, which they have already been studying. She wants to work with them on the theme of colonial exploration and conquest. She wants this lesson to yield an understanding of these ideas but to primarily be a means by which she can introduce her students to ways of extending comparing and contrasting so that they will be led to draw insightful conclusions from the similarities and differences they uncover. She needs to think about how she will structure the lesson so that they will get in the habit of asking and trying to answer the final three questions on the thinking strategy map in Figure 3-1 whenever they compare and contrast anything. Should she present the students with the thinking strategy map for skillful comparing and contrasting, or should she try to draw it out of them? When they apply this skillful thinking procedure to the content she wants them to think about—Europe and Asia—just how should she do it? Should they work individually or team up? Should she give them reference material to work from, or should she give them time to research information in the school library or on the Internet? How should they share their results? Should they discuss their conclusions with each other before they settle on them, or should they draw final conclusions on their own?

Ms. Williams settles on an approach. She will ask the students what questions they ask when they compare and contrast things outside school. She will pose a hypothetical example—shopping for breakfast cereal—in which they are comparing and contrasting two different packaged cereals. Then she will develop a thinking strategy map for skillful comparing and contrasting from these questions, introducing the language of the thinking skill as she does this. She will post a written version of this thinking strategy map on the wall of her classroom in preparation for the next stage of the lesson.

As the lesson progresses and the students review briefly what they've been studying about Europe and Asia, she will ask the students to use this thinking strategy map on their own to compare and contrast the two continents in the 19th century. She will provide some additional written in-class reference material to support this. This activity will be enhanced by the use of a graphic organizer (Figure 3-2) that she bases on the other compare-and-contrast lessons she has observed.[2]

Each student will a get photocopied blank of this graphic organizer and will be asked to work on it individually. When the class comes together, the students will share and can borrow ideas they hear from other students. As they do this, Ms. Williams will develop a PowerPoint slide of the graphic organizer that reflects the ideas that are shared in the class. Then, when she moves them to the last question on the thinking strategy map and is satisfied that they are writing conclusions based on the important similarities and differences recorded on her PowerPoint slide, she plans to do something dramatic. She will engage them in an activity called "Think-Pair-Share,"[3] in which they react to each other's conclusions in pairs by asking questions of clarification, extension, or challenge to help

Figure 3-2. Compare-and-Contrast Graphic Organizer

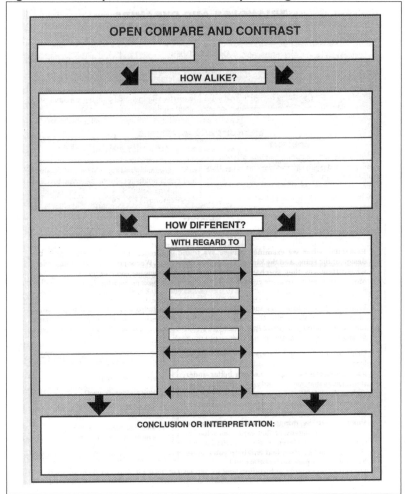

each other, and then are given the opportunity to rewrite their conclusions. Next the students will be asked to volunteer to read their conclusions to the class. Ms. Williams thinks that this will work very well with her students—many of them are very vocal and like to speak in class. She thinks that they will be proud of their conclusions and that this activity will bring that out.

Ms. Williams also intends to weave into this activity the identification and practice of two important habits of mind that she will talk about at the outset: thinking interdependently and communicating with accuracy and precision. She wants to help them to identify Think-Pair-Share as a good technique for the former, and she will raise that question when they've completed that activity. She will also ask them to reflect on what the volunteers who read their conclusions to the class did to make sure that they were communicating these ideas to the class with clarity and precision. So that she doesn't break the flow of that activity, she will wait until it is completed to raise that question. The students in her classroom have already been introduced to the various mental habits that enhance their thinking, and she welcomes this opportunity to help them practice and refine some of these.

When this is completed, Ms. Williams intends to end the lesson by asking the students to step back from what they have been doing and discuss with each other in teams of two whether this way of doing compare-and-contrast is better than just listing similarities and differences, and why. She will refer them back to the thinking strategy map they used to guide them through the activity. Based on this, she will ask them to develop a plan for comparing and contrasting that they will use next time they do this kind of thinking in the classroom. She will have them enter this in their thinking logs in their classroom computer notebooks. She will also engage them in a brief discussion of how the two habits of mind stressed in the activity manifested themselves. Ms. Williams has chosen to engage her students in this episode of reflective metacognition because of the extensive research she's read about that shows how such reflection enhances the development of self-directed skillful thinking on the part of students.

First Grade—Ms. Chen

Ms. Chen opts for a different scenario. She decides to use a simpler version of the procedure for skillful comparing and contrasting. She will not go back to asking her students to simply note similarities and differences. She will prompt them to determine important similarities and differences, but, realizing that even the word *conclusion* is too much for her students at this stage, she will ask them to think about what their similarities and differences "show" about what they are comparing and contrasting. She chooses two stories that she will read to her students: "Goldilocks and the Three Bears" and "Deep in the Forest," a story about a bear that gets into the house of a family and does pretty much what Goldilocks does in the house of the three bears. She will use a simplified thinking strategy map, which she will post and read to the students, illustrating its use with simple things in the classroom like their chairs and her chair. It consists of the questions shown in Figure 3-3.

Ms. Chen also modifies the graphic organizer that was used in the demonstration lessons on comparing and contrasting in which she was involved. She likes the idea of using a graphic organizer, but her children can't yet write, so she will make a large one and post it in front of the classroom, and then write on it what they say in the discussion. The one she's seen is somewhat impersonal, she thinks, so she uses the one shown in Figure 3-4.

Figure 3-3. Primary-Grade Thinking Strategy Map for Compare and Contrast[4]

> **Compare and Contrast**
> 1. How are the things alike?
> 2. How are they different?
> 3. What does this show?

Ms. Chen also decides that she will not have the students work to-gether in groups. When she has tried that in the past with these students she has had a hard time keeping them on task. So she will conduct this lesson with the whole group of students sitting on the rug in front of her. As she reads to the students, she will make sure that she uses the language of the thinking skill from the thinking strategy map and the graphic orga-nizer, so that the students become familiar with it.

Figure 3-4. First-Grade Graphic Organizer

Ms. Chen has just been working with her students on three of the important mental habits that enhance learning. Listening to others with understanding and empathy is one that she has been emphasizing, so she decides that she will make this lesson an opportunity for students to practice this. One activity in which she will engage students in order to reinforce this idea is to periodically ask to repeat what they hear other students say when they report. She will stress that in order to do this they need to listen to what the otehr students say very carefully, as if the ideas were their own.

Finally, Ms. Chen intends to go over the name of the thinking they are doing—comparing and contrasting—and ask the students to repeat the questions they were given for this kind of thinking. She believes that once they master this simplified version of skillful comparing and contrasting, it will be relatively easy for them to move toward the use of the more sophisticated thinking strategy map that the teachers who conducted the workshop showed the teachers in her school.

Direct Instruction

These are two quite different classroom scenarios that fall under the general heading of teaching students a type of skillful thinking using the techniques of direct instruction. These teachers illustrate how, within the parameters of direct instruction in a thinking skill, there are a variety of techniques, tools, and classroom strategies from which a teacher can choose. In this chapter we want to present a comprehensive and systematic look at these various techniques, as well as inform you of what we know, primarily from research, that supports their use. We will present this material in a more formal style than that of most of the rest of this book—a style that one would expect for a study of educational methods and their foundations in educational research—so that it will be easy to grasp the important distinctions that should be made and find the references that support these techniques.

As originally practiced, direct instruction focused especially on subject matter. It consisted of clearly defined learning objectives; highly structured, sequential, didactic, teacher-directed instruction in a specific subject; and of continual content coverage driven by many (often low-level) teacher questions with immediate feedback and continual monitoring of student progress.[5] For example, a science teacher might start a lesson by saying, "Today we are going to learn about the different forms of energy. I will show you how you can distinguish them and the basic principles whereby they produce energy." We all experienced lessons like these when we went to school, so it is not too hard to recognize this technique as a basic instructional norm.

As it has evolved in practice over the years, however, direct instruction has been applied to a wider range of content, including skills of all kinds—for example, in mathematics, writing, artistic composition, scientific investigation, carpentry, and athletics. As a result, some of its original features have diminished in importance, and new features have been introduced. Today, direct instruction has essentially come to mean instruction that (a) has clear, explicit learning goals, (b) focuses on a specific task or content, (c) makes explicit the steps in a learning task, (d) employs carefully structured learning activities, (e) provides extensive practice, and (f) provides continual monitoring of student progress with immediate corrective feedback.[6] Direct instruction in skillful thinking applies these principles specifically to instruction in thinking skills and habits of mind. It is a teaching strategy that seems to mimic the adage that "What is not taught is not learned."[7]

Essential Elements of Direct Instruction in Skillful Thinking

Applying principles of effective teaching,[8] direct instruction makes a specific thinking skill and/or mental habit a "subject" to be learned. As Ms. Fischer started the lesson on the kestrel, her instruction was focused explicitly and continually on the procedures of skillful parts–whole thinking and of a specific mental habit. Ms. Williams and Ms. Chen intend to do the same thing for skillful comparing and contrasting. As these teachers move through the school year, they will emphasize these procedures until students can demonstrate that they can execute or apply them spontaneously with a high degree of proficiency on their own. Their use of direct instruction is typical of the practice by teachers in general. In effective direct instruction, teachers conduct a series of lessons over a period during which, for each skill and/or habit of mind selected for instruction, they move students from an explicit introduction through scaffolded and cued practice to self-initiated, self-directed, and self-correcting application in a variety of contexts. In so doing these teachers accomplish the following:

- Focus student learning and instruction continually and explicitly on the skill or mental habit to be learned in each introductory and scaffolded practice lesson
- Structure each introductory and practice lesson to, at minimum, preview the target skill or habit of mind; engage students in applying it several times; make explicit how to apply it; and review and bridge how, when, and where to use it
- Continually make clear and precise, by explanation, demonstration or modeling, and student reflection, the step-by-step procedures

and rules or heuristics by which the skill or habit of mind is carried out

- Teach any declarative knowledge that informs or guides application of the skill (e.g., criteria established by experts for making judgments, such as those about the credibility of a source, strength of an argument, or bias)
- Teach the value of using the skill or mental habit and how it enables thinking and learning
- Make explicit the conditions, tasks, and situational cues where its use is appropriate
- Teach students how to monitor and assess the application of a thinking skill or habit of mind and how to deal with obstacles to its effective application
- Provide immediate and corrective or elaborative feedback to students about their application of a skill or habit of mind.[9]

Stages in the Direct Instruction of Specific Types of Skillful Thinking

Ms. Fischer does only some of the above in her lesson on the kestrel, because her lesson was introductory in nature. Obviously her lesson would be followed up with a series of guided and then independent practice lessons in the same type of skillful thinking she had introduced. In these she would emphasize the use of the same thinking procedure. This would provide a bridge from the specific example she used in the lesson to other examples for which skillful parts–whole thinking can be used to gain insight.

This type of instruction is referred to as *direct*, in part, because throughout the initial lesson and in parts of subsequent lessons it focuses student attention *explicitly* on the skill and/or mental habit to be learned. This focus is necessary to eliminate or minimize interference from three sources: unfamiliar subject matter to which the skill or mental habit is being applied, the emotion or affect attached by learners to that subject matter, and any recently introduced skill or habit.[10] Digressions from continued attention to the target skill or mental habit at this stage simply interrupt and interfere with learning that skill or habit.[11]

Subsequent thinking-skill lessons, however, put the students in the position of applying and reflecting on what they are being taught about how to do the kind of thinking in the lesson skillfully. This paves the way for additional lessons, which gradually decrease instructional attention to the skill or habit of mind while they increase attention to the content learning generated by the application of the skill, especially as students become more proficient and independent in applying the skill or associated habits of mind. In these guided practice lessons, instructional attention commonly shifts back and forth from how and why a skill or mental habit is operationalized to the subject-matter knowledge and understanding developed in the process of its application. Eventually, in skill lessons in which students are able to apply a newly learned skill or habit of mind effectively on their own, virtually full attention can be given to content learning. In direct instruction in a thinking skill or habit of mind, the focus of instruction thus gradually shifts away from the target skill or mental habit and its attributes to subject-matter learning, as proficiency in applying the skill or mental habit increases.

It is this gradual realignment of the contexts in which we teach content—to include the expectation of the use of an expanded repertoire of thinking skills by the students as they learn, and not just results like those in the kestrel lesson—that gives thinking-based learning its power to enrich and deepen our students' understanding of the subject-matter content we teach them.

It is important to note what direct instruction of a thinking skill or habit of mind is *not*. It is not lecturing about a skill or habit of mind. It is not directing students to do these only one way, the "right" or teacher's way. It is not requiring students to repeatedly apply a newly introduced skill or mental habit without student reflection and self-assessment and continuing student and teacher corrective feedback. It is not drilling, reciting, and then testing and grading a final performance and going on to the next skill or habit of mind. Instead, direct instruction in skillful thinking is continual, explicit instruction in a thinking skill or habit of mind, from a detailed step-by-step or behavioral introduction through frequent repeated scaffolded or mediated applications that provide opportunities for practice and reflection. Over time, these lessons become more intermittent and consist of prompted or cued applications, gradually merging into student self-initiated and self-directed applications in combination with other thinking skills and habits of mind in a variety of contexts and subjects.

If we return to Ms. Fischer's lesson described in Chapter 2 and set it in this broader instructional context, we can see that it is a strong beginning, but it is just a beginning. It now requires continual follow-up, in which she gradually phases out the instructional props provided about parts–whole analysis and the habit of thinking with clarity and precision with an eye to the students ultimately directing themselves in thinking skillfully. This means that Ms. Fischer will follow this lesson with others that provide more practice in parts–whole analysis for the students, based on deep prompted metacognitive reflection on their part about the most effective, efficient, and productive way to engage in this type of skillful thinking; its importance; when it is called for; and how to plan to do it when the need arises.

Research indicates that although it may take 4 or 5 instructional lessons for some students to develop mastery of a cognitive skill, it may take others 50 or more practice lessons.[12] Direct instruction in a single skill or habit of mind must be continual over an extended period. The exact number of lessons required varies, depending on the complexity of the skill or mental habit being taught, the complexity of the subject matter in which it is applied, the ability levels and maturity of the students, and the teacher's knowledge and expertise in applying, demonstrating, and explaining the attributes and application of the skill or habit.

Although the practice of a newly introduced skill or habit of mind is crucial to the success of direct instruction in the tools of skillful thinking and mental habits, this practice is neither mass nor mindless repetition of skill or mental-habit tasks. Rather, in direct instruction, student practice consists of mindful application: Each step in the procedure or behavior being applied is intentionally selected and precisely carried out by the student; made explicit and assessed for quality as or immediately after it is completed; perhaps revised; and then applied again based on the corrective or informative feedback generated by each preceding application. In fact, skill or mental-habit information can often be provided in advance of its application, so as to "feed forward" to inform and organize that application. Although initial practice applications are highly structured, or scaffolded, by teachers and sometimes by students, later applications may be increasingly more intermittent and are prompted or cued rather than highly structured, as students develop increased expertise in applying the skill or habit.[13]

Strategies and techniques like those described here may be used with a wide variety of students at any grade level and in any subject to teach any thinking skill or habit of mind. These lessons may vary in length, from 15 to 20 minutes to 50 minutes or more, depending primarily on the complexity of the thinking skill or mental habit being taught as well as where the students are in the process of learning it. In some cases these lessons will have to be split into two class periods, and some have even been developed into short units. Attention to the skill or mental habit customarily takes longer in introductory lessons and in lessons scaffolding practice than in cued practice lessons.

After an introductory lesson, a teacher may schedule a series of preplanned lessons with scaffolded and then cued practice on the same skill and/or habit of mind, gradually decreasing instructional intervention as practice becomes more intermittent, and finally fading out instruction altogether as the desired level of independent proficiency is achieved. To ensure the achievement of these goals, assessments and documented observations of the application of targeted thinking skills and habits of mind of student thinking should be collected.

Regardless of the strategies employed, the lessons that follow a detailed introductory lesson do not all have to be as long as the initial lesson. However, in direct instruction, all lessons in a single skill or mental habit should (a) preview and review the target skill or habit being taught, (b) engage students in applying it at least several times, (c) engage students in reflecting on and verbalizing how and why they applied it, (d) have students share their procedures with each other and provide each other feedback, and (e) have students summarize or revise how they applied it and what they have learned about its application.[14]

Teaching to Transfer

One of the most important aspects of direct instruction in a thinking skill or habit of mind is teaching students how to apply a skill or habit of mind that has been mastered in one subject or context to another subject or context. Thinking skills and habits of mind are often tied to the context in which they are initially learned or first applied. They rarely transfer on their own, and students do not automatically transfer them beyond that context.[15] *Direct instruction in thinking skills and habits of mind must thus continue beyond teaching in one subject to teaching their mastery in a variety of subjects.* Recognizing the importance of this can help to broaden the kinds of thinking tasks we give students to help them practice a thinking skill after a series of introductory and guided practice lessons in its initial subject-matter context.

It usually takes a number of lessons in the same type of subject-matter content as the introductory lesson—what have been called "near" transfer lessons—for students to become proficient enough to generalize the application of a skill to a new body of content. Although no exact number can be given, this is important, especially in high school subjects. Therefore, once a thinking skill and/or a behavioral pattern that manifests an important mental habit is mastered in one subject area, it is important to introduce variety in the kinds of content-related applications in which the students are asked to engage. In elementary school, a single teacher who teaches across the curriculum can accomplish this rather easily. In secondary school, however, this requires collaboration and coordination by teachers who teach in different subject areas. Whoever engages in such continuing instruction, and whatever their content focus is, continuity in direct instructional techniques is essential. At the very least, the following focal points should be brought out in such follow-up activities:

1. Continue to have the students make and use explicit step-by-step procedures, heuristics, or behaviors by which these skills and mental habits are applied.
2. Use the same language of thinking skills and habits of mind consistently from introductory lessons through transfer applications in all subjects.

3. Scaffold student and cue student application when reintroducing a skill or habit of mind in new subjects until the students demonstrate their ability to apply them on their own.

However, it takes more than simply conducting lessons on thinking skills and habits of mind in a variety of contexts to produce lasting transfer. To teach effectively for transfer—to have our instruction result in students' internalizing and modifying the procedures for applying the thinking skills taught and developing them to the fullest, and for the behaviors that manifest the important generic mental habits we described above to actually become habitual—students must come to value the behaviors and commit themselves to engaging in them whenever the need arises. This requires repeated engagement with their own thinking through well-planned metacognitive activities. Through such activities, students reach a point at which they can describe how they engage in a given type of skillful thinking, reflect on whether and why it is worthwhile engaging in such thinking, and develop their own plans for doing so, based on the experience they have had in the classroom with this thinking skill. Thus, teaching for transfer fits into direct instruction in thinking skills and habits of mind, through teachers prompting students with important metacognitive activities in these lessons. When this happens, students move from teacher dependency in engaging in skillful thinking to taking charge of their own thinking as they practice additional applications of the skill and behaviors of the important mental habits. We will discuss the techniques that teachers can use to accomplish this key phase of direct instruction in the next chapter.

There are three important goals of teaching for the transfer of skillful thinking and mental habits: (a) helping students to identify a variety of contexts—and the use of each—in which the skill should be appropriately applied or the mental habit manifested, (b) enabling students to generalize the procedures by which they enact a skill beyond the limits or conditions imposed by any one content field, and (c) providing students with opportunities to practice these transfer activities with self-reflection and teacher guidance so that they get used to extending the skillful thinking and mental habits they use to these contexts.

Teachers work to accomplish these goals in two basic ways. First, they can incorporate some transfer activities in every lesson they teach on a specific skill or mental habit. In previewing the skill or habit of mind at the beginning of any lesson, for example, they can report (or have students volunteer) instances in the past where the students could have applied the kind of thinking they are working on or the behaviors that manifest the habits of mind that they are developing. A teacher might ask: "What are some circumstances in your life when skillful parts–whole analysis might have been helpful?" or "Describe a time in your life when persisting paid off for you," or "Under what conditions have you found it most difficult to manage your impulsivity?"

After the students respond, the teacher might ask them to describe what it would have been like to make those specific decisions this way or to manage their impulsivity in such conditions. After the main parts of any lesson on a skill or mental habit have been completed, teachers can repeat these prompts but also prompt the students to volunteer other instances in which the application of the skill or habit of mind could appropriately be applied in the future. For example, a teacher might ask: "Besides working through this problem in school, what are some specific instances in your life when you might need to practice persistence in your thinking?" or "In what contexts in your life outside school would it be important to employ the kind of reasoning used in skillful decision making?" or "As you reflect on what you learned today about skillful parts–whole analysis, where might you find it useful to engage in this kind of thinking in other subjects you are studying here in school?"

Teachers can also use a more concentrated direct approach to teaching transfer. They can select transfer examples themselves and present them as contexts in which to apply a thinking skill and/or application of a habit of mind. In this case they would ask students to work on some of these examples, in which the same thinking skill or mental habit is appropriately applied, after the lesson is complete, the next day, or in the next week or month. This could be accompanied with a growing list, developed by the students, of contexts different from the one in which they initially learned the skill and mental habit but to which these can be applied.

Thus the teacher should continually alert students to some of the cues or opportunities that call for the transfer of the skill or habit of mind beyond the immediate lesson, subject, or context, thus "bridging"[16] it to future contexts where it can be applied. These opportunities can be made real by using some of them for practice.

The literature on teaching for transfer identifies two kinds of transfer contexts: those involving near transfer and those involving far transfer. *Near transfer* involves applying a skill or habit of mind in a subject or context that is quite similar to the one in which it was originally introduced and taught. *Far transfer* involves applying a skill or mental habit in a subject or context quite different from any previously encountered setting or subject. Both are important.

Below are some of the near-transfer and far-transfer subjects that have been used by teachers, including Ms. Fischer, who have taught parts–whole lessons. These are activities in which the students engaged anywhere from 1 day to 2 months after the initial lesson(s) introducing them to skillful decision making had concluded.

Near-transfer opportunities include the following (initial lesson is listed in parentheses):[17]

- In social studies you are studying complex societies. Pick a particular example of a society (e.g., ancient Rome) to demonstrate your skill at analyzing parts–whole relationships. Explain the function and roles of the different components that sustained the society over time. Keep at it until you are satisfied that you have produced a good analysis—be persistent! (U.S. government, grade 6)
- List the parts of a dictionary. Then apply your skill at parts–whole analysis to determine how its parts make the dictionary such a useful aid to learning and understanding. Work together with other students on this and make it a real cooperative effort. (Parts of a story, grade 6)
- Select a flowering plant and analyze its parts using skillful parts–whole thinking. (The kestrel, grade 7)
- Perhaps the most important parts of living things are their cells. Living cells are the basic building blocks of all living things. As you know from your studies, living cells have parts that function together to make a cell able to do what it does to sustain the life of the body it supports. Use parts–whole analysis to identify the parts of a cell and how they play this role. Write out your analysis clearly and precisely so that you can help others to understand exactly how cells play this role. (The human organism, grade 12)

Far-transfer opportunities include the following:[18]

- In this classroom what different resources and conditions make it possible for you to learn? How do they all work together to make this happen? (Pots and pans, grade 2)
- Apply the skill of parts–whole analysis to investigate the relationship among teachers, students, staff, the principal, and members of the community. How do all these groups work together for the good of your school and the students in it? Use everything you already know about your school but do not hesitate to get additional information if you need it. (Parts of a story, grade 4)
- Imagine that you are stranded on a desert island and want to make a device for signaling passing airplanes. The only materials you have are a few long branches, a few pieces of clothing, some rocks, some matches, and a mirror. How could you put all or some of these materials together to construct a signaling device? Explain how each part would function. Be inventive and be prepared to construct something unusual. (The kestrel, grade 7)
- In art you've been creating paintings to express certain moods like happiness or sadness. Applying your skill at analyzing parts–whole relationships, examine the parts of your painting and figure out how your painting expresses the mood you chose through its

parts. Take your time before you draw any conclusions about these relationships. (The bar graph, grade 9)
- Just as many natural things make up complex systems in which the parts interact (as in the human body), so do many human-made objects. Identify some complex human-made objects or systems (e.g., a jet plane, an automobile, a computer). Pick one of these and do a parts–whole analysis of it. When you're done, make a diagram to show the parts' interaction. Be sure to consult as many others as you need to get the information. (The human organism, grade 12)

To summarize, once students have demonstrated proficiency in applying a newly taught skill or habit of mind in one subject, setting, or type of media, teachers can and should provide direct instruction in how to apply that skill or mental habit in a new subject, setting, or medium. This can be accomplished by using the techniques described above to introduce it in the new context. Teachers should always provide scaffolded or cued practice in applying a skill in this context; however, the degree to which scaffolding is provided will diminish as students become more quickly adept at applying the skill they are transferring. In addition, these new assignments should always emphasize any ways in which the new context requires modification of the skills or habits. Such transfer lessons may vary in length and complexity, depending on whether they require near or far transfer and on how complex the new content material is.

Continual instruction in a thinking skill or habit of mind—from explicit introduction through scaffolded, cued, and independent practice— serves two important purposes. First, it helps students to achieve highly proficient levels of performance in these thinking tools. Second, it makes such skillful thinking self-actuating and habitual.

The habit of thinking skillfully involves the following characteristics:

- *Valuing it*—choosing to employ a pattern of intellectual behaviors rather than other, less productive patterns. It means that we value one pattern of thinking over another, and therefore it implies conscious decision making about which pattern should be employed at this time.
- *Remaining alert to situations*—being sensitive to and perceiving opportunities for, and the appropriateness of, employing the pattern of behavior. There is an alertness to the contextual cues that signal this as an appropriate time and circumstance in which the employment of this pattern would be useful.
- *Being inclined to use it*—feeling a tendency or proclivity toward employing a pattern of intellectual behaviors in specific circumstances. Greater satisfaction and feelings of efficacy, power, and control are enjoyed when the behaviors are employed.

- *Applying capabilities*—using the basic skills, procedures, and capacities to carry through with the behaviors. A level of skillfulness is required to employ and execute the behaviors effectively over time.
- *Making a commitment*—constantly striving to reflect on and improve the performance of the pattern of intellectual behavior. As a result of each experience in which these behaviors are employed, the effects of their use are reflected upon, evaluated, modified, and carried forth to future applications.

Key Techniques for Direct Instruction in Skillful Thinking

We mentioned earlier that direct instruction benefits immensely from three basic teaching techniques. These are (a) making the skills and mental habits explicit, (b) scaffolding thinking practice, and (c) employing the language of thinking throughout a lesson.

Making Skills and Habits of Mind Explicit

To improve the quality of anything, we need to know two things: first, its present state, and second, its ideal state. To improve the skillfulness of student thinking, teachers and students need to know exactly how students carry out their thinking and how these same operations are carried out by "experts"—those with a demonstrably high degree of proficiency and effectiveness. Comparison of the two can reveal gaps, dysfunctions, and other weaknesses, if any, in the present state of student thinking and disclose what may be done to fill the gaps, correct the dysfunctions, and generally improve proficiency in that thinking. To accomplish this, teachers employing direct instruction continually seek to make explicit how student thinking seems to proceed now and how it might proceed if it were done more expertly, and then to help students close this gap.

Making a procedure or behavior for a thinking skill or habit of mind explicit (such as parts–whole analysis or communicating with clarity and precision) means (a) breaking it into its component parts (i.e., the steps in the thinking process or behaviors by which we exhibit a mental habit and the rules and heuristics we apply), and (b) identifying these parts accurately, clearly, and precisely.

As noted in Chapter 1, the major components of a thinking skill include the procedures and rules (heuristics) by which the skill is applied and the conditional and declarative knowledge that informs the application of these procedures. A habit of mind consists of the behaviors that demonstrate productive generic mental activity as well as the associated knowledge and rules that inform and ground these behaviors. We saw examples of both of these in the thinking strategy map for Ms. Fischer's parts–whole analysis, and in the description of the procedures used to effectively communicate the thinking with clarity and precision. Identifying the components of these procedures and behaviors means articulating with precision and accuracy the features of each discrete part and the relationships of these to one another and to the whole operation.

The problem in making skills and habits of mind explicit is that they are invisible. Their inner workings cannot be seen or touched or held. Nor can these inner workings be precisely or accurately inferred from their products. Thus, to make student thinking explicit, teachers must make it visible by helping students to (a) become aware of what they do mentally to carry out a thinking task or behaviorally demonstrate a habit of mind, and (b) verbalize what they recall or identify doing in each instance.[19] When we help students to do this, they gain more conscious, deliberate control over their own thinking and can more easily modify it. What the students verbalize can be recorded on overhead transparencies, graphic organizers, mind maps, and other similar teaching aids. It can also be put into a computer word-processing program and, if mobility is important, recorded on CDs or memory sticks. When the students hear, see, and reflect on what appear to be better—more efficient, effortless, and productive—ways of applying a skill or mental habit (whether demonstrated by a teacher, a peer, or a so-called expert), students tend to incorporate these into their own thinking behaviors. In time their thinking becomes more skillful and their habits of thinking more mindful.

Six basic techniques can be used to make thinking more explicit in the classroom.

Thinking Strategy Maps

Thinking strategy maps are only one way to explicitly represent a procedure for engaging in a specific kind of thinking process to do it skillfully, but they do so in a very important way. They represent such procedures by casting them as a sequence of questions that are designed to focus our attention and prompt us to specific kinds of thinking that, step by step, will lead us to a natural completion of the thinking process. We call them maps because they guide us through these thinking processes. Their function in instruction is to make sure that our students learn to attend to important mental moves that they ordinarily might not think of whenever they do the kind of thinking in question.

One of the major goals of direct instruction in skillful thinking is to help students get in the habit of, for example, asking and answering the questions on the thinking strategy maps when it is appropriate to do so. Thinking strategy maps play a defining role in this kind of instruction, but these maps should not be taken as "written in stone." They are *suggested* procedures that students should follow to make their thinking more skillful. We should also prompt them to think about whether these maps need any revision or refinement. Despite the maps' appearance, they need to be used with flexibility and in a spirit of open reflection.

Modeling

Modeling is best suited to making visible and explicit the thinking of individuals who are especially proficient in applying a particular skill or habit of mind. It consists of demonstrating, step by step, how to carry out a thinking skill or demonstrate a habit of mind, explaining *as it is applied* how each step or behavior is done and why it is appropriate to employ. If teachers or students are proficient in a particular skill or habit of mind; know in detail the mental procedures, rules, and behaviors by which these are enacted; and can communicate them clearly and precisely to their students, they can model these themselves.

Written or recorded examples or transcripts of experts carrying out certain skills can also be analyzed in class to infer the elements of the procedures or behaviors being applied. Teachers can present and explain expert thinking procedures identified by many researchers in the professional literature.[20] Students can then attempt, with teacher guidance as needed, to replicate the application of these modeled procedures or behaviors or employ them as springboards for improving how they apply these skills or habits.

Oral Use of the Language of Thinking Skills and Habits of Mind

Oral language use is a common technique of teachers who practice direct instruction in thinking skills, and it was exemplified in Ms. Fischer's parts–whole lesson. Using the language of a thinking skill or a habit of mind cues students into the procedures and behaviors that have been identified with these skills[21] and mental habits. This requires accurate and precise use of the language of thinking skills and habits of mind by the teacher. It occurs in contexts in which teachers describe how people actually engage in various types of thinking like decision making as well as in contexts in which teachers guide students in how they might engage in these kinds of thinking skillfully. Ms. Fischer used precise language in the lesson on the kestrel when she guided her students through the activity of describing how the parts of this bird contribute to its hunting ability—for example, when she said straightforward things like, "What is the function of the parts?" and "How do these parts work together to make this bird a good hunter?"

Scaffolding Student Practice With Explicit Skill Guides

Thinking skills can also be made explicit while students practice applying them, without direct teacher intervention or direction. This can be accomplished by providing each student with a printed step-by-step outline of a procedure for executing the skill to which they can refer as they do the skill task. Research indicates that at least three kinds of skill scaffolds prove useful for this purpose: process structured questions, procedural checklists, and skill graphic organizers.[22]

Thinking Aloud

When used to its maximum advantage, thinking aloud can be effective in making student thinking visible and explicit and also in presenting the explicit thinking of an expert. One way of using this technique is to have one member of a student pair report aloud to the other what he or she is thinking as he or she carries out a specific skill-using task. The partner records the mental moves as they are reported and prompts the "thinker" to stay on task and to keep reporting when he or she remains silent. Students then switch roles and complete another task applying the same skill and, if desired, compare their thinking-aloud records with a transcript of an expert executing the same thinking-skill task. They may repeat this process until they have articulated a proficient procedure for applying the given skill. This technique allows students to generate a trail of their thinking and assess and refine it in comparison to the thinking of an expert. This in turn enables them to spot errors in their own thinking, to identify more effective ways to do it from the thinking of the expert, and thus to correct or revise their own thinking. Although this technique might seem at times to interrupt a student's application of his or her thinking or to hold to a line of thinking on which he or she has embarked, it has proven especially useful in remediating and improving on mathematical and analytical problem-solving deficiencies.[23]

Metacognitive Reflection

Metacognitive reflection is especially useful in helping students to make their own thinking visible by engaging them in reflecting on and analyzing what they believe they did mentally to carry out a thinking skill or mental habit.[24] One common process for accomplishing this is to have students individually attempt to recall how, step by step, they carried out a just-completed skill-based thinking task and then share with a partner as clearly as possible what they believe they did and why. Then, several volunteers share with the class the procedures they verbalized to their partners, and the class as a whole analyzes the volunteered procedures to identify potentially useful steps and rules to follow the next time application of the skill is required. This is not a search for the "right way" to apply a skill or mental habit, but simply an attempt to make explicit a variety of ways to do so. Although it takes some time for students to become comfortable doing this, there is no better method for stimulating students to articulate and verbalize their own thinking and to discover other, often better, ways of doing it, which they usually move quickly to adopt.[25] This technique was also used by Ms. Fischer in the sample lesson presented here.

Direct instruction in skillful thinking seeks to make student as well as expert thinking explicit by helping students to become conscious of and articulate as precisely as possible the component parts of a thinking skill and then compare their approaches to those of experts applying the same skill. By doing this, teachers can enable students to become more conscious in the control of their own thinking, less impulsive and more purposeful, and make it more amenable to revision and improvement. Any of these techniques can be used in direct instruction to accomplish these goals. You are invited to reflect on Ms. Fischer's lesson on the kestrel in Chapter 2 to find where they occur.

Scaffolding Thinking-Skill Practice and Application

Although scaffolding is one way of making a thinking-skill procedure explicit, it plays another important role in the direct instruction of thinking. It also structures a skill by using experience. This structure is most useful to novices who aren't familiar with what to do next.

The *sequenced list of questions* presented by Ms. Fischer in her lesson contains key steps in applying the skill of parts–whole analysis. As students answer each question, they actually move through the steps in applying this skill. A checklist of the steps themselves makes them even more explicit, as was shown in Figure 2-8. Students can apply the skill, checking off each step as they complete it. Because a *checklist* presents each move as a step in doing the skill, students are not only made explicitly aware of exactly what they are to do to apply the skill, they are also directed when to take each step. Thus, scaffolds like these allow students to concentrate on actually doing the task skillfully without having to simultaneously rely on their memory of what to do when, something quite difficult to do when just beginning to learn a procedure for skillful thinking. When students have access to personal classroom computers, having these checklists present on a split screen can serve this purpose well.

Thinking-skill *graphic organizers* like the ones presented in Chapter 2 are very useful as scaffolds because they cue the steps in a skill by providing visual prompts. This type of graphic presents a diagram or chart that shows, in the form of linked boxes or circles, the steps in a sequential procedure for carrying out a specific thinking skill. Arrows or numbers are sometimes used to indicate the direction of the steps as well as to correlate with material on a corresponding map or checklist. Many thinking-skill graphic organizers contain verbal prompts within their boxes or circles.[26]

The graphic organizer used in Ms. Fischer's lesson exemplifies this type of visual scaffold. As students respond to each prompt to fill in the graphic, they move through a given procedure for applying a specific skill. Written prompts can be gradually removed from these organizers as students become used to using them. Such graphics can be made for any skill for which authentic, "expert" steps have been identified.

Skill scaffolds are not ends in themselves but are useful aids in structuring and supporting the practice of skillful thinking. These three kinds of scaffolds—questions, checklists, and graphic organizers—are especially useful in the practice lessons immediately following the introduction of a new skill because they relieve students from having to seek teacher help or from struggling to recall "what to do next" in applying the skill successfully. Having these at hand while applying a recently introduced skill enables students to concentrate on developing an increasingly smooth performance in applying it. As they use a scaffold repeatedly, students begin to internalize the specifics of the procedure it presents. In time, just as with a scaffold used to shape the construction of a building, these learning aids can and should be discarded when students can carry out the skill with proficiency on their own.[27]

Some notes of caution regarding the use of these scaffolds are in order here. Not every set of questions, checklist, or graphic is a thinking-skill scaffold. Some question sets, checklists, and mental maps focus exclusively on subject-matter data collection or display. Others, like concept maps, present the results or products of thinking but not the mental procedures that produced those products. To be an authentic thinking-skill organizer, a scaffold must present each step in carrying out a specified thinking skill in the sequence in which these steps are applied by individuals who are proficient in applying the skill.

Scaffolds must also be recognizable as representing a specific skill by the students who use them. This means that the scaffold must use prompts that communicate precisely and accurately every step that constitutes an effective procedure for applying a skill. It must also use as prompts the language that was used in the initial classroom introduction of that skill. Scaffolds that use general words as step labels, such as *think* or ill-defined terms such as *examine*, or the name of the skill itself are dysfunctional and misleading, especially for novices. A useful rule for checking the authenticity of a graphic organizer for a thinking skill is that each step in applying the skill should have its own box.

Scaffolds should not be considered unchangeable. Nor should they remain exactly the same for every student in the class. If the function of these scaffolds is to support the development of student expertise, they should be modified and personalized by the students as they gain experience in applying a skill, because as individuals become more expert in their thinking, they alter how they are executing a skill—by compressing or elaborating some steps, dropping some steps, and/or adding new steps or heuristics. The scaffolding devices that students use to guide their application of a skill should thus be periodically revised to represent how their application of the skill changes as they become more proficient in applying it.

Using the Language of Thinking Skills and Habits of Mind in Instruction

Teachers use words that represent actions, products, and conditions to explain and direct various classroom tasks that involve thinking. Students also use words that represent these actions, conditions, and products as labels for storing them in memory, as cues for retrieving them from memory, as cues for structuring and applying them, and as tools for processing information. Not only does having a shared language of thinking and habits of mind help students to better understand the thinking of others, it also makes their own thinking more precise and more intentional.[28] In order to facilitate classroom discourse and to enable thinking and learning, it is important for teachers and students to use not only the same words but words that precisely and accurately denote the various aspects of thinking being taught and used, and to use these words consistently in classroom discourse.[29] Using a shared language of thinking is an integral part of direct instruction in skillful thinking.

If a teacher wants students to apply the skill of predicting, then rather than asking, "What will happen next?" it is much more helpful to students to use the accepted name of the skill in the question, as "What do you *predict* will happen next?" This is because the name of the thinking skill can trigger in the student's mind which stored thinking skill needs to be called up and applied and what procedures should be used. In teaching thinking skills and habits of mind, it is thus important to use words that denote clearly, precisely, and accurately the thinking operations, behaviors, actions, and procedures that constitute skillful thinking and that have been taught or used in the classroom, and to do so consistently across all courses, grade levels and subjects.

Not just any words will do, however. Self-invented or personalized prompts or labels for commonly used skills or habits of mind or their components are too idiosyncratic to have much meaning to those who do not share them. There are generally accepted words or terms that specifically denote cognitive procedures, actions, conditions, dispositions, and products that have been identified and are shared by specialists in cognition and in teaching thinking.[30] Exclusive, appropriate use of these words—the "language of thinking"—in classrooms brings accuracy and consistency to teaching, learning, and applying the tools of skillful thinking and will facilitate thinking in the larger world outside. Table 3-1 gives some examples.

You can also build the language of habits of mind into your classroom dialogue. Children of a very young age enjoy and can easily incorporate

Table 3-1. Examples of Using the Language of Thinking

Instead of saying	Use thinking terminology
"Let's look at these two pictures together to see how alike they are."	"Let's compare and contrast these two pictures."
"What do you think will happen when...?"	"What do you predict will happen when...?"
"How can you put into groups...?"	"How can you classify...?"
"Let's figure out what this problem is."	"Let's analyze this problem."
"What do you think might have happened if...?"	"What do you infer might have happened if...?"
"What did you think of this story?"	"What conclusions can you draw about this story?"
"How else could you use this?"	"What alternative ideas do you have about how to apply this?"
"Do you think that is the best alternative?"	"How do you evaluate these alternatives?"
"What is your report going to accomplish?"	"What goals do you have in mind for your report?"
"What do you think will happen if you use this approach?"	"What are some of the consequences that you predict will happen if you decide to use this approach?"
"How will you know your project is good enough?"	"What criteria will you apply to evaluate your project?"
"How do you know that's true?"	"What evidence do you have to support that?"
"What ideas do these data suggest?"	"What inferences might these data suggest?"
"Should I be convinced by what he says?"	"Is what he says supported by the reasons he gives?"
"How can you explain...?"	"How does your hypothesis explain...?"
"What thoughts about all things of that sort are you having?"	"What generalizations might you make?"
"What does the author take for granted in saying what he does?"	"On what assumptions is the author basing his claim?"

habits-of-mind terminology into their vocabulary. They think it's pretty sophisticated to use such terms as *impulsivity, interdependence,* and *persistence!* Table 3-2 gives some examples.

As children hear these cognitive terms in everyday use and experience the cognitive processes that accompany these labels, they internalize the words and use them as part of their own vocabulary. Teachers should give specific instruction in those cognitive functions so that students possess experiential meaning along with the terminology.[31]

Using the language of thinking means using the generally accepted terminology associated with thinking and cognition. It also means being precise and accurate in the language used to communicate about thinking. When this language is explained, taught, and used consistently by teachers and students, the quality of student thinking and subject matter learning sharply improves.[32]

Why Direct Instruction Is So Useful in Teaching Skillful Thinking

Teaching the tools of skillful thinking and habits of mind through direct instruction is, in our judgment, by far the most practical and productive way to improve the quality of student thinking and thus of learning. The continuing use of the strategies and techniques of direct instruction can accelerate the development of skilled thinking performances by enabling teachers and students to detect and remediate errors in the procedures, behaviors, and knowledge that inform and guide the application of important thinking skills.[33] Using this approach, teachers can then introduce students to more effective and more expert procedures than they now use to apply these skills and mental habits. When this teaching approach is infused in subject-matter courses it enables students to know and apply these thinking tools to achieve valued subject-matter learning

Table 3-2. Habits of Mind

Instead of saying	Use thinking terminology
"Don't give up on thinking this through!"	"Persist in your thinking!"
"Are you sure you are getting it clear in your mind?"	"Let's strive for accuracy and precision by checking..."
"How do you think John felt?"	"If you were to empathize with John..."

goals.[34] Even more significant, as researchers and specialists in education and cognition have repeatedly stated, teaching thinking skills in subject-matter courses improves student academic achievement as well as the quality of their thinking.[35]

Although it might not at first appear to do so, direct instruction of thinking skills and habits of mind in subject-matter courses also saves teaching and learning time. Direct instruction does initially take some time away from content coverage, but students usually achieve a deeper understanding of subject matter than they would otherwise. More important, in the long run, instruction in thinking skills up front makes more time available later for students to use these skills and habits of mind independently without teacher assistance or remediation, so teaching and learning can eventually concentrate more exclusively on subject-matter learning. Research indicates that in those subject-matter classes where thinking skills are explicitly taught, students achieve higher scores on end-of-course subject-matter assessments than do those students in the same course who did not receive instruction in these skills.[36]

Finally, direct instruction in the tools of skillful thinking enhances the self-efficacy of students. As we described in Chapter 1, many teachers, textbooks, standards, and tests often put students in a no-win situation by assigning learning tasks that require the use of complex thinking, without teaching students the skills they need to complete these tasks successfully. However, by making thinking skills and habits of mind the subjects of continued learning, teachers show an obvious commitment—one that students very much appreciate—to help students master the skills and habits they need to achieve the content learning goals assigned to them. Moreover, the increased student proficiency in skillful thinking that results from such instruction enables students to build an experiential record of success on teacher tests and other measures of learning—what educator Albert Bandura calls "enhanced mastery."[37] The record of success derived from such instruction gives students a greater self confidence in their abilities to engage successfully in future tasks that requires the use of these tools. This in turn enhances student willingness and motivation to tackle more complex and challenging subject-matter tasks and to engage in the subject learning desired by most teachers. Direct instruction in thinking skills and habits of mind thus gives value to learning content and improves the kinds of thinking that are demanded for successful academic performances by both teachers and high-stakes assessments.

Using the strategies and techniques of direct instruction to make student thinking more skillful gives greater value to learning subject matter, increases student motivation to learn the skills and the mental habits, and increases the self-efficacy of students. This leads to higher academic achievement as well as more skillful thinking. What more could students, teachers, or parents want?

Notes

1. Swartz, R., & Parks, S. (1994). *Infusing critical and creative thinking into content instruction: A lesson design handbook for the elementary grades.* Pacific Grove, CA: Critical Thinking, p. 102.
2. Ibid., p. 103.
3. Ibid., pp. 122, 511. See also McTighe, J., & Lyman, F. T. (2001). Cueing thinking in the classroom: The promise of theory-embedded tools. In A. Costa (Ed.), *Developing minds: A resource book for teaching thinking* (pp. 384–393). Alexandria, VA: Association for Supervision and Curriculum Development.
4. Swartz, R., & Parks, S. (1994). Op. cit., p. 106.
5. Rosenshine, B. (1979). Content, time and direct instruction. In P. L. Peterson & H. Walberg (Eds.), *Research on teaching.* Berkeley, CA: McCutchen, pp. 28–56.
6. Doyle, W. (1983). Academic work. *Review of Educational Research, 53* (2), 159–199; Gersten, R., & Carnine, D. (1986). Direct instruction in reading comprehension. *Educational Leadership, 41* (7), 70–78; Rosenshine, B. (1983). Teaching functions in instructional programs. *Elementary School Journal, 83* (4), 335–351; Rosenshine, B. (1986). Synthesis of research on explicit teaching. *Educational Leadership, 41* (6), 60–69; Rosenshine, B. (1997). Advances in research on instruction. In J. W. Lloyd, E. J. Kameenui & D. Chard (Eds.), *Issues in educating students with disabilities* (pp. 197–221). Mahwah, NJ: Erlbaum.
7. Rosenshine, B., & Meister, C. (1992). The use of scaffolds for teaching higher-level cognitive strategies. *Educational Leadership, 49* (7) , 26–33.
8. Beyer, B. (2001). What research says about teaching thinking skills. In A. Costa (Ed.), *Developing minds: A resource book for teaching thinking* (pp. 275–282). Alexandria, VA: Association for Supervision and Curriculum Development.
9. Anderson, R. C., Spiro, R. J., & Montague, W. E. (Eds.). (1977). *Schooling and the acquisition of knowledge.* Hillside, NJ: Erlbaum; Brown, A., Campione, J., & Day, J. J. (1987). Learning to learn: On training students to learn from texts. *Educational Researcher, 10* (2), 14–21; Brown, J. S., Collins, A., & Duiguid, P. (1989). Structured cognition in the culture of learning. *Educational Researcher, 18* (1), 32–42; Doyle, W. (1983). Op. cit; Gersten, R., & Carnine, D. (1986). Op.cit; O'Sullivan, J. T., & Pressley, M. (1984). Completeness of instruction and strategy transfer. *Journal of Experimental Child Psychology, 38,* 275–288; Pressley, M., & Harris, K. R. (1990). What we really know about strategy instruction. *Educational Leadership, 48* (1), 32–34.
10. Posner, M., & Keele, S. W. (1973). Skill learning. In R. M. W. Travers (Ed.), *Second handbook of research on teaching* (pp. 805–831); Nickerson, R. (1988–89). On improving thinking through instruction. In E. Z. Rothkopf (Ed.), *Review of research in education.* Washington: American Educational Research Association, Vol. 1, 3–57. Chicago: Rand McNally; Pressley, M., & Harris, K. R. (1990). Op. cit.; Pressley, M., & Harris, K. R. (1990). Op. cit.
11. Posner, M., & Keele, S. W. (1973). Op. cit.
12. Joyce, B. (1985). Models for teaching thinking *Educational Leadership, (42)* 4–7; Joyce, B., & Showers, B., (1983). *Power in staff development through research on training.* Alexandria, VA: Association for Supervision and Curriculum Development; Kaufman, E. L., & Miller, N. E. (1958). Acquisition of a learning set by normal and mentally retarded children. *Journal of Comparative and*

Physiological Psychology, 5, 614–621; Pasnak, R., Brown, K., Kurkjian, M., Mattram, K., & Yamamoto, N. (1987). Cognitive gains through training on classification, seriation, and conservation. *Genetic, Social and General Psychology Monographs, 113* (3), 295–332.

13. Doyle, W. (1983). Op. cit.; Nickerson, R. (1988–89). Op. cit.; Posner, M., & Keele, S. W. (1973). Op. cit.; Rosenshine, B. (1980). Op. cit.; Rosenshine, B. (1997). Op. cit.

14. Beyer, B. K. (1987). *Practical strategies for the teaching of thinking*. Boston: Allyn & Bacon; Beyer, B. K. (1997). *Improving student thinking: A comprehensive approach*. Boston: Allyn & Bacon; Fredericksen, N. (1984). Implications of cognitive theory for instruction in problem solving. *Review of Educational Research, 54*, 363–407; Nickerson, R. (1988–89). Op. cit.; Posner, M., & Keele, S. W. (1973). Op. cit.; Pressley, M., & Harris, K. M. (1990). Op. cit.

15. Doyle, W. (1983). Op. cit.; Nickerson, R. (1988–89). Op. cit.; Perkins, D. N., & Salomon, G. (1989, Jan/Feb). Are thinking skills context bound? *Educational Researcher, 18*, 16–25; Pressley, M., & Harris, K. M. (1990). Op. cit.

16. Feuerstein, R. (1980). *Instrumental enrichment*. Baltimore: University Park Press.

17. Swartz, R., Kiser, M., & Reagan, R. (1999). Op. cit.; Swartz, R., Fischer, S., & Parks, S. (1999). Op. cit.

18. Ibid.; Swartz, R., & Parks, S. (1994). Op. cit.

19. Astington, J. W., & Olson, D. R. (1990). Metacognitive and metalinguistic language: Learning to talk about thought. *Applied Psychology: An International Review, 39*, 77–87; Brown, A., Campione, J., & Day, J. J. (1981). Op. cit.

20. Beyer, B. K. (1988). *Developing a thinking skills program*. Boston: Allyn & Bacon; Brown, A., Campione, J., & Day, J. J. (1981). Op. cit.; Costa, A., & Kallick, B. (2000). *Activating and engaging habits of mind*. Alexandria, VA: Association for Supervision and Curriculum Development; Hurst, J. B., Kinney, M., & Weiss, S. J. (1983). The decision making process. *Theory and Research in Social Education, 11* (3), 17–43; Marzano, R. (1991). Fostering thinking across the curriculum through knowledge restructuring. *Journal of Reading, 34* (7), 18–24; Swartz, R., & Parks, S. (1994). *Infusing the teaching of critical and creative thinking into content curriculum: A lesson design handbook for the elementary grades*. Pacific Grove, CA: Critical Thinking; Wineburg, S. S. (1991). Historical problem solving: A study of the cognitive processes used in the evaluation of documentary and pictorial evidence. *Journal of Educational Psychology, 83* (1), 73–87.

21. Astington, J. W., & Olson, D. R. (1990). Op. cit.

22. Beyer, B. K. (1997). Op. cit.; Rosenshine, B., & Meister, C. (1992). The use of scaffolds for teaching higher level cognitive strategies. *Educational Leadership, 49* (7), 26–33; Swartz, R., & Parks, S. (1994). Op. cit.

23. Whimbey, A., & Lochhead, J. (1999). *Problem solving and comprehension*. Mahwah, NJ: Erlbaum.

24. Brown, A., Campione, J., & Day, J. J. (1981). Op. cit.; Papert, S. (1980). *Mindstorms: Children, computers and powerful ideas*. New York: Basic Books; Vygotsky, L. S. (1962). *Thought and language*. Cambridge, MA: MIT Press.

25. Beyer, B. K. (1997). Op. cit.

26. See Parks, S., & Black, H. (1995). *Organizing thinking*. Pacific Grove, CA: Critical Thinking, passim; and Swartz, R., & Parks, S. (1994), Op. cit., passim. See also Beyer, B. K. (1997). Op cit., pp. 183–201.

27. Jones, B. F., Amiran, M. R., & Katims, M. (1985). Teaching cognitive strategies and text structures within language arts programs. In J. W. Segal, S. F. Chipman, & R. Glaser (Eds.), *Thinking and learning skills: Vol. 1. Relating instruction to research* (pp. 259–290). Hillsdale, NJ: Erlbaum; McTighe, J., & Lyman, Jr., F. T. (1988). Cueing thinking in the classroom: The promise of theory-embedded tools. *Educational Leadership, 45* (7), 18–24; Rosenshine, B., & Meister, C. (1992). Op. cit.

28. Olson, D. R., & Astington, J. W. (1990). Op. cit.

29. Perkins, D. (1992). Op. cit.

30. Beyer, B. K., Costa, A. L., & Presseisen, B. (2001). Glossary of thinking terms. In A. Costa (Ed.), *Developing minds: A resource book for teaching thinking* (pp. 548–550). Alexandria, VA: Association for Supervision and Curriculum Development.

31. Costa, A., & Marzano, A. (2001). Teaching the language of thinking. In A. Costa (Ed.), *Developing minds: A resource book for teaching thinking* (pp. 379–383). Alexandria, VA: Association for Supervision and Curriculum Development.

32. Cornbleth, C., & Korth, W. (1981). If remembering, understanding and reasoning are important. *Social Education, 45* (4), 276, 278–279; Edwards, J. (1988). Measuring the effects of the direct teaching of thinking skills. *Human Intelligence Newsletter, 9*(3), 9–10; Estes, T. H. (1972). Reading in the social studies: A review of research since 1950. In J. Laffery (Ed.), *Reading in the content areas* (pp. 178–183). Newark, DE: International Reading Association; Jones, B. F., Amiran, M. R., & Katims, M. (1985). Op. cit.; Nickerson, R. (1988–89). Op. cit.; Perkins, D. (1992). Op. cit.

33. Perkins, D. (1987). Op. cit.; Perkins, D. (1992). Op. cit.

34. Bereiter, C. (1973). Elementary schools: Convenience or necessity? *Elementary School Journal, 73* (8), 435–445; Pressley, M., & Harris, K. M. (1990). Op. cit.

35. Nickerson, R. (1989). On improving thinking through instruction. In E. Z. Rothkopf (Ed.), *Review of Research in Education (Vol. 1)*. Washington: American Educational Research Association, pp. 3–57; Doyle, W. (1983). Op. cit; Estes, T. H. (1972). Op. cit.

36. Doyle, W. (1983). Op. cit., (Summer), 159–199; Estes (1972). Op. cit.; Gersten & Carmine (1986). Op. cit.

37. Bandura, A. (1997). *Self-efficacy: The exercise of control* (pp. 212–258). New York: Freeman.

CHAPTER 4

Metacognition: Taking Charge of Our Own Thinking

Your life is the sum result of all the choices you make, both consciously and unconsciously. If you can control the process of choosing, you can take control of all aspects of your life. You can find the freedom that comes from being in charge of yourself.

—Robert F. Bennett, U.S. Senator

SOLVE THIS PROBLEM in your head: How much is one half of two plus two?

Do you hear yourself talking to yourself? Do you find yourself having to decide if you should add the twos first (which would give the answer 2) or if you should take one-half of the first two (which would give the answer 3)? Did you return to your elementary arithmetic class memories and recall the "order of operations (multiply, divide, add, subtract) with the mnemonic "My Dear Aunt Sally"? If you were aware of yourself having an inner dialogue, and if you had to stop to evaluate your own decision-making and problem-solving processes, you were experiencing metacognitive activities.

Meta means "about" and *cognition* means "thinking." So *metacognition* means "thinking about thinking." Located in the prefrontal cortex of the brain are such capacities as use of reason, making sense of ideas and behaviors, planning and future thinking, critical and creative thinking, reflection, and thinking about our own thinking. The capacity for metacognition, therefore, is thought by some neuroscientists to be uniquely human. When we are confronted with a problematic, confusing, or ambiguous situation, we become conscious of what we know and what we don't know. Likewise, we use metacognition to plan a strategy for making careful informed decisions. Metacognition enables us to be conscious of our own steps and strategies during the act of problem solving, and to reflect on and evaluate the productiveness of these strategies so that we can change them if they are not working well for us. These are the brain's "executive functions."

The reason we are devoting an entire chapter to a discussion of metacognition and how to teach it is to explore its role in the third major component of skillful thinking: being aware of the kind of thinking we are going to be doing, planning how we will do it, reflectively guiding ourselves in its execution by this plan, and evaluating the effectiveness of this plan.

We call this component of skillful thinking *reflective self-directedness*. Specifically, we want to encourage you to take the time in classrooms to have students become aware of, direct, and evaluate their thinking processes. If students cannot articulate how they think through problems with success, they cannot, without help, repeat the thinking procedure the next time they need it. That is our ultimate goal in teaching students skillful thinking: We want them to become independent self-directed and productive thinkers.

When teachers ask "How did you solve that problem? What strategies did you have in mind?" or "Tell us what went on in your head to come up with that conclusion," students often respond by saying, "I don't know, I just did it." We want students to abandon this sense of powerlessness and become increasingly aware of, in control of, and reflective on what they do when they strive to draw well-supported conclusions, so that they can continue throughout their lives to reflectively direct their own thinking. Teaching skillful thinking, therefore, includes prompting students to engage in specific forms of metacognition.

Let us explore further what we have just said about the typical way that students approach thinking activities. Students often follow instructions or perform tasks without wondering why they are doing what they are doing. They seldom question themselves about their own learning strategies or evaluate the efficiency of their own performances. They have little or no motivation to do so. Some children have virtually no idea of what they should do when they confront a problem and are often unable to explain their strategies of decision making. For these children, learning is reduced to episodic rote learning and memorization, primarily directed at passing tests and getting through school. Many of them do so, but just barely. They can do better.

There is much evidence to demonstrate that people who perform well on complex cognitive tasks, who are flexible and persevere in problem solving, and who consciously apply their intellectual skills are people who possess well-developed metacognitive abilities.[1] They manage their intellectual resources well—including their basic perceptual motor skills, language, beliefs, knowledge of content, memory processes, and especially their purposeful and voluntary strategies that are intended to achieve certain desired outcomes when they engage in challenging tasks. Central to this complex of self-directed activity is their constant awareness of, monitoring of, and adjusting the thinking that moves them through these tasks.[2]

Thinking About Thinking

I've reached the moment where the movement of my thought interests me more than the thought itself.

—Pablo Picasso

The difference between metacognition and other forms of thinking is in what we are thinking about, not in the thinking we do. In metacognition we think about thinking. On other occasions we think about such things as the events of the day, the book we are reading, and our friends. However, how we think about our thinking is no different from how we think about those other things. Indeed, every kind of thinking we have identified in this book, and that others have identified in writing about thinking, can be done about thinking itself. Thus metacognition is not any special kind of thinking, any more than cognition or ordinary thinking is. We can compare and contrast the thinking we are doing now with the thinking we did an hour ago. We can decide to do a certain kind of thinking (e.g., comparing and contrasting) about two things like plant cells and animal cells in exactly the same way we decide to go to the cinema. We can analyze a thinking episode, such as how we did parts–whole thinking in the kestrel lesson, into its parts (i.e., the questions we asked as we went through the four steps). There is nothing special about the type of thinking that we do when we think about our thinking. What is special is that we are thinking about our thinking and not something else.

Nevertheless, there may well be something special about how we can think about our thinking *skillfully* in the context of learning a thinking skill that will help us to achieve the goals of teaching thinking. Our earlier discussion of the way thinking about thinking progressed in the parts–whole lesson can illustrate this. There the teacher prompted students to think about how they thought about the parts of a kestrel in the lesson; and, based on this, they prepared themselves with a plan for how they would do the same kind of thinking next time it was necessary. When teachers provide students with such focused prompting questions, it helps students focus on their thinking with more specificity. Ultimately, students develop a pattern or structure for thinking about their thinking that they can call on independently in any context.

Some examples will illustrate this. When I have to decide what clothes to wear, I consider my options, think about what clothes would be appropriate, consider the weather, and then decide. I may have to manage some impulsivity and impatience and make sure I raise questions like whether the clothes are too dressy for the occasion, but by and large, this is not a big thing.

On other occasions the thinking we do may be different. I may be investigating the cause of a serious equipment failure. Finding the right cause may be crucial if we are to remedy the situation. I may have to be very careful to explore a range of possible causes before I come to a conclusion, and make sure that I have gathered as many relevant indicators as to what caused the failure. In addition, I may benefit from sharing my thinking with others, as well as asking them to verify some of the evidence. Otherwise, I may come up with a disastrously wrong judgment.

Similarly, I may be a new principal of a school that has had some serious problems in the past. It is an underachieving school, and the different ethnic groups that make up the school population often are in open conflict. I want to transform this school into an achieving school and quell the social and ethnic unrest. To do this I need to think very carefully and very skillfully. The way I tackle the problems can spell success or failure. My thinking about why these problems have occurred may be somewhat similar to my thinking about the cause of the equipment failure, but it also has many other dimensions. I will need to think about the school curriculum and the best way to deliver it, given the needs of the student body and the capabilities of the teachers. And I will want to think about techniques for bringing people of different ethnic backgrounds to situations in which they can work together. And that may merely scratch the surface.

Why do I approach the thinking I do in these three situations in such different ways? This doesn't happen by chance. The behind-the-scenes difference in these situations is my metacognitive sensitivity. If I am a skillful thinker, I have internalized a stock of possible thinking strategies, and there is a variety of mental demeanors that I can adopt. But I will *also* have internalized the process of reflecting on which of these strategies is best under each circumstance and, like many internalized guidance processes in our lives, its operations will seem more or less automatic. Without it, though, what I do will be no better than guesswork—not a very skillful process.

We can teach students so that they learn to guide their own thinking in similar ways.

Why Metacognition Must Be Taught

Violin teachers often get their students to think about how they are holding their bows. "Notice where your thumb is when you hold the bow?" a teacher said to her violin student, an 8-year-old.

"It's on the frog just opposite my first finger," he responded.

"Try putting your thumb opposite your middle finger when you hold your bow, not opposite your first finger," the violin teacher said. "Now play that line again and tell me if you think it sounds better that way."

"Yes, it sounds much better when I hold my thumb there," said the student. "I'll try to hold it that way from now on."

The way we can think about our thinking, as it contributes to developing thinking skills and habits of mind, is no different from this little musical episode, except that instead of thinking about how to best hold a violin bow, we think about how to best engage in specific types of thinking. When students were asked how they engaged in parts–whole thinking, they were being asked to describe what they were thinking about in the episode of parts–whole thinking through which the teacher just guided them. Just as the violin student needs to use the language of his instrument, which he knows all too well, to make a correction for improved performance—he needs to talk about the "bow" and the "frog" (the wooden slide on the end of the bow that is often adorned with mother-of-pearl inlays)—so students need to know the language of the kind of thinking they have done in order to describe how they did it; then they can make specific changes that improve their performance. Most students know this language or pick it up very easily as the teacher uses it. For example, in the kestral parts–whole lesson, one student said the following:

> Well, first we asked; "What are the smaller parts of the object?" and then we moved to thinking about what would happen if some of the specific parts we identified were missing. I tried to picture that in my mind, and doing that helped me to figure out what would happen if those parts were missing. Then I shifted to the question "What is their function?" and tried to answer it. Finally, with my group, I described how the parts work together to make the whole work.

This student is talking about the questions that focused her thinking and prompted mental operations, such as imagining the object without a part. That's similar to the violin student describing where his thumb is on the bow—although, of course, it's about a mental and not a musical episode, and it is somewhat more complex and precise.

The violin teacher had asked her student to do more, however. She asked him whether holding his thumb in a specific way made the line he was playing *sound better*. She wanted him to consider the quality of the sound he produced when he held the bow a certain way and thereby *evaluate* the technique used to produce the sound. The kestrel-lesson teacher also asked this type of evaluative question. After the students had described how they engaged in that kind of thinking, the teacher asked whether they thought that was an effective way to do parts–whole thinking. Students are therefore invited to engage in an evaluation of their thinking, just as the violin student engages in an evaluation of the method of holding his thumb on the bow of his instrument.

Evaluation is sometimes not so easy. The violin teacher focused the student on the quality of the sound. There could be other criteria as well, like how hard it is to hold his thumb there. Maybe his hand muscles tighten up and hurt. There might be more sophisticated types of evaluation in which the student can engage to judge whether this is a good thing to do when playing the violin. Perhaps more than just one line should be played as the basis of it. Musical lines in the piece might sound strong and steady, but maybe when arpeggios are played the sound is not so strong. Thus, perhaps the music teacher should be more precise about the criteria for assessing whether holding the thumb in that spot on the bow is a good idea.

Maybe she should ask the student why he thinks the sound is better and if there are other factors that should be taken into account. Nevertheless, what is described here is a start.

The same considerations apply to what the teacher did in the parts–whole lesson when she asked the students whether this was an effective way to do the thinking they just described. There could be, and perhaps should be, a much more articulate, detailed, and systematic exercise in evaluation. What was done in the lesson can be treated as a start in the development of a more complex evaluative process.

In addition, both the violin student and the parts–whole students do one more thing, which is spontaneous in the violin lesson but prompted in the parts–whole lesson: explicitly planning ahead for how the bowing or how parts–whole thinking will be done next time there is an occasion to do it. This planning is based on the students' evaluations of what they have been doing, but now they are no longer evaluating, they are deciding what they will do the next time they have the occasion to do this kind of activity. They are making this decision quite deliberately and can articulate their plan, explain why they are adopting it, write it down, and do whatever else is necessary to make it likely that they will employ this kind of thinking when the next occasion arises. Then, indeed, they do it! The violin student is taking charge of his own bowing, and the student learning skillful parts–whole thinking is being prompted to take charge of his own thinking. They develop a clear and explicit plan, one for bowing and one for parts–whole thinking. Then, when the occasion arises to implement this plan, both students perform according to it. When they perform their activities enough times, they will not have to think about doing it that way anymore. Good bowing and reflective self-directed parts–whole thinking will become habitual. The violinist will naturally, with ease, and with expertise hold his thumb where it contributes to a beautiful strong tone, and the thinker will do skillful thinking naturally, with ease, and with expertise. That's the power of including metacognition in a thinking-skill and habits-of-mind lesson.

The Ladder of Metacognition

Some of these ideas about metacognition have been organized through the image of a ladder.[3] This ladder represents progressive levels of metacognition that serve the purposes of facilitating the internalization of habits of skillful thinking and their self-directed use by good thinkers (Figure 4-1).

The first rung on the ladder involves being able to identify *what* we have been doing—the kind of thinking we have been doing. When we identify the kind of thinking in the kestrel lesson as "analyzing parts–

Figure 4-1. The Ladder of Metacognition

4. PLANNING how we will engage in the same type of thinking the next time it is necessary

3. EVALUATING whether the way we engaged in the type of thinking was effective

2. DESCRIBING how we engaged in this type of thinking

1. BECOMING AWARE of the kind of thinking in which we engaged

whole relationships," we are on that bottom rung. This is straightforward classification of a thinking episode as a specific type of thinking.

Classifying a type of thinking requires a conceptual apparatus and language that can be used to accurately label thinking processes—for example, predicting the likelihood of something happening, trying to solve a problem, and comparing and contrasting. Most of us have that conceptual apparatus and if our students don't, we can teach it to them through its repeated explicit use or through some more formal introduction of standard thinking terminology.

Climbing onto the second rung of the ladder involves a little more than simple classification. It involves describing *how* we are or have been doing this kind of thinking. Here the episodes or ingredients of the process are articulated. One common way this happens is to identify the prompting questions that move us through this process. In the lesson on the kestrel, the teacher asks the students directly; hence the teacher is trying to prompt this kind of metacognition. This itself is an analytical task. When we are on this rung, the episode of thinking that we are thinking about is broken into component steps if it is a sequenced activity. If not, we can describe it in terms of rules or heuristics to follow. This kind of metacognition thus becomes an example, in itself, of parts–whole thinking.

On the third rung, the thinking shifts from descriptive and analytical thinking to evaluative (or critical) thinking. Is this a good and effective way to do this kind of thinking? For example, in the kestrel lesson a critical

judgment is called for about whether this way of doing parts–whole thinking is a good way to do it.

Finally, on the top rung, we plan how we will do this kind of thinking
in the future, while keeping in mind the previous rungs. This involves
committing ourselves to this way of thinking and, in fact, intending to
do it this way the next time it is required. We are now deciding to deliberately follow the steps we think will work best for us in the future.
When we translate this into action—cognitive action—and actually follow
this thinking plan on a specific occasion, we are taking charge of our own
thinking.

There are a variety of ways that we can think about our own thinking.
We submit the ladder of metacognition as a framework for a sequence of
thinking activities that are metacognitive in character and that lead to the
goal of reflectively taking charge of how we engage in thinking processes
that are important to do skillfully as we make our way through life. This
is obviously an iterative process. As thinkers we should be prepared to
repeat it periodically as a self-corrective mechanism. When this becomes
one of our abiding mental habits, it brings us to the highest level of independent reflective thought that a human being can achieve. The teaching
of skillful thinking does not just help our students to learn some forms of
skillful thinking, it is also a transformative process of developing inde-
pendence of thought and continued reflection on the part of our students.
Helping them to develop the habit of climbing this ladder, and doing it
well, will achieve this loftier goal.

The Ladder of Metacognition in the Classroom

The teaching of skillful thinking does not just help our students learn
some forms of skillful thinking. It also helps them learn a variety of thinking strategies and habits of mind from which they can choose so that they
use the most effective ones appropriate to specific circumstances that call
for skillful thinking. But it is also a transformative process that leads to
their developing the ability to make these choices wisely and with indepen-
dence of thought. Ultimately, that is the goal of thinking-based learning.
Helping our students develop the habit of climbing the ladder of metacognition, and the ability to do it with ease, will achieve this loftier goal.

We know from our own experience that it is not difficult to do this. For
example, a teacher who had been put off by talk about "teaching metacognition" because it seemed like a complex technical enterprise, had an interesting experience that changed her mind. While teaching her students
how to engage in skillful problem solving, she noticed that the students
were working together to develop lists of possible solutions, but every

now and then some of them stopped and said things like this: "That's a ridiculous idea! We shouldn't include that on our list!" So she stopped them
and this little non-planned exchange took place in the classroom:

Teacher: Let's stop for a moment. I want to ask you something.

The students stop and attend to the teacher.

Teacher: What kind of thinking are you doing right now?

Students: Well – brainstorming.

Teacher: What is one of the basic rules for brainstorming?

Student 1: We want to come up with as many ideas as we can.

Student 2: We shouldn't judge the ideas but just lay them out on the
table.

Teacher: You're both right. Why shouldn't we judge our ideas
when we brainstorm?

Student 3: Oh, I see. If we judge our ideas we may not be doing such
a good job of it and we may reject some ideas that might
turn out to be good ones! Hey, we should stop doing that.

Teacher: Let's try to get as many ideas on our lists as we can and
not stop to judge them. We will have plenty of time to do
that later. However ridiculous they may seem, let's accept
them all as equal possibilities to be considered and not
yet judge them.

It was clear to this teacher that in the remaining brainstorming time
the students backed off judging the ideas they were developing and tried
to come up with rich lists of possible solutions. In this exchange this
teacher, quite naturally, and without realizing it, led these students up the
ladder of metacognition as they thought about how to brainstorm ideas
effectively.

To appreciate the generality and power of this framework for metacognitive instruction in teaching skillful thinking, let's see how this plays
itself out in another lesson in which it was planned by the teacher. This
is an extended lesson on the bombing of Hiroshima.[4] The 12th-grade students have learned that to end World War II the United States dropped
two atomic bombs, one on the city of Hiroshima and one on the city of
Nagasaki, virtually destroying these two cities and killing most of their
inhabitants. Shortly thereafter the Japanese surrendered unconditionally
to the United States. The students have seen this photo of one of these
bomb blasts (Figure 4-2).

Was this the best decision for the U.S. government to have made? To
answer this question the teacher, Mr. O'Malley, asks the students to put
themselves back into 1945 and think carefully about the best way to end

Figure 4-2. The Bombing of Nagasaki

World War II, given the information available to them, as if they were President Harry Truman. The students are guided in this lesson to go through the process of skillful decision making. Mr. O'Malley does this by prompting them to follow a thinking strategy map for this type of thinking and to use a graphic organizer that reinforces this strategy and allows them to "download" the ideas generated by its application. This is the thinking strategy map[5] that guides them in skillful decision making (Figure 4-3).

Figure 4-4 shows the graphic organizer that Mr. O'Malley asks them to use to write down their ideas as they answer the core questions (2, 3, and 4) on this thinking strategy map.[6]

The students exchange ideas in open discussion in small groups about specific options that they have previously identified—such as demonstrating the weapon, continuing an air and sea embargo, and negotiating an end to the war with the Japanese—after looking at selected resource material that Mr. O'Malley makes available to them. As they do this Mr.

Figure 4-3. Thinking Strategy Map for Skillful Decision Making

Skillful Decision Making

1. What makes a decision necessary?
2. What are my options?
3. What are the likely consequences of each action?
4. How important are the consequences?
5. Which option is best in light of the consequences?

Figure 4-4. Graphic Organizer to Aid Skillful Decision Making

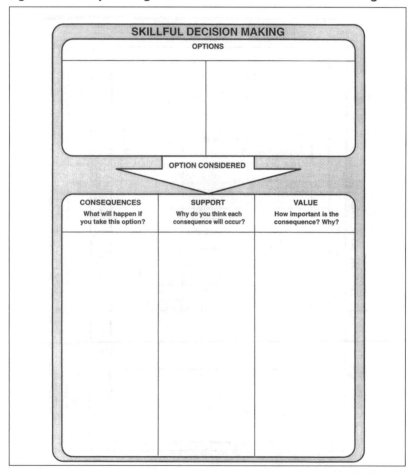

O'Malley guides them to be careful to listen to their follow students and to respect what they are saying even if they disagree with them. In doing this they practice an important habit of mind, listening with understanding and empathy, which Mr. O'Malley has been trying to help them develop.

After all the groups have reported on the option they were considering, each student is asked to choose what he or she considers the best option, then to write a letter to President Truman explaining why this is the best choice. Mr. O'Malley asks some of the students to share their letters in class to prompt more discussion of this issue.

The lesson has been a rich learning experience for the students. It is not yet over, however. Mr. O'Malley now says the following:

> Let's stop thinking about the bombing of Hiroshima, World War II, and the consequences of President Truman's options and shift our attention to thinking about our thinking. You all have told me that you feel pretty good—pretty confident—about your choices, and that this contrasts with the way you used to feel about many previous decisions. So let's think about how you arrived at those judgments about the best option for the United States to end World War II.

So far the students have been attending to issues about the atomic bomb and the situation in the Pacific at this stage in the war with Japan. This statement by Mr. O'Malley prompts the students to shift their attention from what to do to end World War II and to concentrate on the thinking they have just done. He has already peppered the lesson with some brief excursions into metacognition, but now he is preparing the students for a sustained episode in which they are to think about their thinking. His purpose is to guide the students to a point where they will not only be reflecting retrospectively on how they did this kind of thinking but will also be using these reflections to develop a plan for how they will do it in the future and to be alert to situations in which such thinking is necessary. By prompting such metacognitive reflection, Mr. O'Malley is beginning to empower these students to take charge of their own thinking. Here is the rest of what he says as they move along in teacher-student and student-student exchanges; see if you can identify how he takes the students up the ladder of metacognition:

> What kind of thinking did we just do? What are some other examples of this kind of thinking in which you have engaged?
>
> How did you do this kind of thinking? What were the questions we asked?
>
> Is this a good way to think about decisions that we need to make? It has taken us some time to go through this process. Is it worth the time? If so, why? If not, why not? Let's also think about the habit of searching for all the relevant information, which involves persisting, striving for accuracy, and gathering as broad a range of data as we can. Is that worthwhile to do as part of this process? Why or why not?

> We've just had an interesting discussion about how to do skillful de-
> cision making. Think about this now, based on this discussion, and
> try to put into your own words on a piece of paper, in your journals,
> or in your metacognitive computer log your own best plan for skill-
> ful decision making. I want you to put some specific ideas down in
> writing about how to do this kind of skillful thinking next time it is
> required. You should be prepared to explain why you think your
> plan is good.

Notice how Mr. O'Malley prompts the students to write their ideas down, rather than just think about their thinking, or have a discussion.

In practice, many students make alterations as they develop their plan in order to accommodate special circumstances and/or to generalize it so that it can be applied successfully in different types of decision-making situations. For example, after working through the thinking strategy map given earlier, one student modified it as a plan for future use by trans-forming it into a list of directives with very specific details that were not included originally. The student modified the question, "What are the likely consequences of each option?" to read as follows: "List the likely consequences of each option and make sure that you consider (a) cons as well as pros, (b) consequences for others as well as yourself, and (c) long-term consequences as well as short-term ones."

This student recognized that he had a tendency not to consider cons, not to consider consequences for others, and not to think long-term as he tried to make well-thought-out decisions. He thought that a plan for skillful decision making that he could use in the future would be better if it included this way of articulating how he should think about the conse-quences of his options rather than just the simpler question about likely consequences.

Developing a plan for something we will be doing in the future and filing it away in our journals—and eventually in our minds—is risky. It is always a good idea to review the plan prior to actually implementing it and be prepared to revise it each time we apply it as the situation might require. Then we increase the chances that we will actually follow the plan that we wrote down earlier. Many researchers on planning have stressed how effective it is not only to review the plan but also to rehearse it just before applying it. Many athletes, musicians, and performers rehearse as a regular practice; many teachers do, too. Thus, when Mr. O'Malley wants the students to use their plan for another episode of skillful decision mak-ing, he might say the following:

> We're going to be doing some more decision making in class shortly,
> and it has to be skillful. In fact, we are going to take some time to
> think about when this might be a good idea—what sorts of situations

will call for skillful decision making. So go back to your plan and go over it again just to remind yourself what you thought would be a good idea to do when you had to do skillful decision making again. You might even want to run through this plan yet again just before we do the activity. If you think this situation requires it, you may modify your plan, so consider this as well as you review your plan.

This would be very sound advice from the teacher.

The process of repeated self-guidance in skillful thinking, even if initially prompted by the teacher and continued by future teachers, will soon become the driving force for the students to develop the habit to make decisions skillfully, persistently, and with a thorough search for the pros and cons. These students will then be well on the way to becoming skillful decision makers. If their future teachers realize this and help them to turn their good thinking onto the challenging raw material of the regular content curriculum, they will learn what these teachers are trying to teach them in every subject in ways that most teachers only dream of today.

The Impact of Metacognition on Learning

Watch your thoughts, they become words.
Watch your words; they become actions.
Watch your actions; they become habits.
Watch your habits; they become character.
Watch your character; it becomes your destiny.
—Frank Outlaw

These ideas about metacognition and metacognitively based instruction of thinking skills and habits of mind have been backed up by much empirical research. This research adds another dimension to the ideas about metacognition that we have developed in this chapter so far. For example, researchers such as Bloom and Broder[7] found that skillful problem solvers use problem-solving strategies, and they are aware of and can describe these strategies. They can talk about their thinking; in fact, thinking and talking about thinking beget even more thinking! The seminal research of Flavell also indicates this.[8] The crux of this research is that skillful problem solvers employ self-monitoring skills that are necessary for their successful performance on complex tasks.[9] These self-monitoring skills include the following:

- Keeping one's place in a long sequence of operations
- Knowing that a subgoal has been obtained
- Detecting errors and correcting them either by making a quick fix or by retreating to the last-known correct operation

Such self-monitoring occurs in three basic contexts. We monitor our thinking while we are doing it, of course, but we also do monitoring that involves both looking ahead and looking back.

Looking back includes the following:

- Detecting previous errors
- Keeping a history of what has been done to the present and therefore what should come next
- Assessing the reasonableness of the immediate outcome of task performance

Looking ahead includes the following:

- Learning the structure of a sequence of thinking operations to make it skillful
- Identifying areas where errors are likely
- Choosing a strategy that will reduce the possibility of error and will provide easy recovery
- Identifying the kinds of feedback that will be available at various points
- Evaluating the usefulness of that feedback

We can filter out of these ideas an emphasis on how good thinkers use metacognition before, during, and after a thinking task takes place. In each instance they move up the ladder of metacognition to the level of undertaking a deliberate plan for doing the kind of thinking in question. Hence, to help students become aware of, articulate, evaluate, and habituate their thinking through these executive functions, the teacher can do one or more of the following when the students are given a challenging thinking task:

- *Prior* to the learning activity, the teacher can invite the students to develop and describe plans and strategies for the task. Time constraints, purposes, and ground rules under which the students must operate to put their plan into action can also be developed and internalized. When they do this, the students will then keep these in mind during the activity and evaluate their performance during and after the experience.
- *During* the activity, the teacher can invite the students to share their progress, thought processes, and perceptions of their own mental behavior as they are implementing their plan. The teacher can ask the students to indicate where they are in their strategy, describe the trail of thinking up to that point, and list the alternative pathways they intend to pursue next in the solution of their problem.

This helps them to become aware of their own behavior and to modify it if they determine that it is not as effective as it could be. (It also provides the teacher with a diagnostic "cognitive map" of the student's thinking which can be used to give more individualized assistance.)

- *After* the learning activity is completed, the teacher can invite the students to reflect on and evaluate to what extent the plan that they developed was actually followed, how well their strategies worked, and what might be some alternative, more efficient strategies to be used in the future.

One interesting variant on these ideas involves the use of a special classroom strategy that is called "Think Aloud Problem Solving" (TAPS).[10] In this process, the students are invited to describe explicitly to other students what is going on inside their heads as they engage in a thinking task. They do this in pairs, and the partner writes it down and maps it out. The pairs then compare their notes with one another in order to determine if any commonalities have surfaced.

In this process the teacher starts by posing challenging thinking tasks in the content area of instruction. This is made into a metacognitive activity as follows:

- *Before* the students begin to engage in the thinking task, the teacher invites the students to describe their plans and strategies for it.
- *During* the thinking task, the teacher invites the students to share publicly, and in pairs, their thinking as they are implementing their plan.
- *After* the students think they have completed the task, the teacher invites them to reflect on and evaluate the effectiveness of their strategy.

Let us now combine the ideas about the temporal contexts for metacognitive reflection with the concept of the ladder of metacognition. We do this by formulating sample questions that teachers might pose to engage and prompt students to climb to each rung of the ladder before, during, and after the thinking takes place, whether they do this on their own, in pairs, or in the whole class (Table 4-1).

Effective instruction that is aimed at helping students to reflectively self-direct their thinking should not stop part of the way up this ladder, but should move students to the top—to the fourth rung. Table 4-1 represents an elaborated thinking strategy map for skillfully thinking about one's thinking in all its richness. The examples we have used in this chapter can now be identified as examples in which the teachers prompt students to climb the ladder of metacognition after a thinking activity has been completed. You might want to look back at the lessons described in

Table 4-1. Questions That Prompt Climbing the Ladder of Metacognition Before, During, and After Thinking

Rung	Metacognitive Level	Teacher Poses Such Questions as...
4th	PLANNING ahead for future thinking	How might you do this thinking next time? As you anticipate similar problems in the future, what insights might you carry forth about how to think them through? When else in this course, school, life, or work might this strategy prove useful? Why is it important for you to...?
3rd	EVALUATING the effectiveness of the strategy—before, during, and after	How well did your strategy work for you? How do you know your strategy is working? What corrections or alterations in your strategy are you making as you...? What will you pay attention to while you are solving this problem to let you know your strategy is working? What alternative strategies might you employ if you find that your strategy is not working? Why do you think this is the best strategy? What has worked for you in the past? What makes you think that this strategy will work in this situation? By what criteria will you judge that this is the best way to approach this problem?
2nd	DESCRIBING the strategy you use in the thinking	*Before*: What approaches will you employ...? As you approach this problem, how will you try to solve it? *During*: As you consider the steps in the skillful problem-solving process, where are you...? What patterns are you noticing in your approach to solving this problem? What questions are you asking yourself? *After*: As you reflect on your problem-solving strategy, what did it involve? What led you to this decision? What questions were you asking yourself?
1st	Being AWARE of the kind of thinking you have done	Name the kind of thinking you are or will be doing. What type of thinking was going on in your head when...? While you were thinking about_____, what thinking processes were you using?

Chapters 2 and 3, and expand on the metacognitive activities so that they take the students up the ladder of metacognition before, during, and after the thinking tasks.

Evaluating Growth in
Metacognitive Abilities

There are two basic questions that a teacher needs to answer in order to plan metacognitive activities in his or her classroom: (a) To what extent are the students able to reach each rung on the ladder of metacognition? (b) Do the students do this as a matter of habit?

When teachers try to gather information about their students in order to answer these questions, they are evaluating the metacognitive abilities of their students and the degree to which using such abilities has become a habit of mind. What kind of information indicates that the students have developed these abilities and that their use is habitual?

In general, students are becoming more aware of their own thinking if they are able to describe what goes on in their heads when they are thinking. They can identify the kind of thinking they are doing, list any steps or procedures they are using to do it with skill, and can tell where they are in the sequence of steps. They can also trace the pathways they took and the dead ends they met before they got to where they are in the thinking process, as well as any roadblocks they might have come up against and when they needed more information to bring their thinking to a resolution. These are indicators that they can reach the second rung on the ladder of metacognition. Figure 4-5 shows some simple indicators that a group of third-grade students at the Hendricks Day School in Jacksonville, Florida, can reach the first rung of the ladder in mapping cause-and-effect relationships. In this case they are studying dinosaurs and are speculating about how they might have become extinct.[11]

Figure 4-6 shows a more articulated step up to the second rung by students at the same school who are identifying and describing how an important mental habit—communicating with clarity and precision—manifests itself.[12]

It should be clear from these examples that the ability of a student to accurately use the language of a specific thinking skill or habit of mind is a necessary (though not sufficient) indicator of basic metacognitive ability. Inability to use the appropriate language of thinking in these cases is a sure indicator that such abilities have not yet developed.

The third rung of the ladder of metacognition requires that students can not only describe their thinking but also evaluate it; that is, they can engage in critical reflection about it. What does that involve, and what kind of data reveals that they have reached this rung? Let's consider thinking

**Figure 4-5.
The Extinction
of the Dinosaurs—
Cause and Effect**

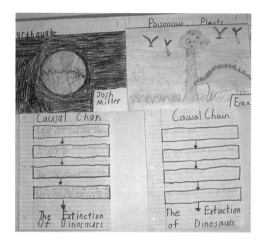

about a variety of options in decision making. Two considerations should be taken into account.

- Will considering a variety of options (in contrast to considering only one option) increase our chances of making a good decision, or the right decision?
- Will considering a variety of options be an efficient and effective way of arriving at a decision?

If we say that thinking of many options makes it less likely that we will miss the right choice, we are responding to the first question in a way that *supports* considering several options in making a decision. In response to

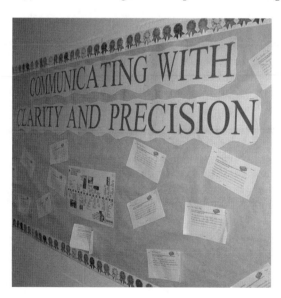

**Figure 4-6.
Descriptions of a
Mental Habit**

the second question, we might say that considering several options takes a lot of time and "the patient may die" before we make a decision if we spend too much time doing this. Then we are producing a reason *against* building such an open-ended step into ordinary decision making. Put together, these considerations suggest that considering a multiplicity of options is a good thing to do in decision making, but perhaps there should be a time limit, or some other limit, to how many are actually processed. And, of course, how we do it will depend on the situation.

Engaging in this kind of thinking about this step in the process of skillful decision making is an example of what is done on the third rung of the ladder of metacognition. Asking students to evaluate whether the procedure they have described on the second rung is a good procedure, and why they think this, is a viable method of gathering data to determine whether these students have the ability to get to the third rung. If their answers to the question "Why?" involve considerations that address both of these key questions, we have good reason for thinking that they have third-rung abilities.

Similarly, if students defend one or more of the broad mental behaviors that we have been discussing, such as listening to the views of other people or communicating their ideas with accuracy and precision, this also demonstrates that they are including habits of mind in their third-rung reflections. They are demonstrating their ability to critically evaluate how worthwhile various types of mental demeanor are in supporting specific thinking goals like good decision making.

Finally, how can we tell if students get to the fourth rung? There we should see students taking more pride in their efforts, becoming self-correcting, striving for craftsmanship and accuracy in their products, and becoming more autonomous in their thinking abilities. We should see students formulating a plan for future engagements with a specific kind of skillful thinking based on their evaluation on the third rung. They should also be able to describe situations in which they might apply their cognitive strategies. Do they have a plan for future episodes of decision making, for example? That should be not too hard to find out. If they are asked why they think this is a good plan, we should be able to find out whether the reasons for adopting this plan lie in the evaluation they engaged in on the third rung.

Reaching the fourth rung means that students have the ability to reflectively direct their own thinking by planning how to do it (see Figure 4-7 for a more detailed rubric). This is the third important trait of skillful thinkers that we articulated in Chapter 1. If you, as the teacher, have information that suggests that your instruction in thinking about thinking has brought this about, and that your students have made this a mental habit every time they engage in a thinking task, you should be proud to have engaged in such teaching!

Figure 4-7. Rubric to Evaluate Metacognitive Reflection

Rubric for Assessing the Quality of a Person's Retrospective/Projective Thinking About Their Thinking

	Level of Metacognition	Excellent	Acceptable	Limited	Unacceptable
Looking Back	*Identifies* Type of Thinking Done	Explicitly identifies the thinking done using appropriate and precise thinking language	Explicitly identifies the thinking done using vague thinking language	Explicitly identifies the thinking done but does not use appropriate thinking language	Does not explicitly identifies the thinking done
	Describes How Type of Thinking Was Done	Describes in detail how the thinking was done using appropriate and precise language and clearly distinguishes the steps in the process	Describes how the thinking was done using thinking language but does not clearly distinguish the steps in the process	Describes how the thinking was done but does not use appropriate thinking; language and does not clearly distinguish the steps in the process	Describes only vaguely or not at all how the thinking was done and does not use thinking language to do so
	Evaluates How Well Type of Thinking Was Done	Provides detailed and significant information about the effectiveness of the thinking judged against explicit and appropriate criteria	Provides some information about the effectiveness of the thinking and shows some awareness of the criteria for judging effectiveness	Judges effectiveness but does not provide information about why or articulate appropriate criteria.	Affirms effectiveness or non-effectiveness without explaining why or articulating any criteria, or *fails* to make any judgment of effectiveness
Thinking Ahead	*Plans Ahead* for Doing Type of Thinking Again	Articulates a specific and explicit plan for using the same kind of thinking in the future, identifies contexts in which it would be called for, and explains why the plan is a good plan	Articulates a specific plan for using the same kind of thinking in the future, but mentions only some reasons why, and/or identifies only a few contexts in which it would be called for	Articulates a vague or general plan for using the same kind of thinking in the future, but does not identify contexts in which it would be called for or explain why the plan is a good plan.	At most only articulates a vague or general plan for using the same kind of thinking in the future and nothing else

Broadening the Concept of
Metacognitive Awareness

We have been discussing how our ability to think about our own thinking processes and habits of mind can be shaped into a powerful tool that can be used to improve these processes and mental habits. There is a strong philosophical tradition that goes back to Plato and includes such great thinkers as René Descartes, John Locke, Immanuel Kant, and Bertrand Russell that recognizes our ability to be aware of our own mental life as a fundamental human trait. They recognize introspective awareness, or "ideas of reflection," in contrast to our sensory awareness of physical things in the world outside us. However, not even Kant recognized what we have spelled out in this chapter about the levels of metacognitive awareness and its ability to give us control over the way we conduct our thinking. Yet we can learn from these philosophers because they treated reflection as a much broader phenomenon that encompasses other aspects of our mental life beyond the thinking processes and mental habits we have been discussing. For them, reflection encompassed every aspect of our consciousness, including the sensations we have when we perceive, our bodily feelings (like pain), and the various emotional states we often experience. In the remaining sections of this chapter we want to advance some ideas on how we might extend the spirit of our discussion of productive and skillful thinking into one of these additional domains, that of emotion.

These philosophers are surely right in embracing this broader conception of reflection. As if standing on a balcony and observing ourselves on the stage, we humans have the capacity to think about our own thinking, as we have elaborated. We also have the ability to be aware of much more about our mental lives, and it is very interesting to think about how much more. At one level we might be aware of ourselves—our senses or our bodies at any given time and in any space, including our kinesthetic movements such as with the violinist. We add another dimension to this when we are also aware of our perceptions of things outside us—as events that take place in time, but events of a greater complexity because they are often enriched with vibrant content, sights, sounds, smells, tastes, and textures lodged in a world of identifiable objects. Similarly, although we can be aware of our moods and emotions as they take place, they, too, bear the complexity of having objects that are crucial components of these states: We are not just sad, we are sad at the loss of a friend, and we are not just angry, we are angry that we are being exploited by our employer. Are there ways of engaging in some or all of these rich aspects of our mental lives more skillfully and more intelligently? Are there other ladders of metacognition similar to the one we have developed for thinking processes and habits of mind that can guide reflection on these mental states?

The final section of this chapter contains some speculative answers to these questions about our emotional lives, which we hope will stimulate further exploration and research.

Meta-Emotional Thinking: Taking Charge of Our Emotions

The sign of intelligent people is their ability to control emotions by the application of reason.

—Marya Mannes

The standard view about our emotions is that they happen to us, that we have little control over them, and that they often control us. They often lead us to do things that calmer, unemotional thinking would not endorse and that are often counter to our best interests. Indeed, when we think of very strong emotions like anger or fear, on the one hand, and love or passion, on the other, we do not have to look very far to find occasions when this characterization seems quite appropriate. Road rage in adults and children fighting on the playground are common examples.

How do these emotions occur? Neural pathways in the brain lead from the rational neocortex to the emotional center of the brain and give us some control over our reactions, allowing us in most instances to respond appropriately to situations. However, these pathways are not in place at birth, which is evident to every parent of a screaming, tantrum-throwing child. In most cases, as the child matures these pathways become more efficient and the child learns to respond more appropriately. The learning environment steps in to play a role as well. The effectiveness of neural pathways is determined to a large degree by experience. If the only response to anger that a child ever experiences is lashing out, then it is likely that the child's brain will become wired to lash out. If delaying gratification is not modeled for or expected of children, they are unlikely to develop this very important characteristic.

When we think about our emotions in general, we recognize two important things. First, emotions serve a function in our lives. For example, the sudden fear that someone feels if he encounters a bear while hiking can save his life. Emotions are immediate, are often triggered by events, and often reflect the significance of these events to our well-being and our life. Second, emotional states are not all like the extreme examples above. Most emotions are not so overpowering, nor do they compel us beyond reason. Our likes and dislikes often play a role in our choices but do not compel them. When we choose one movie or TV show to see over another, or a place to visit, our likes and dislikes are involved, but we also consider cost, time, and other needs that can indicate other courses of action. On occasion, we even exercise some control over whether an emotional state is appropriate: "Should I be afraid of math? Let me conquer this fear—it is thoroughly irrational!" Emotions can be managed skillfully and intelligently.

Even the strongest emotional states are not immune from our exercising skill and intelligence in their advent, experience, and effects. An understanding of the neurological basis of emotional responses helps us to understand why some children do not manage their emotions well. Although the age of the child is an important factor, neuroscientific research discloses that the brain has amazing elasticity, which implies that children can—and should—be taught ways to manage their impulsive behaviors. Let us take a deeper look at our emotional lives to see how this can occur.

Emotional states are typically tied to ideas, just as beliefs are. We don't just believe, we believe that something is the case. If we find that we've made a mistake and it is not the case, we withdraw our assent and belief. I might believe that my car will perform well, but if it doesn't and I find out, I will no longer believe that it does. Likewise, if a child is afraid of monsters in the dark and he realizes that there are no such things, his fear is no longer founded and it usually dissipates. Although emotions can be difficult for us to control, Goleman reminds us that "emotionally intelligent" people mediate and control their emotional reactions and are highly conscious of the impact their emotions have on others.[13]

This is not to suggest that there are not occasions when fear is founded and justified. There are plenty such occasions. Fear, like all our other emotional states, serves an important biological function when we are in danger. Its skillful and intelligent use occurs when we determine, by careful critical thinking, that it is well founded. Then we must take it seriously and skillfully and intelligently determine what we should do vis-à-vis the threatening situation that our fear recognizes.

The same is true of anger, jealousy, hatred, and the other strong emotions that we sometimes experience. They too have their skillful and intelligent use in appropriate circumstances, and they, too, serve important biological functions when they are justified.

At the same time we must acknowledge that it is often not so easy to go through our emotional life skillfully and intelligently. Certain emotions seem to have a staying power despite our ascertaining that they are not justified. With practice, this, too, can be managed.

If being afraid or angry is justified, that does not mean that when we react that way, we will do so skillfully and intelligently. Often we just react and don't think much about it. Another aspect of managing our emotions intelligently has to do with what these emotions lead us to do. When I am afraid because there is a snarling Doberman in front of me, I want to run, but that might not be the best thing to do; I might suffer the consequences of a Doberman attack. Staying perfectly still is probably a better course of action. It's hard, but I do it until the owner comes and secures the dog. Thus, even strong emotions like anger and fear can be led skillfully and intelligently to better courses of expression.

How can a person develop the habit of leading a skillful and intelligent emotional life? Just determining what emotions we are feeling is not enough. In the metaphor of the ladder of metacognition, this is like going up on the first rung only. "Yes, I know I am angry with him, although I didn't want to admit that a few moments ago. So?" a person might say. Let's move to the second rung of emotional awareness: How is this anger manifesting itself? What am I angry about, and what does that make me want to do? At this level what is called for is a description of the details— the structure of the anger. "I am angry with him because he deliberately kept me waiting an hour and it's very cold. That was utterly inconsiderate. It makes me want to never see him again!" We could stop there: "He's a scoundrel and I will never see him again! That's just how I feel!"

You might, however, say, "Maybe there's a better way. Maybe it would be better to be sure. Perhaps I should ask if he really kept me waiting *deliberately*. That's not like him. Maybe I shouldn't be so angry with him." You might also question whether never seeing him again is the best thing to do. You really like being with him and would be giving that up if you ended the friendship. Now you've moved up to the third rung—you are evaluating your emotional state and what it is directing you to do.

The fourth rung of the ladder might be an easy step from there. You decide that you will find out what happened first before you conclude that he kept you waiting deliberately. That will help you to determine whether you should be angry. "If I find out that it really wasn't his fault at all," you conclude, "and he did try to contact me but couldn't, I won't be angry with him anymore." You might even realize that this should be a lesson to *you*. You should ask these kinds of questions whenever you find yourself in a strong emotional state, rather than just accepting things as they appear and doing what your emotions seem to be suggesting you should do.[14]

Obviously, climbing this ladder might not be so easy. This vignette is simplistic, but it has its point. However long it takes to be able to act skillfully and intelligently with regard to our emotions, making the initial climb is bound to be much better than staying on the ground. It can lead us to becoming aware of our emotions and eventually taking charge of them in our own service, just as metacognition can lead us to take charge of our own thinking in our own service. So let's call this the ladder of metaemotion. Besides helping us to think constructively about our thinking, the ladder can help us to avoid falling prey to our emotional impulsivity.

We suggest that in these ideas lie some buds that we should nurture to grow into blossoms that facilitate emotional intelligence in many more people than now have it.

Summary

Thinking about our thinking is not an esoteric or mysterious process. When we think about our thinking, the kind of thinking that we do is exactly the same sort of thinking we do when thinking about things other than our thinking—events that take place in the world, people, and other objects. For example, when we do things like read a novel, teach mathematics, or shop for new clothes, we can usually identify what we are doing. The same mental process of identification occurs when we think about our thinking and identify it as decision making, problem solving, or predicting.

But thinking about our thinking in certain ways is an integral part of skillful thinking. In skillful thinking we use appropriate thinking strategies and procedures (thinking skills) and enhance them with various mental behaviors and attitudes (habits of mind) to effectively complete a thinking task like making a well-thought-out decision or determining the viability of a new idea. These processes don't just happen. We guide ourselves in doing them, just as a good swimmer does in swimming a course, a good engineer in where and how to proceeding with the construction of a new building, a good cook in preparing a meal, and a good artist in the progress and direction of an artistic composition.

In this chapter we have sketched out how to engage in thinking about thinking in a way that will lead to accomplish such self-guidance of our thinking. We need to learn to go up the ladder of metacognition—a four-step process from awareness of the kind of thinking we are doing or are about to do, to endorsing what we think is a viable plan for how to do it again. This can be taught. We, in fact, endorse the idea that it should be taught explicitly like any thinking skill. In mature thinkers, by and large, these processes of guidance are internal and under the level of our consciousness, although sometimes, in rehearsing such events beforehand, we may bring them to the fore. Skillful metacognition is the superordinate guiding force to how we can engage in specific thinking tasks skillfully and effectively.

So it is it not the character of thinking about thinking itself that makes it special, but rather the unique role it plays in helping us to take charge of how we think and monitoring and guiding ourselves to engage in these thinking processes effectively and with skill. That's why we elevate it to the status of the third key ingredient in skillful thinking. To be a skillful thinker such self-guidance is necessary. Going up the ladder of metacognition as we think about our thinking is what shapes the specific procedures and attitudes that we apply on specific occasions, and it is what propels us along through these engagements as they occur. Without metacognition, the way we would respond to a thinking challenge would be to give up and shrug our shoulders; do something that was unthinking, routine, and probably founded on non-productive thinking habits; or make a guess.

Learning to climb the ladder of metacognition liberates us from these possible missteps. *We* choose, direct, and guide our own thinking. Metacognition, as empowerment, is the key to successful thinking-based learning.

The prospects of broadening the impact of these ideas about metacognition to apply to other aspects of our mental lives, in particular to our emotions, carries great promise. We suggest, in fact, that through analogous reflective self-direction, we ourselves, through the power of our thought, can have a profound impact on our emotional lives as well.

Notes

1. See Bloom, B. S., & Broder, L. J. (1950). *Problem-solving processes of college students.* Chicago: University of Chicago Press; Brown, A. L. (1978). Knowing when, where, and how to remember: A problem of metacognition. In E. Glaser (Ed.), *Advances in instructional psychology.* Hillsdale, NJ: Erlbaum; Whimbey, A. (1980). Students can learn to be better problem solvers. *Educational Leadership, 37* (7).
2. Costa, A. (2001). Mediating the metacognitive. A. Costa (Ed.), *Developing minds: A resource book for teaching thinking* (pp. 135–140). Alexandria, VA: Association for Supervision and Curriculum Development.
3. Perkins, D., & Swartz, R. (1989). The nine points about teaching thinking. In A. Costa, J. Bellanca, & R. Fogarty (Eds.), *If minds matter.* Palatine, IL: Skylights.
4. Swartz, R. (2003). Infusing critical and creative thinking into high school and college courses. In D. Fasco (Ed.), *Critical thinking and reasoning* (pp. 207–251). Creskill, NJ: Hampton Press.
5. Swartz, R. (2003). Ibid.
6. Ibid., p. 243.
7. Bloom, B. S., & Broder, L. J. (1950). Op. cit.
8. Flavell, J. H. (1976). Metacognitive aspects of problem solving. In L. B. Resnick (Ed.), *The nature of intelligence.* Hillsdale, NJ: Erlbaum.
9. Rigney, J. W. (1980). Cognitive learning strategies and qualities in information processing. In R. Snow, P. Federico, & W. Montague (Eds.), *Aptitudes, learning, and instruction* (Vol. 1). Hillsdale, NJ: Erlbaum.
10. Lochhead, J. (2000). *Thinkback: A user's guide to minding the mind.* Hillsdale, NJ: Erlbaum.
11. Reprinted by permission of the Hendricks Day School, Jacksonville, Florida.
12. Reprinted by permission of the Hendricks Day School, Jacksonville, Florida.
13. Goleman, D. (1995). *Emotional intelligence: Why it can matter more than IQ.* New York: Bantam.
14. See Swartz, R. (2001). In the grips of emotion. In A. Costa (Ed.), *Developing minds: A resource for teaching thinking*, 3rd ed. Alexandria, VA: Association for Supervision and Curriculum Development, pp. 164–169, for a thinking strategy map for thinking skillfully about our emotions. See also Ong, A. C. (2006). Promoting social-emotional learning, in A. C. Ong & G. Borich, *Teaching strategies that promote thinking* (pp. 145–165). Singapore: McGraw-Hill.

CHAPTER 5

Putting Skillful Thinking Into Writing

To communicate, put your words in order; give them a purpose; use them to persuade, to discover, to instruct, to seduce.

—William Safire, columnist

The ability to express oneself in writing is the quintessential skill for communication.

—Rick Allan, educator[1]

ASK YOUNG STUDENTS "Why do we write?" and they often say, "To tell you some things" or "Because you said we have to." Students also say that writing is not necessary any more because technology is going to take its place. Many find writing to be drudgery.

Detaching writing from its natural contexts and purposes often gives students these superficial and fundamentally misguided views. In our world today, the ability to express one's thoughts effectively in writing is an essential part of the way we relate to others. New technologies often increase the means through which we do this, not decrease them. Like the printing press, the Internet and text messaging are viewed by many as making writing even more of a quintessential skill for communication.

Characterizing writing only in terms of communication, however, is overly simplistic. Writing does often provide us with important information that we never would have uncovered ourselves, but we also use it for persuading, promoting understanding, prompting emotions, and many more purposes. These are often cast in specific circumstances whose impact on the character of the writing depend on our audience, constraints, presuppositions, and goals. Without setting the writing tasks we give students in these broader contexts, we detach writing from what gives it meaning as a human enterprise.

Returning to the lesson on skillful parts–whole thinking in Chapter 2, remember how the teacher set the context for the writing task that concluded the main part of the lesson. She said, "Imagine that you've been hired by the publisher of the *Birds of America* book from which we read the original passage about the kestrel. They now ask you to write one more paragraph describing how this bird gets its prey." This teacher is setting a context for the writing that implies a specific purpose for it and its audience. Remember also how appropriate it became to then include scientific terms like *talons* instead of *claws* in the writing.

Let us think, for a moment, about the importance of knowing your audience before undertaking a piece of writing. Many a writing assignment's downfall has been the failure to recognize the target audience. Although it is important that each student use his or her voice, he or she must realize that one does not write essays and reports as if talking to one's best friend. It would not have been appropriate for the proposed textbook entry on the kestrel to begin with "Hey, Ben," for example. Nor would the conclusion have been as technical if the product were to be a story read by other classmates. The choice of words and phrases is key to reflecting not only the content but also the thinking. There are four basic questions that one should ask oneself in relation to the audience for any given piece of writing:

- Will my intended audience understand what I am trying to tell them, and will they be able to follow my thinking?
- What does my intended audience already know about my topic (so that I don't have to tell it again)?
- What do I believe they want to know about it?
- What do I believe they should know or need to know (that I can tell them)?

By asking and answering these questions, students can identify not only the kinds of words and sentence structures to use but also the kind of content. Research shows that if we have students write to audiences who they know do not know as much about their topic as they do, they will be more inclined to use language and examples that will be understood by their audiences, to be more precise in their explanations, and to provide greater detail.[2]

Writing is not the only way we communicate our thinking and challenge the thinking of others; much of what we have said applies to oral communication as well. However, writing has one big advantage that oral communication lacks and that makes developing skill in writing of paramount importance: The written word is there to be read time and again. This means that it can support ongoing and careful reaction on the part of multiple readers. Writing provides a world of readers with the possibility of a level of sustained reflective, critical, and creative thought that the mere oral expression of the same ideas and points of view cannot usually sustain.

Many writing programs try to address the broader aspects of writing. They emphasize authentic contexts for writing and focus students on the implications of their writing for different audiences and purposes. Nevertheless, this in itself does not guarantee that the students' writing will express or expose deep and provocative thinking. To tap this richer potential, we must teach our students to put their *thinking* into their writing, not just the ideas and information they may gather. An emphasis on thinking and thinking skills, however, usually plays a very underdeveloped role in writing programs. The kind of thinking-based instruction that we have been examining in this book provides an ideal educational context in which to expand this role.

Writing also increases the *scope* of communication dramatically. Reading what is written in today's morning newspaper brings us in contact with the ideas of the journalist, a contemporary. Reading what was written (and has survived) in Greece and Rome 2,500 years ago brings us in contact with the ideas that were promulgated at that time as well, and as long as the writing survives, it will continue to bring future generations in contact with these ideas.

This chapter describes how we can teach our students to communicate their thinking in effective writing for the authentic purposes for which we undertake such interpersonal communication. Paper-and-pencil examples as well as computer writing are cited. We presume that students have already learned the basics of sentence construction and paragraphing, perhaps through thinking-based learning. The main question that we answer in this chapter is: What is the role of skillful thinking in effective writing, and how can we teach students to construct pieces of effective writing that utilize this connection?[3]

Thinking About What You Will Write

As a nation we can barely begin to imagine how powerful education might be if writing were put in its proper focus. Facility with writing opens students up to the pleasure of exercising their minds in ways that grinding on facts and information never will. More than a way of knowing, writing is an act of discovery.

—National Commission on Writing
in America's Schools and Colleges[4]

Time for organized thinking *prior* to writing is crucial for effective writing. We do not mean thinking about how to write but rather thinking about the topics on which we are going to write. Teachers often ask students to write without providing time for organized thinking beforehand. Let's look at some examples of what three fourth-grade students from a rural school in South Carolina wrote when asked to do a compare-and-contrast essay about Abraham Lincoln and Frederick Douglass, based on their textbooks. The first example is from Eric (Figure 5-1a). Stephen, as we noted in Chapter 1 (Fig. 1-2), wrote, "Compare and Contrast. Lincoln wanted fredom [sic], Douglas [sic] wanted fredom [sic]." Justin's example (Figure 5-1b) may stir a smile, but it carries a serious message to us in its honesty.

Figure 5-1a. Eric's Response

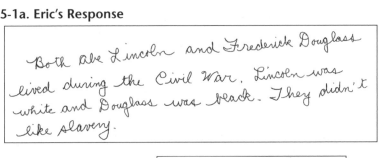

Both Abe Lincoln and Frederick Douglass lived during the Civil War. Lincoln was white and Douglass was black. They didn't like slavery.

Figure 5-1b. Justin's Response

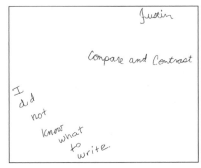

Justin

Compare and Contrast

I did not know what to write.

Eric, Stephen, and Justin are students on whom many teachers often give up.

Now let's look at samples from the same students after they have been given an opportunity to do some organized comparing and contrasting of Lincoln and Douglass in class before the writing. Figure 5-2 shows Eric's new response.

This essay has more detail as well as some organization—in this case chronological. Although it has a way to go, there is obviously much more thinking behind it than in Eric's initial attempt.

Now let's look at what Stephen wrote (Figure 5-3). The teacher obviously needs to work with Stephen on some of the mechanics of writing, especially spelling and capitalization. Notice, however, that he does know how to construct a sentence and even a paragraph. We attribute the sketchiness at the beginning of the writing to laziness or inertia rather than lack of skill. Once Stephen perks up, out come full sentences! More important, notice that the compare-and-contrast activity prior to the writing really got this student thinking; his second paragraph is a reflection of this. This is by no means a polished piece of writing, but it is a good start. Feedback and editing will take it far.

One important thing that this teacher did in the activity prior to the new writing was to use the graphic organizer (shown in Figure 3-2, page 56) for comparing and contrasting.[5] She had the students write their similarities and differences on this graphic. Then she had them focus on which similarities and differences are important and what conclusions can be drawn from these about the two men.

Figure 5-2. Eric's Essay

> Abrahan Lincoln and Federick Douglas were both leaders. They both worked on farms when they were little There mothers both died when they were little. Lincoln and Douglas both liked to read. Their family were poor. Douglas was born a slave. Douglas had no rights as a slave. He taught his selve how to read and write. Lincoln had rights to go to school. Douglas never new how his father was. Lincoln now his father well. Lincoln was against slavery and so was Douglas. But Lincoln was not a aboltionist and Douglas was. Douglas made speeches for black rights and women could vote. Lincoln was president. Lincoln was assinghtned at a theater. Douglas had a heart-attack and died.

Figure 5-3. Stephen's Essay

> Stephen
>
> <u>compare and contrast</u>
>
> both leaders. ther morethers died, lived in same time both against slavery one was free the other was not. one was president other was writer. One was an aboltionist onther was against slavery
>
> Thos are some things difrent and alike about frederic dongles and Abe lincoln. I think they were both good pepal becuas they wanted all men to have the same rights.

Insofar as what they write on their graphic organizers reflects the students' thinking, it represents prewriting that becomes very helpful when the students work on their essays. It enables them to perceive the mere similarities and differences between two things from the conclusions and inferences that they make about the two things based on these similarities and differences. This plays out in Stephen's essay, however primitive it may otherwise be.

Now let's look at what Justin wrote after the same class (Figure 5-4).

Although this piece of writing is certainly not as articulate and detailed as Stephen's, and it is somewhat more superficial, Justin, too, shows us that he knows sentence structure; more important, he has thought about some of the similarities and differences between the two men. What he has not yet understood is how to choose what is significant as he lists the comparisons; however, he has started. The flourish with which he ends this piece of writing shows his pride in this accomplishment. In contrast to his first effort, this piece of writing has some substance. With feedback and editing, it, too, could lead to much higher quality writing. For the teacher it is a beginning, in stark contrast to what Justin wrote earlier. There should be no giving up on students like these—guidance beforehand by a teacher in skillful thinking can bring this out dramatically.

Figure 5-4. Justin's Essay

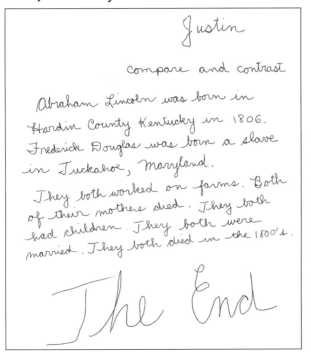

Justin

compare and contrast

Abraham Lincoln was born in Hardin County Kentucky in 1806. Frederick Douglas was born a slave in Tuckahoe, Maryland.

They both worked on farms. Both of their mothers died. They both had children. They both were married. They both died in the 1800's.

The End

Translating Good Thinking
Into Good Writing

Now let's look at another piece of compare-and-contrast writing from a student in a fifth-grade classroom. Students have read the book *The Sign of the Beaver* by Elizabeth George Speare, which is often used in the language arts programs of upper elementary classrooms.[6] This novel is set in the 18th century, when the state of Maine was still part of Massachusetts and was opened to settlement by the American colonists. The book focuses on two main characters: Matt, the 13-year-old son in a family from Quincy, Massachusetts, and Attean, the 14-year-old grandson of the chief of the Beaver tribe of Penobscot. After building a cabin on their new land in the woods of Maine, Matt is left alone while his father returns to Quincy for the rest of the family. Attean and his grandfather save Matt's life when he is attacked by bees. These boys, who hail from very different cultures, have to first overcome their prejudices before they can establish a bond founded on mutual appreciation of each other's survival skills. It is an awakening for both Matt and Attean as they cross a wide cultural barrier to become "brothers."

Like Lisa Williams, the teacher we mentioned in Chapter 3, this teacher gives her students classroom time to think through a comparison and contrast of these two characters. This lesson is the start of her program to implement one of her thinking goals: to teach the students to engage in *skillful* comparing and contrasting. Also like Lisa Williams, she bases this on an extended conception of what skillful comparing and contrasting involves. It is more than just listing some similarities and differences. She uses the same thinking strategy map as in the Lincoln-Douglass example to guide her students, she enhances their thinking by having them share their conclusions, and she helps them to start to learn how to plan their thinking ahead of time so that next time they compare and contrast they will be able to follow their plan.[7]

Here is a piece of compare-and-contrast writing that one fifth-grader did when the students were asked to write an essay about Matt and Attean based on the thinking they had just done.

Blood Brothers

Matt and Attean are two boys from two very different cultures who discover friendship through sharing their knowledge and skills with each other. In the book *The Sign of the Beaver*, these young men learn how to survive on their own in the woods of Maine. There are similarities and differences between the two boys that show this.

Matt and Attean are different but have many similarities. They were both very quick thinking. When they saw the bear, by quick thinking they killed it. Both of them were highly intelligent. Attean was a smart person because he knew the way and signs of the wilderness and knew how to get back. Matt knew how to cook, build a cabin, and read. The two boys were both without parents, which made them be more resourceful. Attean's parents were killed by white men, and Matt's parents were in Massachusetts.

Although Matt and Attean have similarities, they also have several differences. One way the boys are different is their culture. Attean's culture has spirits, clothes made from skins, dancing ceremonies, and wigwams. Matt's culture has a belief in God and Christ, clothes made from cloth, and log cabins. Another way in which they are different is their survival skills. Attean fishes with a spear, makes good bows and arrows, and know his way out of the wilderness. Hunting with a gun until it is stolen, Matt cooks his own food, fishes with a pole, and farms. The last way in which they are different is their background and race. While Attean is a Native American from the woods of Maine and believes that no one can own the land, Matt's race is White, from the town of Quincy, Massachusetts, and he believes that land may be bought and sold.

Matt and Attean prove that friendship can exist without prejudice. They learned from each other by sharing their skills and experiences. They looked beyond their differences and became friends through their similarities.

Arthur Whimbey and his colleagues state that "good writing demands clear thinking. Good thinking often results in concise, clear prose."[8]

Writing is the "hard copy" of thinking, yet the three Lincoln and Douglass examples speak against Whimbey et al.'s idea. The essays do show that time for careful thinking beforehand can have a dramatic impact on the substance of a piece of writing, but they have a long way to go for them to become "concise, clear prose."

Unlike those three examples, the organization and depth of this piece of writing about Matt and Attean stands out. This student has advanced a thesis and supported it with the relevant similarities and differences that he uncovered when guided by the thinking strategy map for open comparing and contrasting. He has comprehensively written his thinking explicitly into this piece of writing; the previous students did not (yet). How has this come about?

Figure 5-5 shows the completed graphic organizer developed by this student prior to his writing his compare-and-contrast essay about Matt and Attean.

As in other lessons we have described in this book, the use of a graphic organizer in this lesson provides students with an organized way to record their thoughts. They may do this on their own or in small collaborative groups. Although this technique of recording thoughts is not new, this specific graphic organizer has some special features. As we have commented in Chapter 2, it is not just a place to record ideas, like a journal. It is, like the other graphic organizers for skillful thinking that we have

Figure 5-5. Open Compare and Contrast

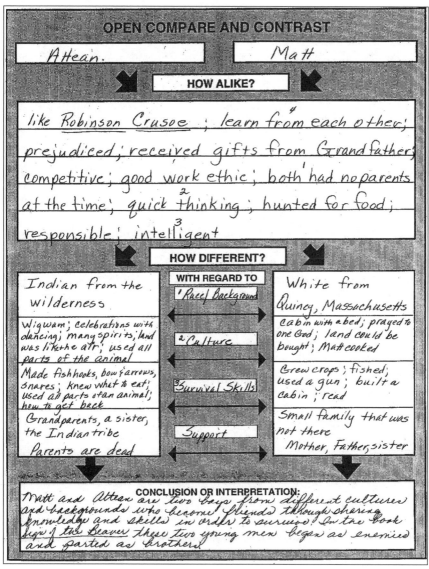

OPEN COMPARE AND CONTRAST

Attean. | Matt

HOW ALIKE?

like Robinson Crusoe ; learn from each other; prejudiced; received gifts from Grandfather; competitive; good work ethic; both had no parents at the time; quick thinking ; hunted for food; responsible; intelligent

HOW DIFFERENT?

WITH REGARD TO

Indian from the wilderness — ¹ Race/ Background — White from Quincy, Massachusetts

Wigwam; celebrations with dancing; many spirits; land was like the air; used all parts of the animal — ²Culture — Cabin with a bed; prayed to one God; land could be bought; Matt cooked

Made fishhooks, bow & arrows, snares; knew what to eat; used all parts of an animal; how to get back — ³Survival Skills — Grew crops; fished; used a gun; built a cabin; read

Grandparents, a sister, the Indian tribe. Parents are dead — Support — Small family that was not there. Mother, Father, sister

CONCLUSION OR INTERPRETATION:

Matt and Attean are two boys from different cultures and backgrounds who become friends through sharing knowledge and skills in order to survive. In the book Sign of the Beaver these two young men began as enemies and parted as brothers.

looked at in this book, *cognitively dynamic*. It is structured to prompt the movement of thought with built-in directionality to guide the students as they employ the thinking strategy embodied in the map.

Note also the depth and breadth that occur when the students are asked to categorize the types of differences and to find any patterns that show up in the similarities and differences that were identified. These subepisodes of thinking are introduced to enhance the process of comparing and contrasting so that it leads to deeper insight about what is being compared.

As students share the similarities and differences that they have noted, many teachers use the important technique of asking extending questions. For example, when a student reports that one similarity between Matt and Attean is that they both had no parents with them at the time, the teacher might ask: "When a child is without his parents, what might that mean for the child?" The student might answer, "He'll have to do a lot of things on his own and especially for himself." Prompting such thoughtful responses is especially important. It activates relevant background knowledge and thereby deepens the students' understanding of the significance of the similarities and differences that they note. It also requires students to think and communicate with accuracy and precision, a necessary habit of mind to carry over to the actual writing process.

The results of the organized and deep pattern of thinking done by this student show up in the graphic organizer. He has actively engaged in skillful comparing and contrasting prompted by his teacher and the structure of the graphic organizer. Now he must transfer this thinking, as recorded in the graphic organizer, into an organized piece of effective writing. He utilizes what we call a "Thought-Full Writing Map."[9] This is the writing map that he uses for compare-and-contrast writing (Table 5-1).

Using devices such as writing maps to guide writing is controversial. When students use a writing map like this to guide their writing, it seems to immediately transform the dynamic of the writing activity into a mechanical formulaic exercise. The result might be nothing more than a "paint by numbers" applied to writing.

This is a misconception. Let's consider an analogy. Suppose that when I go shopping I don't just randomly go into stores and buy things. Rather, I do it in an organized and thorough way, guided by a written shopping list that is organized geographically—that is, it starts with the things I need to buy at one place, then adds to the list things in the next closest store, and so on. I follow it religiously. Does this mean that no thought has gone into how I will do my shopping? On the contrary—the shopping list is the product of very careful thought. This was my shopping map; that's what writing maps are in the "thought-full" classroom.[10]

How does this happen in the classroom? In this case the teacher had prompted the students to think about what they might want to accomplish in writing a compare-and-contrast essay, and whom they would expect to read such an essay. They decided that the essay would be written for people interested in the two characters being compared and contrasted— hence for people who had some knowledge of these characters already through their reading of at least some of the novel. They then decided that the purpose of their writing would be to show that their conclusions, which were not stated in the novel, were supported by specific informa-

Table 5-1. Example of a Writing Map

Open Compare-and-Contrast Writing Map
Expository

(This writing map is to be used with the completed open compare-and-contrast graphic organizer)

Paragraph 1 – This paragraph is an introduction to your writing.

Sentence 1: Write the conclusion or interpretation from the graphic organizer. It should include the names of the two things that you are comparing and contrasting.
Sentence 2: Write a sentence to elaborate on the first one, giving more information about your topic.
Sentence 3: The last sentence should relate to your reader that the two things you are comparing have similarities and differences.

Paragraph 2 – This paragraph will explain the similarities that the two things share.

Before you begin this paragraph, you need to choose the three best similarities from your graphic organizer. Number them in order of importance from best (1) to least (3).

Sentence 1: This is a topic sentence to tell the reader that the paragraph will contain similarities.
Sentence 2: State the second most important similarity that you chose.
Sentence 3: Give an example of how the two things you are comparing meet the similarity.
Sentence 4: State the least important similarity you chose.
Sentence 5: Elaborate on how the two things you are comparing meet the similarity.
Sentence 6: State the most important similarity.
Sentence 7: Elaborate on how the two things share this commonality.

Paragraph 3 – This paragraph will discuss the differences between the two things.

Choose the three best categories (listed under the With Regard To box) and number them from best (1) to least (3).

Sentence 1: This is a transition sentence between the two paragraphs. It should connect the last sentences of paragraph 2 to the topic of paragraph 3. For example, "
Although ___ and ___ have similarities, they also have differences."
Sentence 2: Write a sentence using the second most important category.
Sentence 3: Give an example of how each of the two is different in this regard. (You may also write additional sentences giving specific examples.)
Sentence 4: Write a sentence using the third most important category.
Sentence 5: Give an example of how each of the two is different in this regard. (You may also write additional sentences giving specific examples.)
Sentence 6: Write a sentence using the most important category.
Sentence 7: Tell the reader how each is different in this regard. (You may also write additional sentences giving specific examples.)

Paragraph 4 – This is your concluding paragraph.

Sentences 1, 2, and 3: This is your opportunity to impress the reader with your conclusion. However, it should be worded differently from the first paragraph. The last sentence, the clincher, is what the reader will remember the best.

Reread your entire essay. Then answer the question "So what?" in your mind. This will help you to generate a closing statement.

tion given in the novel about the characters. How, then, should their writing be organized to convey this to those who would read it? And how can they make sure it is clear and precise?

At this point this teacher divided the class into small working groups of three and told them that they should outline a four–paragraph essay that they thought would serve this purpose. They then shared their results and tried to reach a class consensus, guided by the teacher. The writing strategy map that was used by the student above was the result. The ideas for what should go into this four-paragraph, sentence-by-sentence structure came from the students working interdependently.

After the writing the teacher intended to raise this question with the students: "In what ways did this writing map work for you in composing your compare-and-contrast essay about Matt and Attean? If it did not, how would you modify it, and why? Restate it in your own words."

Teachers of children in grades 2 and 3 who are concerned with thinking often find this approach too advanced and impractical. They frequently give their students writing maps that they have designed. An example of a primary writing map for comparing and contrasting is shown Figure 5-6. Usually, such writing maps are simpler than the fourth-grade example we have just looked at, for obvious reasons. The approach of using them is in the same spirit, however. The teachers want their students to think about the usefulness of these writing maps, but with younger students this is prompted in process or after they use what the teacher has designed. For example, such teachers often ask their students, while they are using the maps, to think about whether they help them to show other students how they reached their conclusions.

After using this writing map the children are encouraged to suggest changes, and the teacher guides a discussion of whether these are good changes. If the class agrees, then the changes are made in the writing map.

Figure 5-7 shows an example of writing done by a second-grade student using this writing map. The comparison and contrast that she has done in preparation for this writing is with regard to bats and birds.

Making Explicit the Products of Skillful Thinking in Our Writing

Good writing presupposes that skillful thinking, supported by powerful mental habits, lies behind the writing. As a general rule, we suggest that when achieving the purpose of the writing depends in part on the soundness of the thinking behind it, and when the readers need guidance to follow the thinking, it should be made as explicit as possible without compromising the force of the writing. The typical paradigm for this is writing persuasive prose.

Figure 5-6. Grade 2 Writing Map[11]

Open Compare-and-Contrast Writing Map for Grade 2

- *Sentence 1*: State the name of the two things being compared and contrasted in a sentence that tells the reader that there are ways the two things are alike and different. This is your topic sentence.

    1)_____

    _____

- *Sentences 2–4*: These should tell some important ways that the two things are alike. Make sure that you give details about the similarities.

    2)_____

    _____

    3)_____

    _____

    4)_____

    _____

- *Sentences 5–7*: These should tell some important ways that the two things are different. Make sure that you give details about the differences.

    5)_____

    _____

    6)_____

    _____

    7)_____

    _____

- *Sentence 8*: This is your last sentence. It should tell something important about the conclusions that were made about the similarities and differences.

    8)_____

    _____

The following persuasive letter was written by a fifth-grade student to Mrs. Preston, a main character in the novel *Shiloh* by Phyllis Reynolds Naylor. In this Newbery Award winner, Marty Preston longs for a dog, but his father has made it clear that due to a lack of money there will be no dog in the Preston household. When a cruelly treated young dog runs away from his master and follows Marty home for the second time, the boy hides the animal, which he has named Shiloh, in the woods. His mother is suspicious and discovers his hiding place. Marty knows that if

Figure 5-7. Bats and Birds[12]

Sample Student Expository Writing • Grade 2 • Bats

Bats are like birds in some ways but they are different in other ways. They use their wings to fly just like birds. They have to be old enough to fly alone just like birds. They have two feet like birds do. But bats hang upside down with their feet and birds sit on branches. Bats have different faces from birds because they have a nose and a mouth and birds have a beak. A really important thing is bats have fur because they are mammals and birds have feathers because they are birds. The most important thing to remember is bats can't be birds because they have mammal body parts and are really mammals.

he returns Shiloh to Judd, the cruel owner, the dog will probably be killed. His mother does not believe in lying by omission. Thus, in this letter, the student recommends what Mrs. Preston should do when she is asked by Marty to keep Shiloh a secret from his father for at least 24 hours.

Dear Mrs. Preston,

You have discovered Marty's secret. He is keeping the dog Shiloh from Judd because he fears that Judd will kill it. You are faced with a tough choice. The purpose of this letter is to recommend what I think you should do. It may seem to you that you have to decide whether to tell Marty's father or not. However, there are many options other than just those two. You could keep Marty's secret and tell no one, make Marty take Shiloh back to Judd and not tell your husband, or take Shiloh back to the house and show him to Marty's father.

If you make Marty take Shiloh back to Judd and not tell Pa that you found him, there are several negative consequences and not too many positive ones. Most likely your husband would find out. After all, he is a postman, and they visit with everyone. He feels strongly about the fact that Shiloh belongs to Judd and he would be embarrassed in front of Judd. Being so mean and cruel, Judd might have Marty arrested, although he often breaks the law by killing deer out of season. Judd might even kill Shiloh. He has a history of abusing his dogs and has threatened to break Shiloh's legs if he found him.

Another option you might consider is to keep Marty's secret and tell no one. It is obvious that you believe that telling the truth is extremely important. It is part of your deep faith in God. When you made Marty tell the truth about eating Dara Lynn's treat, you showed how you felt about lying. Omission is another form of lying. You might even feel so guilty that it would change your relationship with your husband and family. Pa also might find out since he often goes hunting. He would probably be mad at you at first, but you seem to have a strong marriage so he most likely will forgive you. However, there would be some pretty miserable moments first. Guilt is hard to live with.

Probably the best option of the three is to take Shiloh back to the house, show it to Marty's father, and explain the situation to him as best you can. You have a very good relationship with your husband and he listens to you. Even though he feels strongly about property, he might help to think of another solution besides giving the dog back to Judd. Because you have told the truth, you would not feel guilty. Marty would see that the truth is very important because you are a good role model. Although Shiloh might have to go back to Judd, Marty's father might be more understanding about the situation and he might tell Judd that he is going to be watching to see if he hurts Shiloh.

If you look at these three options, each has both positive and negative consequences. Because you value the truth so highly and more good things can come out of taking Shiloh back to the house and talking to Marty's father, that is the option that I recommend to you. It will deepen the trusting relationship that you have with your husband and show Marty that a truth is of great value. Thank you for your consideration and attention. Please think carefully before you make a decision. The future of your family could depend on it.

Sincerely,

Matthew

Table 5-2 shows the writing map that was developed by the students after they were prompted by the teacher to engage in skillful decision making about this issue and asked to decribe a good persuasive letter that would reflect skillful decision making.

Notice how this writing reflects the style of writing in which the substantive results of the student's engagement with skillful decision making are structured into his letter in accordance with the writing map and the thinking he engaged in is written explicitly into the letter.

Let's look at another example from a 12th-grade student. This letter, too, makes various aspects of skillful decision making explicit through the use of the terminology of the thinking in which this student has engaged.

Table 5-2. Five-Paragraph Persuasive Letter Writing Map

Decision-Making Writing Map: Recommending the Best Option
Persuasive Letter

This letter will be used to convince your reader to take an action that you recommend. You will use at least 3 completed Decision Making graphic organizers that have each explored a different option. Before you begin writing rank the options from strongest to weakest, state your purpose, and think how best to communicate with your audience.

Paragraph 1—This paragraph is your opportunity to gain the attention of the person to whom you are writing.
Explain the situation that makes the decision necessary, state the purpose of the letter, and list the options that you are going to discuss.

Paragraph 2—This paragraph is to inform your reader about the option you ranked second strongest.
State the second strongest of the options. Discuss it with regard to its positive and negative consequences. Support each consequence with evidence and explain its importance. (8-10 sentences)

Paragraph 3—This paragraph is to inform your reader about the option you ranked weakest.
State the weakest of the options and discuss it with regard to its positive and negative consequences. Support each consequence with evidence and explain its importance. (8-10 sentences)

Paragraph 4—This paragraph is to inform your reader about the option you ranked the strongest.
State the strongest of the options (this is the one you think is best) and discuss it with regard to its positive and negative consequences. Support each consequences with evidence and explain its importance. (8-10 sentences)

Paragraph 5—This paragraph is your recommendation.
Review the options you have discussed and recommend the one that you think is best in light of the consequences. Explain why the option you are recommending is better than the others. Close your letter with something like this: *Thank you for your consideration* or *Please consider my recommendation*. (4-5 sentences)

This is the world history lesson described in Chapter 4 in which the students try to decide the best tactic to end the war with the Japanese in the Pacific in 1945.

August 1, 1945
Dear President Truman,

I understand that you must make a decision about how to end the war. From the information I have, you have five basic options. You may use the atomic bomb on a strategic military city, demonstrate the bomb, invade Japan, continue conventional bombing, or negotiate peace. I am going to lay out the consequences of each option to assist your decision.

Recently, you have been given information about a top-secret weapon, the atomic bomb. From the test at Los Alamos we understand that this weapon could devastate an entire city. This fact in itself should be given heavy consideration. An entire city will be reduced to nothing. Any people or buildings within a certain radius of the bomb will disappear. This not only includes military weapons and personnel, it also contains civilians who work and live in the targeted city and the buildings that they inhabit. This total destruction must be discussed further before making this sort of decision. On the other hand, our secret weapon may save millions of American and Japanese lives in the long run. Right now, many soldiers are dying on behalf of both countries due to conventional fighting tactics. Therefore, the atomic bomb could put a quick end to the war, saving many military casualties.

However, most of the scientists I have corresponded with have made it very clear that they do not think we should use the bomb against a populated city at this point. They suggest that a demonstration of the bomb be given the Japanese. In this way, the Japanese will witness the power that the United States possesses. This may intimidate them enough to surrender and end the war and save lives. Yet they may not surrender even if a demonstration is given. Or perhaps the demonstration won't work properly. There is a lot of uncertainty about this. Nevertheless, a demonstration of the bomb will reduce some of the guilt that the United States will have to face if it is necessary to use the bomb on a military target.

Previously, the United States had been planning to invade Japan with two million soldiers. We estimate over a million casualties on both sides as a result of this invasion. These numbers do seem plausible because of the reports we have received regarding casualties from recent attacks. The negatives seem to far outweigh the positives in this alternative. Besides loss of life, we could lose the battle. In addition, this invasion may not end the war quickly. If the war is prolonged, it will cost the U.S. more money. More men may be drafted in order to revive the force from losses. All of these factors may also cause you to lose favor with the American people and therefore lose the next election. On the other hand, there is a slim chance that we may win the war quickly by invading. The Allies may join in. We may then be able to spare many civilian lives and keep the atomic bomb as our "secret" weapon.

While an invasion may have drawbacks, continuing conventional bombing seems to incur just as many. First this process is costing us many American lives and dollars. Also, there is no guarantee that the Japanese will surrender anytime soon. We are receiving reports that the Japanese soldiers will fight until all of them are dead. On the other hand, we have also received reports that tell us that the commanders are talking about a way to negotiate an end to the war through Stalin as a mediator. If this is the case, we need to consider carefully the last option—negotiate peace.

The final choice is my recommendation to you. I suggest that the United States try to negotiate peace with the Japanese at this stage in the war. We may gain a resolution to end the war quickly. Leading Japanese intellectuals support negotiations. Also, we know that the Japanese military wanted to negotiate an end if they won the Marianas. Knowing that the Japanese leaders also consider surrendering under conditional terms, we may be able to achieve peace quite easily through compromise.

Yet there are people who believe that Japan will never surrender, due to their immense sense of national pride. In addition, Mr. Stimson believes that the United States should not change its position about Japan's unconditional surrender. He thinks that if the Japanese do not surrender unconditionally, then they will rise up and begin another war. He does not want to see the Japanese repeat what the Germans did in World War I and World War II.

There is also the fear that if we begin negotiations with Japan, the talks may take too long or that nothing will be decided from the talks. Finally, there is the danger that the Japanese may have time to become stronger during these peace talks. Nevertheless, it is my earnest opinion that peace arbitration is the best choice for you to make at this time. It is in the United States' best interest to win the war quickly. We may not have to concede anything very serious that could leave Japan still a threat; there is some indication that the Japanese will surrender if they can retain their emperor. If the Japanese stall, on the other hand, to rebuild their armed forces, we must remember that we still have the atomic bomb. We should then consider more seriously either demonstrating the weapon or using it on a city. We have little to lose and much to gain if we give peace talks a chance.

Sincerely,
Rebecca Price

This letter is based on the writing map shown in Table 5-3, which was developed by the students and the teacher, who has prompted them by asking what in a letter like this would give them confidence that its writer had thought carefully and skillfully about this issue.

This writing represents the epitome of instruction in skillful thinking infused into content instruction and enhanced by powerful habits of mind. The development of an organized framework for the writing in the form of the writing map gave the students another essential component in the composition of powerful pieces of persuasive writing.

Table 5-3. Six Paragraph Persuasive Letter Writing Map[13]

Persuasive Letter
(Decision Making)

(This writing map is to be used with at least three completed skillful decision-making graphic organizers.)

This persuasive letter will be used to convince your reader to take an action that you recommend. You will use at least three completed decision-making graphic organizers that have each explored a different option. Before you begin writing, rank the options from strongest (1) to weakest (3).

Paragraph 1 – This paragraph is your opportunity to gain the attention of the person to whom you are writing.
Explain the situation that makes the decision necessary.
State the purpose of the letter.
List the options that you are going to discuss.

Paragraph 2 – This paragraph is to inform your reader about the option you ranked second strongest (2).
State the second strongest of the options. Discuss its positive and negative consequences. Support each consequence with evidence and explain its importance (8–10 sentences).

Paragraph 3 – This paragraph is to inform your reader about the option you ranked the weakest (3).
State the weakest of the options and discuss its positive and negative consequences. Support each consequence with evidence and explain its importance (8–10 sentences).

Paragraph 4 – This paragraph is to inform your reader about the option you ranked as the strongest (1).
State the strongest of the options (this is the one you think is best) and discuss its positive and negative consequences. Support each consequence with evidence and explain its importance (8–10 sentences).

Paragraph 5 – This paragraph is your recommendation.
Review the options you have discussed and recommend the one that you think is best in light of the consequences. Explain why the option you are recommending is better than the others (6–8 sentences).

Paragraph 6 – This paragraph is your last chance to convince the person to whom you are writing that the option you are recommending is the best one.
Make your recommendation again. Give the strongest reasons why it is the best one. Close your letter with something like this: "Thank you for your consideration" or "Please consider my recommendation" (4–5 sentences).

Including the Products of Skillful Thinking in Writing (but Hiding the Thinking)

So far we have been examining classroom strategies for instances in which a writer uses the language of thinking to write about some aspect of that thinking. In other cases, however, a writer has engaged in thinking before writing (or while writing), but what is written is the *result* of that thought, not an explicit description of all or even part of it.

Here are two excerpts from Shakespeare's plays that will help to illustrate this point:

Romeo and Juliet

But soft! What light through yonder window breaks?
It is the East, and Juliet is the sun!
....

Two of the fairest stars in all the heaven,
Having some business, do entreat her eyes
To twinkle in their spheres till they return.
What if her eyes were there, they in her head?
The brightness of her cheek would shame those stars
As daylight doth a lamp; her eyes in heaven
Would through the airy region stream so bright
That birds would sing and think it were not night.

                                   Act II, Scene ii, 2–3, 16–23

As You Like It

Jaques:
All the world's a stage,
And all the men and women merely players;
They have their exits and their entrances,
And one man in his time plays many parts,
His acts being seven ages.

                                   Act II, Scene vii, 139–143

Shakespeare obviously put some thought into the metaphors used in these selections. The power of his writing depends in large part on these metaphors. However, his thinking about what metaphor to use is not described at all in these plays, nor does Shakespeare even use the word metaphor. In fact, if he did that would seriously detract frrom the force of his words.

When we don't think much about the kinds of metaphors we use, they often are mundane and shallow rather than deeply evocative like those in these poems. Careful and skillful thinking clearly went into these poems.

Here is an example from a fourth-grade student in which the thinking that preceded the writing involved choosing the most powerful metaphor to convey thoughts about reading a book.[14] (This was taught in the same way as the other skillful thinking activities described in this book, through the techniques of direct instruction.)

Reading

A book is a roller coaster
Taking you up and lifting your spirits to the sky
Making your stomach churn
Something you will never forget
Taking you through different emotions, reaching the top
The next step is unknown, like the next page in a book
Surprised by where it takes you and where it might leave
    you
You're nervous, hands trembling, fists clenched as you
    wonder
What will happen next.
A book is a roller coaster.

Thinking Infused in the Writing Process

Process writing is an instructional approach to writing that involves students in a process of the development of a piece of writing from draft to final version. Typically, peer editing, self-editing, teacher editing, and feedback are all involved, with the rewriting of two drafts or more leading to a final polished piece of writing. Such organized programs for students have had generally good results in upgrading the quality of student writing and improving students' motivation to write. How can the introduction of explicit instruction in skillful thinking as a prelude to writing, the prompting of explicit reflection on the purposes and audience for the writing, and the creation and use of writing maps fit into this program?

Process writing has been identified as one of the most effective approaches to teaching and learning writing.[17] Skilled writers are involved in five stages: prewriting, drafting, revising, editing, and publishing the final product. Fletcher and Portalupi identify a three-part process: conceive, craft, and correct.[18] How do these stages fit in with teaching thinking strategies, habits of mind, and the use of writing maps? By what process can what we have described earlier in this chapter lead to "thought-full" writing?

Skillful thinking is a self-planned, proficient, and purposeful application of appropriate thinking skills without skipping any key operations, using relevant skill-related knowledge, and supported by appropriate and important mental habits. However, "thought-full" writing does not automatically flow from this process. Downloading these thoughts, as we have illustrated, is facilitated by the use of various graphic organizers and can serve as focused prewriting. This must now transition into more formal written works as a writer works through the writing process. Using a writing map facilitates learning how to make this transition. As we have described them, writing maps provide a structure for translating these thoughts into various forms of written expression. What emerges is a written draft of an organized piece of writing designed to serve a specific purpose for a particular audience.

As we have affirmed earlier in this chapter, without prethought of this sort it is unlikely that more than superficial and sketchy writing will result. Our earlier examples illustrate this clearly. In our experience, there are myriad other examples across the curriculum that illustrate this point. Many teachers who work with students on writing lament this fact also. Hence we suggest that the term *"thought-full" writing* be used only when skillful thinking precedes the writing.

Note-taking is often mentioned as a paradigm of prewriting. Graphic organizers such as those used in the kestrel, Hiroshima, and *Sign of the Beaver* lessons can be effectively used as note-taking devices. These graphic organizers give students a structured and focused way to record their thinking and allow the students to look back at their notes in order to structure their writing. When students were asked to write a textbook entry on the kestrel using what they knew about parts-to-whole relationships, they were able to authenticate not only their writing but also their thinking by going back to their graphic organizers on which they had written the names of the parts of this bird and had recorded the function of these parts. Journals and diaries are just two other examples of authentic vehicles for prewriting. When the writing process is preceded by skillful thinking, habits of precision and clarity are encouraged.

We have referenced three more standardly accepted stages in the writing process: revising, editing, and publishing. Is there anything in instruction in skillful thinking that can enhance these stages in the process?

Revision is one of the basic steps in effective writing. It is a direct result of feedback from either a peer or a teacher. "If high school students don't develop the habit of writing and revising, they pay the price when they arrive at college."[19] Phyllis Katz says that most of the students she teaches do not understand what revision entails. She says that they believe it means

> incorporating the teachers' corrections and handing in the paper for a new grade. But when students revise, they should ask themselves: "What is my argument? Have I developed it coherently and supported it with sufficient evidence? Does my paper sustain its focus?"[20]

We want to suggest, as Hurwitz and Hurwitz do, that significant revision should grow out of standards set by the pre-thinking that has been done as a basis for the writing.

It is difficult for teachers to walk the fine line between giving students helpful feedback on their writing and taking away the ownership of the product by giving them too much input. Most students are so insecure about writing that they want feedback in which the teacher suggests words, phrases, or sentences that make it "better." It can even become the teacher's assignment instead of the student's, and the teacher will end up assessing him- or herself. Writers need feedback that stimulates them to think and make changes within their own level of expertise and to persist through the rather lengthy writing process. In order to focus students on their own writing and not on what you as the teacher must do for them, good questioning strategies can be employed: "How can you say this differently to make your reader understand more completely?" "What else can you tell about … so that your reader will know what you know?" Such questions help the student to understand that asking for feedback does not mean that the teacher will rewrite the assignment. This is difficult because, as teachers, our level of sophistication is so much higher and we naturally want our students to reflect the same level.

Teachers must also consider when to give feedback. Barak Rosenshine points out that feedback must be continual, supportive, and occur during or immediately after the performance—no three-day delay between writing and feedback.[21] When students are slow or hesitant, feedback should be sustaining (e.g., hints, alternatives, suggestions). Those who make errors need corrective feedback and options for revision.

Thinking-Based Peer Editing

The most frequent uses of collaboration in the writing process involve peer editing and revision. Students are not born peer editors; they must be taught the art of collaborative writing. Here is a peer-editing technique that teachers have taught students to use. It promotes one student listening or reading a fellow student's writing with empathy and understanding. The "editor" is allowed to ask questions that deal with the hard copy of thinking and not with the mechanics of spelling, grammar, and sentence structure, unless they interfere with meaning and understanding. In an activity called Think–Pair–Share, students are asked to pair with another student. There are two variations.[22]

- Each partner reads his or her product to the other, which requires good listening.
- Each partner reads the product of the other, which requires focused reading.

The following kinds of questions may be asked:

- *Clarification*: If you don't understand what a word means in context, you may ask questions that help you understand what is being said. For example, you may ask, "What do you mean when you say…?"
- *Extension*: If you think your partner is saying something interesting, but is too brief, you can ask for more details about the idea. You might say something like "What more can you tell me about…?"

- *Challenge*: If you think the writer is misled or confused, you may ask questions that you think will prompt your partner to reframe his or her thinking and perhaps realize that the statement needs further consideration. Such questions might begin with "Why do you think…?"

There is another way that standards of skillful thinking play a role in peer editing. Sally Rogers has worked with her third-grade students to identify the functions of the various parts of the human ear and to determine how they work together to make it possible for us to hear. She has asked the students to write about how the ear works based on this example of parts–whole thinking, making sure that they mention all the parts and that they make use of what they have learned about the function of parts like the eardrum, or anvil, to explain to someone who doesn't know how a person can hear. After each student has written a draft, Ms. Rogers pairs the students together, gives them a checklist of the parts that they covered, and asks them to read each other's writing. If they think that a part is omitted, they are to check it off on the checklist and make a suggestion as to where in the writing their partner can add it. They then share these ideas. Ms. Rogers then asks each student to revise what they have written based on these suggestions.

This is an example of peer editing, which makes use of a checklist that flags the important things that students have thought about that should be in their writing to make it more "thought-full." It is one way of fostering constructive revisions based on the standards set by the thinking goals behind the writing.

Other teachers have used Ms. Rogers' technique with other types of writing, asking the students to use their writing maps for comparing and contrasting, or for writing a persuasive piece, as standards for the writing they are helping their partners with. Remember the teacher who asked her students to think about what they would want to see in a piece of persuasive writing that would show that the writer had thought carefully about the issue and that what he was recommending was based on careful and skillful thinking? The writing map they developed, in fact, served three purposes in the process of writing a persuasive letter:

- An initial writing map to guide the students in developing their first drafts
- A checklist for peer editing and suggested revisions
- A basis for each student to self-edit his or her writing

Such self-editing involved more than just watching for typos, misspellings, and grammatical errors. It was also based on the thinking strategy map as a standard for the organization of the piece of writing to best reflect the thinking that went into it.

Figure 5-8 shows one example of a writing map restructured as a tool for peer editing. This is a 12th-grade version used in the lesson on the bombing of Hiroshima.

These classroom activities show us how teachers can use the connection between skillful thinking and writing to enhance their instruction on an effective writing process.

The final stage of the writing process is publishing. This is not to be taken literally; it merely represents the need to bring the writing to completion by having each student produced a polished piece in the appropriate authentic format: a book, a letter, a poem, or a report with recommendations.

We have seen many such products in this book so far. Let us look at some writing that is a little different from the compare-and-contrast essays and persuasive letters that we have examined. Below are two polished pieces of poetry in diamante form produced by fifth-grade students. One is about Matt and Attean of *The Sign of the Beaver*, the other is about Abraham Lincoln and Frederick Douglass. These are finished products that resulted from a process that started with comparing and contrasting the two people and concluded with peer editing, revisions, and final editing.

A diamante poem is structured like a diamond, blending characteristics that give us contrasting insight in one unit. Such a structure lends itself to contrasting two items, whether they are characters in a story or pyramids and triangles. The writing represents the deep thinking behind it, and, conversely, the thinking that stands behind it enhances the writing.

Here are the two examples. Think of the understanding represented by each of these words, and the way the whole creates something more than just the sum of the individual parts:

Matt
Responsible, Alone
Cooking, Farming, Surviving
White, Christian, Indian, Manitou
Hunting, Fishing, Trapping
Resourceful, Stubborn
Attean

Lincoln
Free, Caucasian
Farming, Lawmaking, Disapproving
President, Constitutionalist, Newspaperman, Abolitionalist
Escaping, Leading, Representing
Enslaved, Determined
Douglass

This, too, is "thought-full" writing.

Figure 5-8. Adapted Writing Map

Editorial Checklist for Well-Thought-Out Persuasive Letter

Initial Background Task: (1) How would you answer the following question: If you were President Truman and were receiving letters recommending what to do to end the war with the Japanese, what characteristics of the letter would make you confident that the writer had thought carefully about this question. (2) Transform your answers into a checklist that can be used to judge the quality of any piece of persuasive writing.

Suggested Checklists: Below is the set of items you suggested for a checklist of factors to attend to when reading a piece of persuasive writing in order to be assured that it is well thought out. Check the box if the factor is present, leave it blank if it isn't, then make whatever suggestions you have for improving the letter in the "suggestion" boxes.

☐   The letter states the conclusion (recommendation) clearly.
   a. If this was not your original conclusion, explain what it was and why you changed.

> Suggestions

☐   The letter indicates an awareness of the circumstances or facts that make a decision necessary.

> Suggestions

☐ The letter indicates that a number of options have been considered.

> Suggestions

☐ The letter shows an awareness of the cons as well as the pros in discussing the consequences.

> Suggestions

☐ The letter supports the importance of controversial consequences with statistics or hard facts.

> Suggestions

☐ The letter explains why this recommended option is better than the others.

> Suggestions

☐   The letter uses nonloaded language.

> Suggestions

☐   The letter is well organized.

> Suggestions

Conclusion

Writing-process instruction, enhanced by thinking strategies and tools, takes time. Students must be given ample opportunity to think before they write. The deeper the thinking, the more elaborate the writing will be. This will invariably take longer than if the students simply read the chapter and answer the questions at the end. In fact, two or three class periods might be necessary to complete the thinking portion of the lesson before the teacher asks the students to do any organized writing. That, too, will take time. If we want to achieve the objectives of a well-conceived thinking-based curriculum, we need to spend the time. Time spent on the writing process is time well spent.

Every teacher knows that good writing about content that is central to the learning objectives in a curriculum enhances the achievement of those objectives. When such writing is the culmination of a process of infusing instruction in skillful thinking into content instruction, the learning potential it represents is inestimable. We cannot fail to appreciate the power of this kind of instruction when we look at the insights of the students whose writing samples we have used here. We should note that the students who wrote these are not gifted and talented students; they represent every student we teach. We cannot fail to see how widely this potential extends.

This kind of instruction is within the reach of every teacher. The door is open, the pathway easy to follow, and guides are accessible and ready. Cross that threshold!

Notes

1. Allen, R. (2003, Summer). *Expanding writing's role in learning, 1–8. Curriculum Update*. Alexandria, VA: Association for Supervision and Curriculum Development.
2. Hayes, J. R., & Flower, L. S. (1981). Writing as problem solving. *Visible Language, 14*, 388–399. See also Scardamalia, M., & Bereiter, C. (1986). Research on written composition. In M. C. Wittrock (Ed.), *Handbook of research on teaching* (pp. 778–803, esp. pp. 785–787). New York: Macmillan.
3. Reagan, R. (2001). Developing a lifetime of literacy. In A. Costa (Ed.), *Developing minds: A resource book for teaching thinking* (pp. 337–342). Alexandria, VA: Association for Supervision and Curriculum Development. See also Sinatra, R. (2000). Teaching learners to think, read, and write more effectively in content subjects. *The Clearing House, 73* (5), 266–276.
4. See http://www.writingcommision.org.
5. Chapter 3, p. 56.
6. Speare, E. (1983). *The sign of the beaver*. Boston: Houghton Mifflin.
7. Swartz, R., Kiser, M. A., & Reagan, R. (1999). *Teaching critical and creative thinking in language arts: Lessons, grades 5 and 6*, pp. 77–84. Pacific Grove, CA: Critical Thinking.

8. Whimby, A., Lochhead, J., Linden, M., & Welsh, C. (2001). What is write for thinking? In A. Costa (Ed.), *Developing minds: A resource book for teaching thinking* (pp. 298–302). Alexandria, VA: Association for Supervision and Curriculum Development.

9. Swartz, R., Kiser, M. A., & Reagan, R. (1999). Op. cit., p. 359.

10. According to substantial research, there are three thinking tasks students have trouble with in writing expository essays: a) generating a topic sentence or thesis statement; b) arranging content in logical sequences, including structures for arguments (both inductive and deductive), descriptions, explanations, and narratives; c) generating a concluding statement that carries the writing forward—for example, by inventing or creating a new statement that answers the question "So what?" (as opposed to restating the topic sentence). Notice how the writing map for compare/contrast essays remedies this without actually telling the students what to write. See Hayes, J. R., & Flower, L.S. (1981). Writing as problem solving. *Visible Language, 14*, 388–399; and Scardamalia, M., & Bereiter, C. (1986). Research on written composition. In M. C. Wittrock (Ed.), *Handbook of research on teaching* (pp. 778–803, esp. pp. 785–787). New York: Macmillan.

11. Swartz, R., Larisey, J., & Kiser, M. A. (2000). *Teaching critical and Creative thinking in language arts: Infusion lessons, grades 1 & 2.* Pacific Grove, CA: Critical Thinking, p. 399.

12. Ibid., p. 94.

13. Swartz, R., Kiser, M. A., & Reagan, R. (1999). Op. cit., p. 357.

14. Swartz, R., Whipple, T., Blaisdell, G., & Kiser, M. A. (1999). *Teaching critical and creative thinking in language arts, grades 3 & 4.* Pacific Grove, CA: Critical Thinking.

15. Flower, L. S., & Hayes, J. R. (1981). A cognitive process theory of writing. *College Composition and Communication, 32* (4), 365–387. See also Unger, J., & Fleischman, S. (2004). Is process writing the "write stuff"? *Educational Leadership, 62,* (2), 90–91.

16. Fletcher, R., & Portalupi, J. (1998). *Craft lessons: Teaching writing K–8.* Portland, ME: Stenhouse.

17. Hurwitz, N., & Hurwitz, S. (2004). *Words on paper.* Available online at http://www.asbj.com.

18. Ibid.

19. Rosenshine, B. (1997). Advances in research on instruction. In J. W. Lloyd, E. J. Kameenui, & D. Chard (Eds.), *Issues in educating students with disabilities* (pp. 197–221). Mahwah, NJ: Erlbaum.

20. Swartz, R., & Parks, S. (1994). Op. cit., pp. 511–512. See also Swartz, R., Kiser, M., & Reagan, R., (1999). Op. cit., pp. 76–77.

CHAPTER 6

Assessing Skillful Thinking

How much do students really love to learn, to persist, to passionately attack a problem or a task? ... to watch some of their prized ideas explode and to start anew? ... to go beyond being merely dutiful or long-winded? Let us assess such things.

—Grant Wiggins, Author and Consultant

IMAGINE THAT YOU ARE DRIVING to work in the morning and there is a traffic jam due to a breakdown in the next block, so you take a side street and go around the traffic. You wouldn't have done that if you had not assessed the situation and judged that you would never make it in time if you stayed on the street with the traffic jam.

Skillful assessment of this sort is fundamental to living an effective life. Most of us do this to some extent every day, even when we engage in very routine tasks. We need to know how well we are achieving our goals and be able to shape what we do accordingly. In so doing, we try to gather information on which to base these judgments, making sure, to the best of our abilities, that this information is accurate and complete.

Assessment plays the same role as we are learning. To learn continually, we all need feedback to know how well we are learning. Have we understood the most important content and concepts that we need to master in order to function well in the world outside school? Have we developed the skills we need to apply this understanding to tasks that require it?

Skillful thinking is basic in this mix: Do our thinking abilities enable us to access, analyze, interpret, understand, assess, and apply relevant information to complex tasks? Do we have a highly developed set of intellectual habits that will sustain this as we meet continued challenges both in school and in our lives outside school? Can we manage all this ourselves as we work to accomplish tasks that require us to practice thinking with skill?

Although such practices appear to be automatic when people are accomplished at them, in most cases they grow from continual feedback from others and deliberate efforts by learners to grow. Such feedback must be reliable and accurate, of course, but ultimately it is the learner who needs to be motivated to grow. Hence, the mental habit of remaining open to continual learning must be nurtured in a child's life in school. Although our evaluative judgments can serve as gatekeeping events for students—telling them whether they can get into certain classes, identifying them for particular interventions—the most significant role of these judgments is in their meaning to the learner as he or she acquires useful knowledge and skills. If these judgments signify a growth pattern, show strengths, and provide honest feedback for new learning, then the learner can be empowered to make those changes in his or her route to future learning. This is true of both content learning and thinking instruction. The learner will be a knower and a thinker with a sense of efficacy to be an active respondent to these judgments.

The power of this kind of assessment-learning spiral can be dramatically enhanced by including opportunities for students for self-assessment, supported by teacher guidance, in the course of the regular instruction that teachers provide. This, again, is true of content as well as thinking. When teachers infuse instruction in strategies for skillful thinking and in intellectual behaviors that manifest productive habits of mind into content instruction, this dramatically enhances both content learning and the development of skillful thinking abilities. Teachers can also help students develop skill at assessing their own thinking abilities in ways that direct them to self-improvement.

We have already seen examples of this in the lessons we have used in some of the chapters of this book. For example, we explored lessons in which the students develop a thinking strategy map to guide them in skillful decision making, then use this to guide their thinking, monitor it as they do it, assess its viability, and plan how they will do it again. This didn't happen in private—in fact, if teachers structure into these activities episodes of open discussion or small-group work, this adds an interactive dimension to assessment issues that can broaden students' perspectives on how to monitor and evaluate their thinking.

The ultimate purpose of this chapter is to explore how skillful thinking can be assessed effectively so that it serves its purpose of pointing the way to growth, development, and the effective management of our lives. It is usually the teacher and other educators who are charged with conducting such assessments and gathering this information. We will discuss how this can be done effectively. Teachers can use such assessment-based information to make decisions about what they will teach and how they can best help their students to achieve what they or other educators determine to be meaningful learning. The primary purpose of assessment, however, should be to inform students so that *they* become motivated to play a role in guiding their own progress. Thus we also want to explore how teachers can help students to gather as well as use such information in this context for themselves. That is the force of the driving metaphor with which we began this chapter.

Feedback Spiral for Continuous
Learning and Growth

A feedback spiral provides a graphic representation of assessment as a significant part of remaining open to continuous learning, one of the dispositions that is critical to a student's capability to receive and make use of assessment feedback. Figure 6-1 shows such a spiral.

The process represented in this feedback spiral suggests a dynamic lifelong learning enterprise that can be applied to organizations intent on continual improvement, to groups desiring greater productivity, and to individuals who are continuous learners, such as teachers and students. It is easy to see the role of assessment in this process in a school context, whether it is the teacher or the student who conducts the assessment and whether it is student learning or teacher growth to which it is applied. The spiral suggests an evolution of continuous growth in the following example of how a teacher concerned with instruction geared to infusing the teaching of a particular type of skillful thinking into content instruction might use the spiral as a planning tool. Let's operationalize these stages in the spiral in terms of questions that guide the teacher through the process.

The spiral begins by *clarifying goals and purposes*. The teacher answers the following question: Why do I want my students to become better thinkers? What is it that I am observing in my students that suggests that they need to become better thinkers? What specific set of thinking skills and habits of mind have I identified to work on with my students? Why have I chosen these skills and habits? What do I hope students will be able to do as a result of having learned these skills and habits?

Once the teacher has clarified her purpose, she *develops a plan*. As the teacher considers implementation, she plans for lessons that focus on the skills and habits of mind she has selected. How do these skills and habits fit into the units of study that she is teaching? How will she provide time for students to practice the skills and habits? What are some indicators that will provide evidence that the students are achieving the goals? How will she assess the work the students produce to know if they are becoming better thinkers?

The teacher then will *take action*. Too often teachers want to perfect their plans for a prolonged time, dotting every *i* and crossing every *t*. In so doing, they prevent action. Yet we all know that it is when we implement our plans that we learn the most. Although planning is critical, when teachers become too exacting with their plans, they are less receptive and responsive to the students' reaction to the work. How can they counter this? The feedback spiral suggests that there is an evolutionary growth

Figure 6-1. A Feedback Spiral for Learning[1]

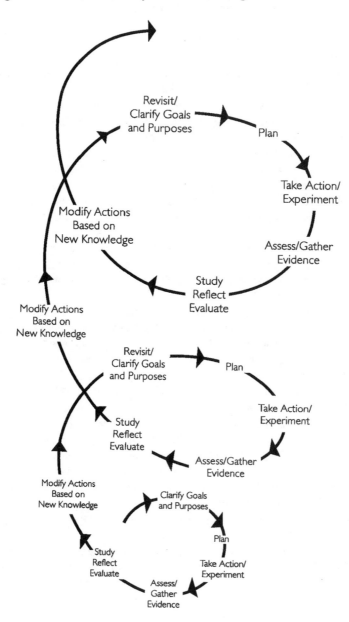

in learning and that the first loop of the spiral might be considered a first draft of learning. So the suggestion is "just do it." However, feedback from assessment is critical to the revision of this draft.

In order to know about student learning, the teacher must *assess and gather evidence*. In this phase, the teacher is using her assessment plan to gather data. How can she make sure that the data are reliable? She will be concerned with both formative and summative assessments, depending on the nature of the tasks.

Once assessment data have been collected, the teacher must take the time to *study, reflect, and evaluate*. The results from the assessment data must be analyzed in light of the anticipated outcomes. The teacher asks questions of the data such as these: How well did the students perform? How does what I observed students doing compare with what I had planned? How effective were the lessons? What have I learned about the difference between students who learned and those who did not? For those whose learning was not what I had expected, what is the most likely cause? What alternate strategies might be considered for those who have not learned? What new questions arise?

As the teacher answers these questions, she sees how to *modify actions based on new knowledge*. The teacher considers what changes should be made in the learning activity based on the assessment that was conducted. What changes should be made in the unit of study or thinking-skills lesson for next time? What modifications have to be made for the future direction with the students? What new insights will she carry forth to future lessons?

Now the teacher has completed her cycle of learning and she can return to *clarifying goals and purposes*. The teacher might ask at this point: Do I still have the same goals and purposes as when I first initiated my work on thinking? How might I clarify those goals based on what I have learned thus far? The next cycle in the spiral is then initiated.

This example illustrates clearly that the energy source that vitalizes this continuous learning spiral is feedback data that are collected at the assessment stage. That is what this chapter is about: gathering data to activate and engage the feedback spiral for teachers, students, and the school as a continuous learning organization.

Toward a Balanced Assessment System

Suppose that you are about to get on an airplane for a short flight. As you are walking on the jet bridge you notice that the pilot is getting on also. He looks rather young to you, so you ask him, "How do I know that you can fly this plane?" He replies: "I went to flying school, and just last week I passed the multiple-choice test on how to fly an airplane." Which way would you go?

Now suppose that he didn't say he had passed a multiple-choice test, but rather, he said he had passed an essay test on how to fly an airplane. Would that make any difference?

Obviously, such paper-and-pencil tests are not sufficient. In addition to content knowledge, we want good performance. One hundred satisfactory hours in a flight simulator under the watchful eye of a qualified supervisor would give us greater confidence in the pilot's capability. Even greater assurance would come from knowing that the pilot has had many experiences over time actually co-piloting and piloting this and other airplanes in a wide range of conditions—landing and taking off in different weather situations, responding to emergencies, and flying to and from many different airports. Is this a good analogy for how we should try to assess the development of students' abilities at skillful thought? Do we need paper-and-pencil test results at all?

We suggest that there are various methods of gathering assessment information about student thinking that are reliable and informative. In the best of all educational programs these should all be used in a balanced assessment system that gives us information about how skillful students are thinking on specific occasions and that also tracks changes and the evolution of students' skillfulness in thinking over time. Such assessment can be integrated into, or set side by side with, content assessment, but it has to be kept focused on what specifically we want to find out about student thinking. For example, when students are presented with problems in which they must apply their knowledge in situations where the answers are not immediately apparent, what thinking steps do they take? What mental behaviors do they exhibit? How do these measure up against the models of skillful problem solving and mental demeanor that inform our instruction? Are these internalized to the extent that they are habitual and adopted by the students without external prompts? In particular, are students internalizing important thinking strategies and habits of mind that enhance the skillfulness of their thinking, as we discussed in Chapter 1?

Some of the ways we can gather information about student learning in general are formal and data driven, while others are very informal and at best anecdotal. We suggest that all can be put to service as thinking indicators. The next section itemizes the variety of information-gathering techniques and opportunities that teachers have used as assessments. Some of these opportunities are more limited than others. We should also note that some of these focus on collecting data during the process of learning (formative), and some focus on the final product of learning (summative). The choice of which technique and context are dominant, and whether you engage in formative or summative assessment, depends on what you want to learn about student thinking and about the impact of your instruction in skillful thinking, and at what stage.

Types of Thinking Assessments and Opportunities for Gathering Assessment Data

Performance

Evidence of the performance of skillful thinking might be gathered through observing how students produce such products as storyboards, labels, thinking maps and graphic organizers, interviews, story lines, graphs, charts, observational drawings, note cards, artifact analysis, photo essays with text, comparative observations, blueprints, models, posters, dioramas, museum exhibits, debates, forums, choreography, anthologies, games, musical compositions, and projects.

Constructed Written Responses

Teachers may also prompt thinking that students explicitly express in writing through engagement in composing answers to quizzes, tests, short stories, newspaper articles, extended research reports, simple research reports, persuasive essays, analytical essays, descriptive essays, personal essays, plays, position papers, business plans, criticisms of film or videos or TV programs, advertisements, literature, poetry, political speeches, electronic games, work-study analysis, case studies, legal briefs, and senior projects.

Direct Observations of Informal Activity and Personal Communication

Anecdotal data can be collected through observation of students during informal conversations, independent work (including research in the library or on the Internet), book work, discussions, process coaching, conferences, interviews, journal writing, letter writing, and e-mail communications.

Selected Responses

In addition, how students respond on certain of the following can also be indicators of the skillfulness of their thinking: multiple-choice test items, true-false questions, and standardized tests.

Some of the techniques may yield numbers as reporting tools, whereas others may be in narrative form, revealing qualitative differences. Some may be less tangible and more impressionistic but nonetheless significant. How we manage these measures will help to create a picture of how well students are improving in their thinking, and it should point to how we can help them to become even better at it.

How can the techniques listed above, which have traditionally been used to assess content learning, be used to assess what we teach students when we teach them skillful thinking? The following questions help us to focus on assessing skillful thinking directly:

1. When given a familiar task and asked to engage in a specific kind of skillful thinking to accomplish this task, is the person able to engage in this kind of thinking and apply it to the task?
2. Is the person able to apply the requisite type of skillful thinking when faced with a more complex task that he or she is not familiar with and that he or she is told calls for this kind of thinking?
3. Can the person explain his or her process of thinking accurately using the terminology associated with the thinking skill?
4. Does the person use the requisite type of skillful thinking spontaneously when faced with a situation that calls for it?

Notice that items 1 and 2 focus on thinking abilities, although 2 focuses on the ability to transfer the use of skillful thinking to new situations. Item 3 focuses on the metacognitive process of describing how the thinking is being done, and item 4 focuses on whether a person has developed the habit of engaging in skillful thinking when it is required. What kind of information can we gather that will help us to answer these questions in specific instances?

We will start by looking at some of the traditional paper-and-pencil tests, including both selected-response (e.g., multiple-choice) and extended written-response tests. We will then take seriously the analogy of assessing the abilities of airplane pilots and look at the ways in which student performance beyond paper-and-pencil tests can reveal information about student thinking, what kind of information it is, and how we can gather it. These are, traditionally, ways of gathering information about student learning at specific periods. We will conclude the chapter with a look at systems, like portfolio systems, which are designed to provide assessments of change and development over time, which show extended patterns of thinking, and which have bearing on whether skillful thinking has become habitual.

Multiple-Choice, or Selected-Response, Testing of Thinking Skills

Teachers, of course, are not the only ones who conduct assessments of student knowledge and abilities. Schools, school districts, states, and national departments of education all engage in similar practices. They do this for a variety of reasons, from accountability to back-door influence on instruction and instructional practices. Such large-scale testing raises special issues when we consider its relationship to classroom teaching and classroom-level assessment of student performance. It is bound to have an impact on the luxury of individuality that the classroom provides to teachers, who usually have a certain amount of freedom in what they emphasize in the classroom and who can pay attention to individual students easily. It can also provide useful information to teachers about their students' abilities, however. So let's look at what has been done on a large scale to assess student thinking abilities and habits of mind.

The most common way that student learning is assessed in large-scale testing is through the use of selected-response, or multiple-choice, test items, which can be scored using answer sheets and electronic scanners. Electronic versions of such tests often are used, some on local school or college Web sites, some more generally accessible. Some educators have argued that such test items, as product-oriented items, can tell us only what answer students choose; the way the students made their choice— that is, any thinking they did—remains hidden. Indeed it does. Nevertheless, it would be a mistake to dismiss multiple-choice testing as a way to gain information about students' thinking. Let's take the following example of a multiple-choice question:

Q. There are six New England states in the United States. Which of the following is not in New England?
   A. Massachusetts
   B. New York
   C. Rhode Island
   D. Maine

This will not tell us much about the thinking of the person who chooses an answer. However, multiple-choice test items do not have to be—and often are not—constructed to prompt mere recall. Choosing a correct answer can require students to use procedures or strategies that they have learned, such as mathematical operations or special procedures in the sciences. The results then provide indirect evidence that students know, understand, and can use these operations or procedures. The same technique can be used to provide us with information about students' thinking skills and habits of mind. Consider the following multiple-choice test item[2]:

Q. The 4,000 km of Britain's coastline are under threat from the rising sea levels as never before. Storms batter cliffs, and in parts of eastern England, sea levels rise by 5 mm per year. This is partly because of global warming, but largely because geological processes are causing much of the coastline to sink. However, the construction of sea walls to protect the coastline would be expensive, using up money for other worthwhile purposes. In addition, the natural mud flats and salt marshes of the coast are havens for tens of thousands of birds and other wildlife. These havens will be lost if a barrier of sea walls is constructed and the natural areas where the sea meets the land are destroyed.

Which one of the following conclusions can be drawn from the information in this passage?

A. The construction of sea walls to protect the coastline would be unacceptable in financial and environmental terms.
B. Strong sea walls should be built around Britain's coastline to prevent the sea from encroaching farther onto the land.
C. We should spend money investigating the causes of global warming rather than constructing expensive sea walls.
D. Thousands of species of birds and other wildlife will be lost forever if sea levels continue to rise at the current rate.

Choosing A and rejecting B, C, and D takes some thought and careful reading of the passage. The thought involves recognizing that the information given about sea walls and their impact are negative consequences (cons) with regard to the option of building sea walls, a key component in skillful decision making. So even though the choice of A gives us no direct indication that the person is thinking skillfully, it seems to provide us with perfectly acceptable indirect information to this effect.

Such multiple-choice items can even be used with children in the primary grades. Here's something that a teacher did to check students' grasp of the relationship between evidence and conclusion in a first-grade lesson on causal explanation, a lesson based on the story of "Henny Penny."[3] In this lesson the teacher had been helping the students to reconstruct the beginning of the story so that Henny Penny would be doing skillful causal explanation—that is, judging what caused the bump on her head based on evidence rather than jumping to a panicky conclusion that the sky is falling. One of the teacher's goals was to help the students develop the mental habit of looking for all the evidence before impulsively judging what caused something. She also wanted to help them distinguish between circumstantial and direct evidence (although she did not use these words). She used the thinking strategy map in Figure 6-2 to guide her students in learning how to think skillfully to answer the question "What caused this?"[4]

Figure 6-2. Thinking Strategy Map for Skillful Causal Explanation

---

Finding Causes Skillfully

1. What are some possible causes of what happened?
2. What are some clues or evidence that you might find for these?
3. When you gather clues or evidence, what do you find?
4. What do the clues show is probably what caused this to happen?

Before she gets to item 2 she says to the students: "Suppose you were Henny Penny and you were thinking about what clues or evidence you might find about these possible causes. Which of the following would be a clue that it was an apple that hit her on the head?" ("An apple hit her on the head" was one of the possible causes that the children had identified.) The teacher then taped four sketches she had made on the wall: one showing other hens pecking corn, one showing the farmer eating an apple while sitting on a chair in his house, one showing some apples on the ground near Henny Penny, and one showing some apples growing on the branch of a tree. Some students chose the third, which is what the teacher had in mind, and some students chose some of the others. She then explained to the class why the third answer was the best answer.

This use of a multiple-choice item was for instructional purposes, but this does not diminish its usefulness as a quick way of getting information about these students' ability to identify evidence that supports a conclusion. The technique is perfectly generalizable for use in the classroom. A teacher can say the following after a lesson like this: "Suppose some new evidence was found in the barnyard the next day. Here is a list. Would any of these be more evidence that what we chose as the cause of the bump is what really happened?" She then produces a list of pieces of evidence (or more pictures). The teacher could also say: "Suppose you were still thinking about this question and you got this information: Two other animals said that they found apples on the ground in the barnyard. Which of the following possible causes would that evidence count for?" The teacher could then list four possible causes, only one of which had anything to do with apples hitting Henny Penny on the head.

These, of course, speak to only the first of the four important focal points for thinking assessment that we listed earlier: that the student employs the type of skillful thinking in question in the learning context. It is easy to see how the same technique can be used for the second and third focal points: extending the use of this thinking procedure to a new situation and being able to explain the thinking process. It is not so easy to see how it can be used to assess the disposition or habit of doing skillful thinking that is implied in the fourth focus. We suggest that you take this as a challenge and see if you can construct some multiple-choice items that do that.

When you consider multiple-choice test items, it is important that the thinking-skill focus be made explicit in them by using thinking terminology in the item stem (see Chapter 3 for ways to use the language of thinking skills). In this case the teacher asks such questions as "Which of the following would *be a clue that*...?" "Which of the following *possible causes* would that evidence count for?" and "Would any of these be *more evidence* that what we chose as the cause of [the event] is what really happened?" The language of the thinking skill is used directly in the prompt in these items. This is a key feature of multiple-choice test items designed to give us information about a person's thinking. It makes these items very specific to a type of skillful thinking.

Thus, at least with regard to the types of skillful thinking that involve drawing conclusions from other information or from evidence (i.e., some of the key critical thinking skills), there are ways to construct multiple-choice test items that can be used to get information about these thinking skills. We have looked at two models for such test items.[5] Table 6-1 is a chart that includes both.

Let us summarize what we have said so far about multiple-choice assessment of student thinking. It is possible to construct multiple-choice test items in which the question (the "stem") provides information, and the answer choice provides a number of statements from which students are asked to pick the one that is best supported by the information in the stem. Multiple-choice test items can also be constructed in which the stem contains a conclusion and the possible answers contain information; the student is then asked which piece of information best supports the conclusion.

There can still be problems with this way of assessing skillful thinking. If our goal is to gain information about student thinking from individual responses on such test items, they are always inferences. Yet any inferences we make about how students arrived at their choice must be weak ones, because there is always the possibility that students have

Table 6-1. Two Types of Multiple-Choice Test Items

Two Types of Multiple-Choice Test Items for Critical Thinking Skills	
Starting with Evidence	**Starting with a Conclusion**
Stem: A body of evidence	Stem: A conclusion
Select One Correct Answer (Out of Four or Five for Each Question)	
What conclusion is best supported by the evidence?	What evidence best supports the conclusion?
What conclusion is least supported by the evidence?	Which evidence most weakens the conclusion?
Assigning Credibility or Support Values to Answers	
Is (A) more, less, or as credible as (B), given the evidence?	Does (A) support or weaken the conclusion, or is it neutral?

guessed and have not used any thinking at all to get the answer. So these items cannot really tell us how the students arrived at this knowledge, either directly or indirectly.

This is not quite right. We can admit that making judgments about student thinking based on these kinds of responses is always indirect. These judgments are inferences based on the choices that the students make and the assumption that they have read and understood the question. Of course, students might guess at the answer to any multiple-choice test item and get it right without doing much thinking. We have no direct way of telling this just from their answer sheets, but there is a way to make this highly unlikely: by relying not on any one single test item but on *a battery* of different test items and assessment tools, as described in this chapter, thereby minimizing the likelihood that students will guess correctly on all or most of them.

Even the best multiple-choice assessment of student thinking remains an indirect measure of students' thinking abilities. Is there a way to bridge this gap?

There is a way that multiple-choice testing has been redesigned to contain more direct measures of student thinking. It involves using a very simple device: Students can be asked "Why?" when they choose an answer. In effect, a short extended-response prompt can be added to any multiple-choice test item that is designed to provide information about student thinking.

Note that scoring such responses cannot now be achieved by feeding student response sheets through a scanner. Nor can we expect immediate results if these test items are accessible on a computer. Someone has to read them and assess what they show about the thinking of the respondents. This is true even of short answers. In addition, cross-style scoring becomes an issue. What if the student gets the multiple choice item right, but his answer to why misses the point and fails, or vice-versa?

Designing Assessment Prompts for Extended Written Responses That Invite Student Thinking

Prompts that require extended written responses can be designed to bring out directly the way students engage in thinking. Here's an example:[6]

> Suppose that you were trying to gather information about the feeding habits of the animals that live around a nearby pond, and you go there to observe these animals. What would you do to make sure that the reports of your observations were accurate and reliable so that others could trust them? Write out a plan for your observation describing how you ensure its trustworthiness.

This prompt was given to an eighth-grade class in which the teacher had been working with students to help them develop skill at determining the accuracy of information by ascertaining the reliability of its source. They were working on what could be determined about the reliability of observation reports of the sort found in eyewitness testimony. Earlier they developed a checklist for the reliability of a source in general, either primary or secondary. Now they were looking at some primary source material.

In their study of history, the teacher had provided the class with some eyewitness accounts of conditions in the textile mills in 19th-century New England in relation to the impact of the industrial revolution in the United States. This was leading to the topic of the development of the trade union movement in this country, but right then they were looking at the textile mills in Massachusetts and New Hampshire. Some of the accounts about conditions in the mills were from the mill owners, some from activists, some from newspaper reporters, and so forth. In the course of this activity, the students developed a checklist of factors to take into account in judging the reliability of the sources in producing accurate descriptions. This checklist was quite similar to those developed by students in science classes, in which observation reports are used to provide information. The thinking map they developed is shown in Figure 6-3.[7]

The students were given reports to review from observers of the specific textile mills they were investigating. The students were asked to systematically record what they could find out about the observers, the way they conducted their observation, how they recorded their data, and whether there were any corroborating reports. They judged the report indicating very poor working conditions as likely to be accurate, whereas the other two, they thought, were probably distortions. If challenged, they could easily explain why they made these judgments by referring to the information they had gathered and written down on their checklist.

After this activity, the students practiced using these same criteria to support their judgments about the accuracy of direct reports in science and local newspaper reports.

Finally, the teacher asked the question above about planning an observation of a nearby pond. She was interested in assessing the degree to which her students had learned and internalized a procedure for critically assessing the reliability of sources. Her purpose was to determine whether the whole class needed more practice with the skill or whether only specific students needed more practice. She can get that level of differentiated information about student thinking only when she provides an individual task for the students.

This teacher is giving her students a task—planning an observation—and setting it in circumstances that call for determining the reliability of an observation. Notice how she tries to prompt this type of skillful thinking by stating its goal using the language of the thinking skill itself ("make

Figure 6-3. Thinking Strategy Map for Determining the Reliability of Eyewitness Observers

---

Determining the Reliability of Eyewitness Observers

1. Who is the observer and what is the observation?

2. What do we know about these factors:

   The Observer
   The background of the observer?
   How much does the observer know about what is being observed?
   Does the observer have biases or prior expectations about what he is observing? Explain.
   Does the observer have good vision? Explain.
   What is the reputation of the observer?
   Is the observer going to get some benefit if you accept what he says he's observed? Explain.

   The Observation
   How long was the observation?
   Was the observation repeated?
   Were any observation-enhancing instruments used? Explain.
   Was it light enough to see?
   Was the observer close enough to see well?

   The Report
   When was the report recorded?
   Where was the report recorded?
   Does the report use emotional language?
   If it was published, did someone else work on it (and perhaps change it)?
   If published, what is the reputation of the publisher?

   Others
   Did anyone else observe the same thing? If so, what does she say she saw?

3. When we take the factors present into account, is the observation reliable, unreliable, or uncertain?

---

sure that the reports of your observations were accurate and reliable so that others could trust them").

When the students were learning the skill, they were studying the work of outside observers of conditions in the mills. When they were asked this assessment question, they reflected on themselves as observers. Moreover, this teacher cleverly built in another variation. They have been reflecting on observations that were already made. In this case they were being asked to reflect on an observation that has not yet been made—a future observation. So this teacher raised the level of assessment a notch to try to determine whether these students could draw forth this thinking skill and apply it to a new and more complex situation. This is a good example of an assessment item with the second focal point in the list of questions on page 146.

In addition, by asking the students to "write out a plan for your observation," she was attempting to see how well they use the language of this type of skillful thinking, and in particular how they describe the criteria for the accuracy of an observation that they have been using in their learning activities.

Finally, she assesses the habits of mind in which the students are expected to check for accuracy and communicate with clarity and precision.

To summarize: You can bring out student thinking so that you can evaluate it by doing the following:

- Describing a task in which the specific type of thinking you are interested in is required in order for the task to be accomplished
- Prompting the students to employ that type of thinking by explicitly using the language of the thinking in question
- Identifying the habits of mind that would be most important to use when addressing the problem presented

Evaluating Extended Written Responses From Students Who Are Prompted to Show How Skillfully They Are Thinking

Let's now look at a response of one of the students, who wrote the following answer to the question of the pond:

> I would bring binoculars and make sure I was close enough to get a good view when I was not using them. And it would have to be daylight. In addition I would make sure that I read up on what I was going to be observing beforehand so I knew what I would be looking at and could identify the things I saw correctly. And of course I would bring a pad and pencil along so that I could write down what I saw. I would also bring someone else along who would take note of these things.

Does this student demonstrate mastery of this critical thinking skill? What is this teacher looking for? In order to develop a scoring rubric for this task, the teacher has considered these questions:

- How has the student used the thinking map that was described above?
- How much of the thinking map should be represented in the student response—all of the factors?
- Is reference to only some of the categories sufficient as a demonstration of understanding?

Figure 6-4 is an example of the scoring sheet the teacher used for accuracy of observation. It is a simplified structure that combines the features of a checklist with those of a rubric. In the left-hand column, the factors indicative of skillful thinking about the reliability of observations are listed. These should be present the writing. In the right-hand column, a number will be entered on a scale of 0 to 3, where 3 indicates expertise and 0 indicates a complete lack of knowledge. Then the numbers are added together.

Figure 6-4. Scoring Sheet

Scoring Sheet for Task That Involves Skillfully Determining the Accuracy of an Observation	
Teacher: _____ Student: _____	
Grade: _____ Subject: _____ Date: _____	
Task: <u>Planning an observation</u>	
THINKING FOCUS	**SCORE**
Considers factors related to the <u>observer</u> that contribute or detract from accuracy	
Considers factors related to the <u>conduct of the observation</u> that contribute or detract from accuracy	
Considers factors related to the <u>writing</u> that contribute or detract from accuracy	
Considers factors related to <u>additional corroboration</u> by others that contribute or detract from accuracy	
Makes judgment of accuracy based on <u>weighing the factors</u> identified	
Clearly identifies the factors considered and clearly articulates the conclusion in appropriate language	
Scale: 3 = expert (all factors), 2 = apprentice (some factors), 1 = novice (one factor), 0 = does not yet show evidence.	

It is up to the teacher to indicate overall scoring levels and what they mean based on the sum. Thus, 15–18 might be considered skillful thinking, 9–14 somewhat skillful but in need of more work, 6–8 weak and in need of significant work, and 0–5 poor and in need of a major effort.

How would you score the student response to the question of the pond on page 154?

Designing Rubrics to Use in Assessing Student Thinking

A rubric provides a clear statement of the standards by which students will be judged. Clear and easily applied standards for scoring or grading minimize subjectivity and build consistency from student to student, over time, and from scorer to scorer.

Thinking strategy maps play a crucial role in rubrics and scoring-guide development. Thinking strategy maps define what the teacher is trying to teach the students to help them become more skillful thinkers. In fact, you could say that these maps provide us with definitions of the important forms of thinking done skillfully, operationalized into question-strategies. Hence, they provide parameters for what the teacher should expect to encounter if the instruction is successful. A thinking strategy map provides the substance of what is translated into scoring criteria when scoring rubrics are developed to guide the evaluation of students' abilities in skillful thinking.

Table 6-2 shows a rubric for skillful decision making expressed in a written piece of persuasive prose. Note the criteria are derived from the thinking strategy map for skillful decision making introduced in Chapter 4.

The standards for grading the responses (i.e., from novice to expert) are set by the teacher and depend on what the instructional goals are in his or her particular classroom. Some rubrics of this sort are developed, and the standards set, by the consensus of a group of teachers. Notice that even if student writing is done on a computer, and rubrics for scoring are programmed into the computer, their use to produce actual grades will depend on input from readers.

We started this chapter by emphasizing the importance of feedback in guiding us in what we do in our lives. When our goal is the development of skillful thinking and we find, based on an evaluation of our thinking abilities, that we are not yet thinking very skillfully, we know we have a ways to go to achieve this goal. How can we get there? If we just have the result of the assessment—"not yet thinking skillfully"—that will provide us with little guidance on what we should do to improve. Scoring rubrics for skillful thinking, or derivative scoring sheets of the sort that we have described, have an additional function in educational settings: They can fill this gap. If they are returned with the students' scores, they will pro-

Table 6-2. Rubric for Persuasive Decision-Making Essays

RUBRIC FOR PERSUASIVE DECISION-MAKING ESSAYS

Indicators	Expert	Practitioner	Apprentice	Novice
Main Idea	Starts essay with a strong recommendation that is chosen from at least three other options and does not repeat the consequences used as support.	Starts essay with a strong recommendation that is chosen from at least three other options and does not repeat the consequences used as support.	Starts essay with a recommendation that is chosen from fewer than three other options and does not repeat the consequences used as support.	Does not start essay with a recommendation or starts by repeating the consequences used as support. Does not mention options considered.
Evidence	Cites at least three positive and negative consequences each relevant to the recommendation as evidence of and against the recommendation.	Cites some, but less than three, positive and negative consequences, each relevant to the recommendation as evidence of and against the recommendation.	Cites some consequences as evidence of the recommendation, some of which are not relevant.	Cites few positive and/or negative consequences in the main body of the essay.
Examples	Supports each consequence with at least one example. Provides details in the examples. Well organized.	Supports some, but not all, consequences with at least one example. Provides some detail in the examples. Organized.	Rarely uses examples to support the consequences cited.	Uses no examples to support the consequences cited.
Concluding Paragraph	Returns to recommendation and, based on the body of the letter, explains why it is best despite the negative consequences.	Returns to the thesis, elaborates it, but does not explain why it is best despite the negative consequences.	Returns to the thesis, but merely repeats main idea.	No concluding paragraph.
Conventions of Writing	Has few (if any) errors and follows appropriate conventions, including spelling, paragraphing, and punctuation.	Has some errors mainly and follows conventions, including spelling, paragraphing, and punctuation.	Has some errors in spelling and punctuation.	Has many errors in spelling and punctuation.

vide students with very specific information about the areas that need further work in their development of skillful thinking. Thus we recommend that teachers always share scored rubrics or the derivative scoring sheets for skillful thinking with the students who are being scored.

More Extended Response Prompts to Bring Out Student Thinking

So far we have developed a framework for constructing extended written response prompts for bringing out student thinking and for scoring them. Let us now look at an example that is somewhat more complex.

It includes a teacher's assessment prompt about the same critical thinking skill—determining the accuracy in observation reports—but this prompt is embedded in a longer series of questions that are designed to prompt students to write short extended responses that can reveal information about their problem-solving abilities as well as their skills at determining the accuracy of observational data by judging the reliability of the source. In this case, accuracy of observation is flagged as an important critical thinking skill to be used in such problem solving.[8]

Let us look at the whole set of prompts. This is an assessment developed by a teacher for her seventh-grade students.

1. Imagine that you've been hired to help with a problem. When prairie dogs are near farms, they eat the farmer's crops. Because of this, farmers have killed thousands of prairie dogs. Black-footed ferrets eat prairie dogs. Explain what problem this poses for the ferrets and why this is a problem.

2. What ways can you think of that people can save ferrets and still control prairie dogs? Explain what you might do. How might you determine that your solution will work? What knowledge can you bring forth that has bearing on this?

3. Suppose that you were also asked to observe the feeding habits of black-footed ferrets so that you could gather some data about this problem. Describe what you would do to make sure that your observations were as accurate as possible and that you brought back data that other people could trust. Write out a plan listing all the things you would think about beforehand.

Note how these prompts are constructed to elicit student responses to problem identification and then to the consideration of multiple possible solutions and the need to consider the pros and cons of the consequences of these options based on relevant information in order to decide if a solution is a good one. The last prompt is, of course, about determining the accuracy of observation skillfully. The reason it is in this trio of prompts is that this teacher recognized how important it is to base problem solving on accurate information. She has also been teaching her students ways of thinking skillfully about the reliability of sources in general and in particular the reliability of observation as a means by which to gather accurate information.

The background to these questions is that the students have been studying endangered species, extinction, and food-chain relationships in science. They have been reading a chapter on these topics in their textbooks. In addition, this teacher has introduced them to the strategy for skillful problem solving described earlier in this book, and she has taught them about determining the reliability of sources of information in other lessons. They have not previously learned anything about prairie dogs and black-footed ferrets.

As you analyze these questions, you might ask: Is their design consonant with the principles of extended-response prompt design that we outlined earlier in this chapter? How? If not, how might you modify those principles to relate to what you find here?

Assessing Student Responses About Prairie Dogs and Black-Footed Ferrets

Here are some responses from the seventh-grade students to these questions on a response form that a teacher gave them (Figure 6-5). Let's consider the responses to questions 1 and 2, which are designed to give us information about students' problem-identification skills and their skills at the core of problem solving. How do these responses fare? Don't just make a snap judgment here—please use some of the techniques we have described earlier to make these judgments. You decide what standards you would apply to these responses, then formulate a basis for scoring these responses.

Simple things sometimes bring about unexpected results. This sample gives us a sense of how to evaluate the thinking embedded in the student response with some degree of confidence. Obviously, the criteria for skillful thinking that the teacher is looking for in this extended response are derived from the problem-solving strategy being taught to the students: the teacher is looking for the consideration of a number of options and a sense that specific consequences, pro and con, are relevant to determining which solution is best. These define the thinking focus that should be flagged in any scoring rubric or guide. We should also note that what is *not* called for is a defense of any particular solution.

Let's look at another set of student responses to questions 1 and 2:

Question 1: "If there aren't enough prairie dogs for the ferrets to eat many of them will starve to death. That's because prairie dogs are their main food. If the farmers kill most or all of the prairie dogs, this will be a big problem because most of the ferrets might die. This would mean that their population would become very low. This would mean that they could become an endangered species. And if they all died they would become extinct. Then there would never be any other ferrets. And maybe this would not just be a problem for the ferrets. If other animals depended on the ferrets for their food, they could become extinct, too."

Question 2: "I suppose they could move all the ferrets away and feed them something different while they keep on killing prairie dogs. Or they could protect the ferrets from the animals that kill them so that

Figure 6-5. Prairie Dogs and Ferrets

Prairie Dogs   Black-footed Ferret

Answer the following questions in complete sentences and in paragraph form. Please include any diagrams that would further illustrate your answer.

1. When prairie dogs are near farms they eat farmer's crops. Because of this farmers have killed thousands of prairie dogs. Explain what problem this causes for the ferrets and why.

The prairie dogs are being killed by the farmer's poisons. This means that there is less food for the ferrets. Without food, a living thing can't survive so this is a problem.

2. Think of ways that people could save ferrets and still control prairie dogs. Explain what you might do. What would you have to make sure of in order to be certain your solution will work? Is there anything you already know that has bearing on this?

To save the ferrets it is possible to bring them away from the wild and breed them. They could live there. It's been done by scientists before and is still being done today.

3. Suppose you were asked to observe the feeding habits of black-footed ferrets so that you could gather some data about this problem. Describe what you would do to make sure that your observations were as accurate as possible and that you brought back data that other people could trust. Write out a plan listing all the things you would need to think about before collecting data.

I would have to get rid of all possible variables (except the one I plan to study). These would include time of day, location, climate, weather, etc. To get data for others to trust my data I would get reliable witnesses to witness my data and videotape any event included in my data.

more and more of them would survive and they would eat more and more prairie dogs. This would solve the farmers' problem for them and they wouldn't have to kill the prairie dogs. Or they could find some other way to keep the prairie dogs from eating the crops.

"I'm not sure any of these will work. Maybe the ferrets won't like to eat other things besides prairie dogs. How do we know that they will? And if there are more ferrets and they eat more and more prairie dogs, that may save the farmers for a while, but what then?

If there are more ferrets won't the ferrets eat up all the prairie dogs and then not have any food left? And how can prairie dogs be kept from the crops? I learned that they burrow in the ground, so a fence won't help. They'd just go under. Maybe the farmers should move and leave the prairie dogs and ferrets alone."

How would you rate these, and why? Neither of the teachers who developed these assessments used rubrics like those we have looked at for rating these answers. Their ratings were more or less "intuitive." However, it is far more viable to base such judgments on a formal scoring rubric for the reasons we mentioned earlier in this chapter. Most people who compare these say that the second set of responses is far more articulate and detailed than in Figure 6-5; it shows the student's thinking much better, so it should be given a higher score. This type of comparative judgment is not justified in our view. We say this not based on a scoring rubric that we have, but rather on a more basic consideration that applies to any comparative judgment of this sort.

In any test situation, there are variables that impact on the results to which we need to be sensitive. These might include the knowledge or skill of the student who is being tested, the fact that some assessment items are worded in such a way that they lend themselves to a number of different interpretations, or that the language is so advanced that many students don't understand the test items. Item writers try to avoid these circumstances by controlling these variables, but if there is a variable that is not controlled, it may well make a difference.

If a teacher were to abandon the form used in Figure 6-5 and ask the students to write their responses on a blank piece of paper, would that make a significant difference in their responses? In this case it is not altogether clear. Think, for a moment, about time. The answers given in the second sample are longer and more articulate on key points. Maybe the teacher gave that student double the time to write than she gave the first student. We don't know, but we do know about space. The student who wrote in the Figure 6-5 was given less space to write in than the student in the second sample was given. Perhaps the first student would have written something longer and more articulate with more space in which to write, perhaps not. We just don't know. Thus any comparative scoring that we advance could be tainted by these uncertainties. When we give students extended-response items and do comparative scoring—whether it be with other students' responses or with their own, later in the school year—we should make sure that the variables in the test situation that could affect the quality of a student's answer are as closely controlled as possible.

We should now have a basic sense of how to conduct extended (or constructed) response assessments that can be used to make well-founded judgments about the quality and skillfulness of the particular episodes of thinking that the students engage in as they respond to our extended-response prompts. We leave it to readers to develop rubrics and scoring guides for problem identification and problem solving based on the thinking strategy maps provided and the models for such rubrics and scoring guides identified earlier in this chapter.

Performance Assessment of Skillful Thinking

Do paper-and-pencil assessments restrict us too much? A fourth-grade teacher keeps a log with notes of students' thinking as they work on an extended project in their school that involves missing library books. At the end of every year, the school library has a problem. It gets back only about 25% of the books it has lent out during the school year. The librarians then go around to the classrooms after school is over, and they retrieve another 20% of the books. This is very costly and takes a lot of time on the part of the librarians.

The students have been introduced to a basic thinking strategy for skillful problem solving in their social studies class earlier in the year and have been practicing it to some extent, along with deliberate attempts to be metacognitive and to manage their impulsivity as they solve problems. They are learning not to jump to conclusions when they have a problem to solve but to follow a plan that helps them to take the time to gather relevant information and base their problem solving on it. They are doing this by learning to ask and answer important questions as they work their way through a problem. The thinking strategy map that we introduced in Chapter 1 (Figure 1-3) summarizes the strategy they are learning. Without prompting them with these questions, this teacher now asks her students to try to solve this problem for the school.

This is not just another activity for practicing and honing this type of skillful thinking. Now the teacher is assessing the students' problem-solving skills. She will observe the students' behavior as they work to solve the problem. She must now exchange her "teacher" hat for an "assesser" hat. She needs to be careful not to make inferences about what is happening based on the students' general behaviors. Rather, she must specify in advance what she will be looking for and make certain that the students are aware of her observation targets. Table 6-3 shows an observation checklist she might use.

As this teacher observes the students working on this problem, she makes notes on each of the 25 students in her classroom. Her purpose is to ascertain the level of development of the students' performance and determine the need for more directed work on this type of thinking. If she thinks most of the students have mastered the skills of careful problem

Table 6-3. Observation Checklist

Problem-Solving Skills *Are the students considering:*	Often	Sometimes	Not Yet
A variety of possible solutions			
Pros and cons			
The reliability of sources			
Making a plan			
Monitoring thinking			

solving and have developed the requisite habits of mind to support and propel these, she can move on and concentrate on another cluster of thinking skills. At the same time, she can determine which students need more help, and she can provide differentiated lessons to reinforce the necessary thinking skills.

The authenticity of this example matches the authenticity of logging in flight hours in our earlier example of the pilot. There is no substitute for real, serious problem solving as a context that provides the opportunity to engage in the skillful practice of the types of thinking and habits of mind that go into skillful problem solving! At the same time, we also want to note that the authentic contexts that provide students with these opportunities might not be so plentiful and/or accessible to the students. However, teachers who are mindful of the opportunities that arise in their classes take advantage of the opportunities when they do arise.

In addition, the analogy to assessing the skill of airplane pilots can broaden the range of contexts for this sort of assessment by reminding us that flight simulators can provide us with information as well, so it may not be too difficult to construct *simulated* problems for students to use. If simulation is used to provide such contexts, however, teachers need to make sure that they can also provide students with simulations of the array of information they need to do good problem solving (e.g., factual reports).

Another point of importance about such performance assessment is that although it is informal, it should not be merely impressionistic. In the case described, the teacher has some definite and specific things she is looking for—such as considering multiple possible solutions and considering the pros and cons of the proposed solutions—based on the types of instructional objectives that are recorded on the thinking strategy maps. It might be wise for a teacher to make a written checklist to guide his or her observation, or even develop more complex assessment rubrics analogous to the rubric we have shown you for decision making.

Even then, however, if this teacher relies solely on the observation of student behavior, her judgments could be risky as providers of reliable data, depending on the observation circumstances. If a student says, without prompting, things like "Let's be sure we take some time to consider a range of options," and then writes down the options that his classmates suggest on a graphic organizer, the teacher can be pretty sure that he respects the need to think carefully about possible solutions in problem solving and that he strives for accuracy and precision in his thinking. On the other hand, if the teacher observes that other students don't say things like this, the students might still be thinking about possible solutions, but the indicators of their thinking could be much more subtle and more easily misinterpreted. This suggests that teachers who engage in such observations of performance must assure themselves that they are conducting these observations in ways that will yield data that can be trusted to be reliable and accurate. In short, teachers who practice the kinds of assessments that we are describing need to use their own skills at ensuring the reliability of observational data.

Even if these points are accounted for, it can still be quite difficult to do this kind of performance assessment with thoroughness and reliability. If the teacher we have described has 25 students and wants to record information about the thinking of each of them, this is not an easy task for one person to do. Attending to one student and recording information about that student's thinking can distract the teacher from other students who are displaying important behaviors indicative of careful thinking. If the teacher is also involved in giving some direction to the activity and helping students learn how to do it well, her records might turn out to be just a spotty impression and not a good comprehensive in-depth record. Many teachers resolve this dilemma by acknowledging these difficulties and creating a system for long-term observation. They tab an observation notebook with each student's name and choose to observe only five students in depth during such activities. This means that they must make certain to provide enough opportunities for problem solving so that they have information about all their students. Although teachers are constantly making observations about their students, this can provide systematic documentation about individual students that focuses solely on their thinking performances. Videotapes also provide an excellent opportunity for teachers to study student work.

This kind of data can be collected and be helpful, but it is possible that supplementing it with paper-and-pencil tests is necessary to achieve any degree of comprehensiveness, consistency from student to student, and real depth.

Assessing Growth in
Skillful Thinking Over Time

So far we have looked at two major complementary ways that classroom teachers have tried to gather data to assess the quality of their students' thinking: paper-and-pencil responses from the students and observation of their performance. We have discussed instances of these that have been geared to providing information about specific episodes of thinking. However, the information we want to gather about students is more extensive. We are concerned with the habituation of these processes: Do they persist over time, and has skillful thinking become spontaneous? These are part of another dimension of assessment: assessing a student's growth over time in becoming a more skillful thinker and sustaining it. We can have many "snapshots" of student performance. Each assessment can be considered as a single event, but if we want to see the full family album, we must see those snapshots accumulated over time and in varied contexts.

Many teachers use portfolios for that purpose. A portfolio can be organized around thinking skills and habits of mind. Students can enter the best examples of their capacity to solve problems, persist with a project, become increasingly more flexible in their thinking, and use thinking strategy maps to organize their thinking. The categories for collecting work for the portfolio can be determined by the teacher alone or by the teacher and the students. Students can collect work samples and organize them according to the agreed-upon thinking categories. At conference time or reporting time, the students can select a few key examples that they put into the portfolio. They can then reflect on why they chose those pieces and how they are examples of thoughtful work. Finally, they can set goals for their next quarter of work. Portfolios provide an excellent opportunity for students to become more conscious of their growth in thinking. In fact, portfolios can be a great vehicle for demonstrating engagement with the process of the feedback spiral that we introduced earlier.

Figure 6-6 shows a portfolio cover sheet designed by a seventh-grade science teacher and her students.

Figure 6-7 shows an evaluation sheet that students attach to selected pieces in their portfolio.

This portfolio system was developed before computers became a regular feature of the classroom scene. Its adaptability for inclusion in a student's computer files should be obvious. With the advent of memory

Figure 6-6. A Thinking Portfolio

Portfolio: A Learner's Mirror

A portfolio is a selective, ever-changing collection of your work. It should contain pieces of work that show you (and others) something about yourself as a learner. It should show how you are changing over time. A portfolio will help you chart your progress.

It should include pieces of work that show you:

You as a thinker/scientist
1. Observe, ask questions and inquire into things
2. Solve problems, make decisions, think
3. Understand scientific knowledge

You as a self-directed learner
1. Set and accomplish goals
2. Keep working (persist) on tasks
3. Do quality (best) work

You as a collaborative worker
1. Work with others
2. Consider different viewpoints
3. Try various roles

What to include
Samples for your portfolio can come from:
*1. your yearly or quarterly goals
 2. all science work:
    a. lab work
    b. group work
    c. quarter projects or research papers
    d. selections from your "thinking journal"
    e. feedback or evaluation sheets
    f. free work, sketches, poems, audio or video tapes
    g. homework, extra credit
 3. work in other subjects
 4. work from nonschool areas
 5. questions you have been thinking about
 6. any other items you feel are important to you as a learner

Note: (*) means these <u>must</u> be included.

Name: _____ Period: _____ Date: _____

YOU

Figure 6-7. Evaluation Sheet

Evaluating Growth

Portfolio Evaluations

Student Name _____ Date _____

Title: Piece #1 _____ Block _____

Me As a Thinker and Problem-Solver

Select one piece of work from your portfolio that shows how you are improving as a thinker/problem-solver. (You may wish to place it with an earlier piece in order to show some change.) Write about why you selected this piece, and what it shows about you. Be sure to cite in which kind of thinking (creative, analytical, critical) you are improving and explain why.

Parent Comments

Teacher Reflections

Student _____

Parent _____

Teacher _____

---

sticks and CDs, the possibilities of students' maintaining an electronic record of their work have been dramatically enhanced. Note, however, that collecting projects and exhibitions—even though they are additional rich opportunities to observe growth in thinking—will not reveal growth in thinking unless they are processed with an explicit framework for skillful thinking as a guide. The critical factor in making certain that the collection becomes an evaluative tool that focuses on thinking is the reflection on what was selected and why. In the absence of such reflection, the collected work becomes merely a very good scrapbook.

An Example of a Project

Table 6-4 is an example of a sixth-grade teacher using a multiplicity of assessment techniques as she teaches a social studies lesson aimed at helping students to become more skillful in their decision making and develop the habit of taking time to think (thereby managing their impulsivity). We suggest that you add the assessment ideas to the sample lessons developed in earlier chapters.

Table 6-4. Dress-Code Project

<u>**Dress Codes in School**</u>   <u>**Grade 6 Social Studies**</u>

Lesson Preliminaries

<u>Content Objectives</u>**:** *What is the content that you will associate with the thinking skills that you will infuse? What are the important ideas that you want the students to know as a result of this lesson?*

Students will draw on previously researched information about the effects of dress codes used by public schools. Students will understand why people make rules and create laws.

<u>Thinking Skill Objectives</u>: *What specific thinking skill are you infusing? What do you want the students to focus their attention on as they think skillfully? What mental habits will you stress in this lesson?*

Students will learn to think about options, consequences, and the importance of consequences as they make a decision. They will learn how to manage their impulsivity when making a decision.

<u>Resources And Materials</u>**:** *What will you need in order for the lesson to be successful? Do you need to connect to any Web sites? Books? Other materials?*

Materials are available regarding use of dress codes in schools. Use a text on making laws in U.S. government. Graphic organizers for skillful decision making can also be used.

Table 6-4. *continued*

The Lesson

Introduction: *What will you do as a teacher to introduce the skill? What will you have the students do to define the skill?*

Gather responses. "We can all think of a time when we've had to make decisions. Can anyone think of a decision you made today? Can you think of a time when you have made a bad decision?" (Give examples if the students have difficulty coming up with these).

"Sometimes we make decisions without thinking things all the way through. Maybe we don't have enough information before we make a decision, maybe we make decisions too fast, maybe we don't think about the consequences."

"What do good decision makers do?" Write the responses. Develop a thinking strategy map for skillful decision making based on these responses.

Active Thinking: *How will you help the students to activate the use of this thinking skill in thinking about the content material they are learning in social studies? How will you promote the mental habit of managing impulsivity?*

Since the students have done the research on the dress code, it will be possible to move quickly to the graphic organizer. They will be asked to use the graphic organizer for skillful decision making as they practice thinking as good decision makers think. Observe which students are able to manage the decision-making matrix on the graphic organizer. Walk around the room and ask students who are having problems what they are finding hard about the activity and make suggestions that will help them.

Students list the pros and cons for having a dress code as well as a number of other options and report orally on what they think the best choice would be, explaining why. The teacher has organized sheets with student names and a place for notes. She moves about the room with a clipboard for note-taking. She makes note of which students are using the language of the thinking skill (decision making), to what degree, and which are not. She will stress the way the language of decision making can be used if students show that they have difficulty using this language. The teacher collects the graphic organizers used by the students (to be returned to them later) and checks to see which students were not able to use the organizer. She makes note of this and develops a plan to remedy it.

Students are then asked to take the perspective of the principal and write a persuasive letter to the school board either for or against having

(continued overleaf)

Table 6-4. *continued*

a dress code in the school. A decision-making rubric is used to evaluate the student writing. The rubric focuses on how well students give an opinion, justify the opinion based on the consequences, and consider multiple points of view. A graded copy is attached to the writing when it is returned.

Thinking About Thinking: *What will you do to help students reflect on the thinking that they have engaged in?*

The teacher asks the following questions for reflection and asks the students to discuss these with their partners: What steps did you take in your decision-making process? What did you need to consider to develop your final writing product? If you were to face another situation in which you needed to make a decision, what steps that you just took would be most helpful to you? The teacher asks the students to write out plans for future decision making in their notebooks. The students write out their plans and turn them in to the teacher, who records the facility with which they use the language of decision making to articulate a plan for doing this kind of thinking skillfully.

 Applying the Thinking: *What will you do to give the students more practice in skillful decision making so that they do it more spontaneously when they have to?*

A new case scenario is created built on the assumption that there is a dress code in the school. "Pretend that a student attends a school that has a dress code. This student comes to school wearing a T-shirt that has a swear-word written on it. What should the principal do?" The teacher asks the students to work in groups. The thinking strategy map is on the wall of the classroom and the graphic organizer for skillful decision making is available in the classroom, but the teacher does not give it to the students. The teacher makes note of which groups look at the thinking map as they work together and which groups either find or draw the decision-making matrix as a graphic organizer that they use in doing the activity. The students are asked to write a recommendation to the principal showing that they have thought carefully about the matter when they decide the best thing to do. Students are paired and present their thinking to one another. They become critical friends for each other's work. What is meant by critical friends is that they are prepared to provide honest critique and feedback because they are a friend to the success of their partner. Students have learned how to use a protocol for this purpose.

Finally, individual work is turned in. The teacher checks the work to see whether students are able to effectively note options and consequences in supporting their choices. Informed by these results, the teacher plans more decision-making activities for the students.

There are three basic activity points for teachers that sum up what we've said so far, and a fourth that we are adding. These describe what you can do to develop an assessment program to provide continued monitoring of student thinking so they can learn from your assessment and utilize it in their continued growth as thinkers:

- Assess the skill directly with a balanced assessment program, preferably using the content as a vehicle for the thinking skill.
- Use the data from the assessment to identify the needs of the students.
- Provide continued practice of the skill, informed by identified student needs, with ongoing assessment and feedback to students.
- Provide opportunities for students to become self-assessing, observing their growth over time.

Self- and Peer Assessment of Thinking

Students' abilities to assess their own thinking can be enhanced by practice in assessing the thinking of their fellow students. Remember the activity in which a teacher asked his students to develop a checklist of what they would like to see in a piece of persuasive writing to give them confidence that the recommendation being promoted was the product of careful thought? This was integrated into the lesson on the bombing of Hiroshima we described in Chapter 4.

In this lesson the teacher, Mr. O'Malley, asked his students to write a letter to President Truman recommending what they think the best course of action is to end World War II. Before he gave the students this assignment, he said the following:

> I'd like you to get together with a partner now and think about something. Suppose you were President Truman and you had been receiving letters and other written communications from your advisors about this situation. What would you want to see in these letters that would give you confidence that its writer has put the kind of careful thought into this question that you are engaged in? What will make you perk up and take what this person says seriously and not consider it just an "off-the-top-of-the-head" comment?

In this activity, Mr. O'Malley wants the students to do some thinking together that will create a set of standards for good persuasive prose, standards that derive from reflection on the kinds of authentic contexts in which people write such prose and the function of such writing and based on the standards of skillful decision making.

He now asks the teams to share what they have come up with and develops it into a checklist of standards for good persuasive writing (Figure

6-8). It is clearly based on what the students know about writing and on the thinking strategy map for decision making that they have been using.

These students have now developed a set of standards that they can use to judge how well thought out and well expressed a piece of persuasive writing is. Mr. O'Malley might wish to add to what the students have developed. If the students have left out something that he thinks is important, he could say to his students, "I notice that you didn't mention that the writer should indicate why the main information provided to support the recommendation is from a source that is credible. Do you think it would be a good idea to include this?" Students often add such suggestions, and the enterprise becomes a cooperative one between the teacher and the class.

Now Mr. O'Malley says the following to these students:

> I am going to ask you each to write a persuasive letter to President Truman about this issue. When you have done this, I will ask you to share your letter in your pairs and use these standards to assess your partner's letter. I also want you to do more than that. If you find, for example, that your partner has not indicated that a number of options have been considered, I will want you to make some recommendations to your partner in writing about how he or she might do that. You can use this simple form to make these comments.

Mr. O'Malley is now helping his students to assess the work of their colleagues. This is an empowering activity that can have dramatic effects on students' own self-esteem. See Figure 5-8 on page 136.

Mr. O'Malley does more than this. He tells the students that he wants them to rewrite their letter to President Truman and to use this checklist to guide them and to assess their own writing as they revise it in light of their partner's suggestions and before they submit it. Mr. O'Malley is blending assessment conducted by the students in this activity with instruction. These students are learning how to develop assessment standards and then use them to monitor, assess, and improve their own work.

This does not mean that Mr. O'Malley has abandoned his role in assessment. He uses the same checklist to grade the students' writing. He

Figure 6-8. Criteria for Persuasive Letter

Criteria for a Well Thought Out Persuasive Letter

- The writing should clearly indicate the options that the writer has considered.
- It should show that the writer has considered the cons as well as the pros of these options.
- It should indicate why the option recommended is a good one despite its cons.
- It should show why this option is better than the others.
- It should be well organized.

---

could, in fact, use the same type of grading chart that we showed you when we discussed assessing skill at determining the accuracy of an observation or the reliability of sources of information. In cases in which the students' grades are low, he could ask them to take his checklist and use it as a basis for rewriting their letters to try to improve their grades.

What we have just discussed can be used as a model for the elementary and middle school grades. When students go through a decision-making process in the second or third grades about what Mr. Arable should do about the runt pig in the book *Charlotte's Web* by E. B. White, they can be asked to write a letter to Mr. Arable to convince him of the option that they think is best.[9] They can also be involved in the development of standards for such letters, just as the older students were. When fifth-grade students read the book *Shiloh* by Phyllis Reynolds Naylor, they wrote a letter to Mrs. Preston recommending what she should do about her son and the dog, Shiloh. The same technique of peer assessment can be used in this case as well. When students have studied alternative energy sources in the seventh grade, they have been asked to write a recommendation to the government of their country of what the best source of energy would be for their country. These students could also be involved in the process of developing standards for planning, monitoring, and assessing these recommendations to make sure that they will have the force they deserve.

Teaching students how to conduct careful, responsible, and constructive assessment of the quality of their own thinking is essential if we are to help them become independent, self-sufficient thinkers. The blending of assessment with instruction is a powerful classroom technique that enhances student learning and deepens student motivation. It also gives them a set of skills that, if properly reinforced, can be used throughout their lives to improve the quality of whatever they are doing.

Assessing Growth in Habits of Mind

When we are serious about students developing important habits of mind that accompany and support the use of specific strategies for skillful thinking like those we have discussed for skillful parts–whole thinking and skillful comparing and contrasting, we can find ways to make them the subjects of techniques of assessment and feedback, which we can extend over time to assess the growth and development of these habits. We can also provide opportunities for students to build the skills of self-evaluation of mental habits.

Self-evaluation of habits of mind develops from internal and external reflections and observations. Feedback from teachers also serves as a rich data source. Teachers, for example, often give feedback on thinking habits by focusing on the student's disposition or attitude toward learning in general. Evidence for these dispositions can be collected in ways similar to those that we have described for specific forms of skillful thinking like decision making and judging the reliability of sources of information. Teachers can use student writing, portfolios, metacognitive journals, exhibitions, and performances as their data. In each of these domains, information can be gathered about students' use of strategies for skillful thinking about the content they are learning, but it can also be gathered about students' mental behaviors in using these strategies and their attitudes or disposition to manifest such behaviors as they engage with the work. It can then be used to document change in these behaviors over time. So, for example, a student may show a great deal of skillfulness in solving a math problem. However, as in the examples in Figures 6-9 and 6-10, the student might show a change in his disposition on how he conducts his math problem solving. He is evidencing drawing from past experience as well as persistence in problem solving.

Figure 6-9. Student Journal Entry, September

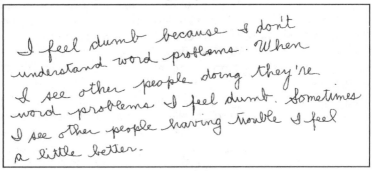

Figure 6-10. Student Journal Entry, January

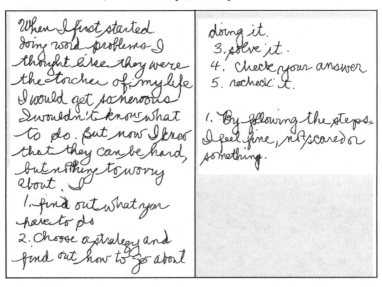

Collecting Evidence of Habits:
A Planning Matrix

The matrix in Table 6-5 can serve in planning how to collect evidence of mental habits, like persistence and respecting the ideas of others by using a variety of assessment strategies.[10]

Table 6-5. Planning Matrix for Various Habits of Mind

	Assessment	Checklist	Portfolio	Rubric	Interview	Anecdotal Record	Performance	Exhibition	Journal	Writing
Habits Of Mind										
1. Persisting										
2. Managing impulsivity										
3. Listening with understanding and empathy										
4. Thinking flexibly										
5. Thinking about our thinking (metacognition)										
6. Striving for accuracy and precision										
7. Questioning and problem-posing										
8. Applying past knowledge to new situations										
9. Thinking and communicating with clarity and precision										
10. Gathering data using all the senses										
11. Creating, imagining, innovating										
12. Responding with wonderment and awe										
13. Taking responsible risks										
14. Finding humor										
15. Thinking interdependently										
16. Remaining open to continuous learning										

The following examples will amplify the potential for how to collect evidence that can be entered on this matrix.

Checklists

Invite students to describe how they can determine if they are becoming more aware of their own thinking (metacognition). When students become skillful at recognizing their use of the habits of mind, they can do the following:

- List the steps and tell where they are in the sequence of a problem-solving strategy
- Trace the pathways and dead ends they took on the road to a problem's solution
- Describe what data are lacking and their plans for producing those data

Checklists can be developed through a facilitated conversation in the classroom that serves as a model for students who are developing the capability for self-evaluation. Students are asked, "What would it look like if a person were a good listener?" and "What would it sound like if a person were a good listener?" Students generate a list of positively constructed observable behaviors. For example, in the "looks like" category there might be responses such as "establishes eye contact" or "nods head when agreeing." In the "sounds like" category there might be responses such as " builds on the other person's ideas" or "clarifies when does not understand." Finally, the students and teacher agree to observe for these behaviors as students work individually or in groups. Table 6-6 is an example of a student-teacher checklist. It uses the phrase *How are we doing*, implying that this is used for group work. It can also be changed to *How am I doing* or, from a parent's perspective, *How is my child doing*? This checklist is used primarily for self-evaluation, with data added by the observations of the teacher, parent, or peers.

Building Scoring Rubrics for Assessing Habits of Mind

Another tool for assessing habits of mind is a scoring rubric. The descriptions for each scoring category can be developed with students, as we illustrated with strategies for skillful thinking earlier in this chapter. Each category should be sufficiently clear so that students can learn from the feedback about their behavior and how to improve. Tables 6-7 and 6-8 (pp. 178-179) show examples of scoring rubrics for some of the mental habits. In each case, students were involved in their development.

Table 6-6. "How We Are Doing?" Checklist

Habit of Mind: Flexibility	Often	Sometimes	Not Yet
Restates or paraphrases a person's idea before offering personal opinion.			
Clarifies a person's ideas, concepts, or terminology.			
Expresses empathy for others' feelings and emotions.			
Takes an allocentric point of view:"If I were in your position" or "Looking at it from your point of view, I would…"			
Changes mind with addition of new information. "As a result of our discussion, I'm seeing it differently now."			
Approaches problems from different perspectives.			
Generates multiple and alternative statements of a problem.			
Displays a sense of humor.			
Laughs at him- or herself.			

Maintaining Portfolios

Various habits-of-mind designations may be used as an organizer for a student's portfolio. The portfolio could be sectioned with folders, each with an attribute as a heading. Students would choose work based on their best example of when they were persistent in their work, or when they felt that their work reflected their flexibility. The work is put in the

Table 6-7. Rubric for Thinking Interdependently

Level	
4	Demonstrates interdependence. All members contribute. Shows indicators of cooperation and working together, compromising, and staying on task. Disagreements are welcomed as learning opportunities. Completes task with accuracy and within time limits. Members listen to others' points of view. Paraphrasing, clarifying, and empathizing are in evidence.
3	Members disagree but reach agreements through arguing and debate. Some paraphrasing and clarifying are in evidence. Group sometimes strays from task. Some members remain silent or refrain from participating.
2	Some members are off task. Group rushes to complete task in the most expeditous way due to the pressure of time. Evidence of arguing or encouraging others to get it over with.
1	Few on task. Evidence of arguing and uninterest. Some members occupied with other work.
0	Chaos. Task not completed. Many put-downs. Some members leave before task is complete. Complaints about having to participate in task.

portfolio and the student reflects on why that work has been chosen, writing this in a way that will inform the reader of the contents of the portfolio. Documentation of these mental behaviors and attitudes over time in such portfolios will provide information about whether such behaviors have become habitual. When portfolios are developed around habits of mind, they become more powerful if they are transdisciplinary—that is, one portfolio includes artifacts from all subjects. This is an especially useful design for high school students and broadens the students' and our insights into whether the mental behaviors exemplified in the portfolios have become genuine *habits* of mind. Students can coach one another as they build these portfolios by having peer conferences. A teacher can ask the other students to read the work in the portfolio to confirm, and thereby help the learner reflect on, what these particular pieces show about their mental behaviors and the degree to which their thinking is skillful.

Performances

In addition to focusing on the content and form of a student's work, teachers focus on the process the student was involved with to arrive at the final presentation. One science teacher uses the habits of mind as part

Table 6-8. Rubric for Thinking Flexibly

Domain	In Repertoire	In Perspective	Open Mindedness	Creativity of Approach
Expert	Uses time and resources creatively to find and evaluate as many ways as possible to look at a situation.	Consistently explores as many diverse and useful alternatives as time and resources will allow and analyzes how the identified alternatives will affect outcomes.	Expresses appreciation and value for others' points of view. Changes mind and incorporates others' points of view in own thinking.	Generates a variety and range of innovative and unusual definitions and/ or ways to approach tasks.
Practitioner	Finds a variety of ways of looking at a situation and evaluates how useful they are.	Consistently generates alternative ways of approaching tasks and analyzes how the alternatives will affect those tasks. Some alternative shows originality in the approach.	Describes some ways others' points of view are found to be new and different from his or her own.	Generates several novel and original approaches to tasks.
Apprentice	Describes different ways of looking at a situation from own perspective.	Sporadically generates alternative ways of approaching tasks and analyzes how the alternative will affect those tasks.	Realizes and considers others' views but must be persuaded to change mind.	Some alternatives show originality in the approach to the tasks.
Novice	Looks at a situation in only one way, and that way is often his or her own. Looks no further even when it is clear that it would be helpful to do so.	Rarely generates alternative ways of approaching tasks.	Discounts others' perspectives and points of view while clinging to his or her own.	Is unable to generate alternative solutions and adopts a single, first, and banal approach to a task.

of student goal setting. She asks the students to choose one habit in which they feel especially strong and one on which they need to work. When they are engaged in lab work, she has them consider how they are doing. Which of the habits was most important? They write a reflection on their behaviors as they solve the problems presented in preparation for their final performance. She then maintains a record of how students are doing with the goals they set. Finally, she has the students plot graphs describing their growth and learning in the development and demonstration of the habits of mind.

Exhibitions

Exhibitions are displays of student work compiled and organized around one or more of the important habits of mind. Building a set of criteria with the students before they construct their exhibits causes them to apply a set of standards to evaluating their own and each other's design. Visit an exhibit, such as at a fair or in a museum, and ask students to describe what makes the exhibit visually appealing. What is it that captures their interest? How is the viewer drawn into the exhibit? What has the exhibitor done to engage learning in the viewer? Invite the students to observe other viewers to discover in which exhibits do the viewers become most involved and which exhibits hold the viewer's interest for the longest time.

Anecdotal Records

As students demonstrate particular habits of mind, teachers document their work. The most significant part of this strategy is to be systematic about record keeping. One teacher found that she was able to observe all the children in her class when she designed a notebook, tabbed each section with a student's name, and used sticky notes to record information about the child's intelligent behaviors. At the end of the first marking period, when she wanted to write narrative comments about students, she had a good database from which to draw.

In addition to the anecdotal records a teacher keeps, there are also the anecdotal records from home. Many teachers send a copy of the habits of mind home and ask parents to notice when the child is using the behaviors in the home environment. When conference time comes, the parents share their observations with the teacher.

Interviews

Teachers can use the interview to encourage students to share their reflections and the accomplishment of their mental habits. By creating an atmosphere of trust and by constructing well-designed questions, students can reveal their insights, understandings, and applications of these mental demeanors. The following questions may be posed:

- "As you reflect on this semester's work, which habits of mind were you most aware of in your own learning?"
- "Which habits of mind will you focus your energies on as you begin our next project?"
- "What insights have you gained as a result of employing these habits of mind?"
- "As you think about your future, how might these habits of mind be used as a guide in your life?"

Interviews provide teachers with opportunities to model their listening with understanding and empathy, precise language, and questioning strategies. Teaching students to conduct interviews provides situations in which they must practice these habits of mind themselves.

Journals

Consciousness about the behaviors often begins with journal entries designed to help students focus on how they are developing. Thought starters can help students use the lens of the habits as a way of documenting their learning. Some examples are as follows:

- One thing that surprised me today was…
- I felt particularly flexible when I…
- I used my senses to…
- As I think about how I went about solving the problem I…
- A question I want to pursue is…
- When I checked my work I found…
- Because I listened carefully I learned…

The Role of Assessment in
Becoming a Skillful Thinker

We believe that one powerful and crucial contributor to students' continuous learning as a lifelong disposition is assessment. Individuals who are open to feedback from the environment, from themselves, and from others employ and apply the results of assessments to clarify and modify their own goals, establish their own personal learning, and initiate change. A major purpose of this chapter is to shift the paradigm of assessment from being external and critical without sufficient feedback for change to being descriptive, providing a good road map for the further development of skillful thinking, and encouraging the student to take responsibility for following that road map.

In Chapter 1 we developed a concept of skillful thinking that has three basic ingredients: utilizing a strategy for engaging in a thinking task, supporting this activity with appropriate mental behaviors, and directing oneself to engage in the task in these ways. We have argued that teaching skillful thinking should be an explicit goal of education, and that when this is accomplished by infusing direct instruction in skillful thinking into content instruction, powerful dual learning objectives can be achieved: deep content understanding and the habitual practice of skillful thinking. In this chapter we have presented a picture of how we can assess the thinking abilities and the habituation that are the yield of such instruction. Teaching for skillful thinking and the development of thoughtful habits of mind requires skillful planning and design work from teachers in order to maximize chances that the instruction provided will lead to improving the quality of thinking of all students in a classroom. The explicit assessment of thinking skills and habits of mind should be an integral part of this venture.

The ultimate sign that this classroom labor has been successful is that the classroom becomes full of skillful thinkers. Each student has integrated the strategies, skills, and intellectual habits to such a degree that he or she knows what strategy or skill to use when, is motivated to do so, and is alert to and carries out these engagements of skillful thinking as needed in a wide range of situations. The students are motivated because they have developed the reflective habit of "thought-full" work. In this mix there is more of a role for assessment than just a final measure of classroom success or failure. Assessment, whether conducted by the teacher, the student, or both, can point the way to improvement and hence should become part of the learning process itself. Only then will we be doing our students the service they deserve, because only then will we be empowering them to make use of the results of informative assessments to continue to learn and improve. That's what teaching should be.

Notes

1. Adapted from the work of Stiggins, R. J., Arter, J. A., Chappuis, J., & Chappuis, S. (2004). *Classroom assessment for student learning*. Portland, OR: Assessment Training Institute. See also Costa, A., & Kallick, B. (1995). *Assessment in the learning organization*. Alexandria, VA: Association for Supervision and Curriculum Development.
2. Cambridge Examination Syndicate (2000).

3. Swartz, R., and Parks, S. (1994). Op. cit., pp. 396–402.

4. Ibid., p. 393.

5. Here are three such tests. Each one tests somewhat different critical thinking abilities: Ennis, R. (1985). *The Cornell critical thinking test, level X*. Pacific Grove, CA: Critical Thinking (credibility of sources, deduction, observation, generalization, and assumption identification); *The Watson Glaser test of critical thinking appraisal* (1980). San Antonio, TX: The Psychological Corporation (deduction, assumption identification, argument evaluation, generalization); *The California test of critical thinking abilities* (1990). Milbrae, CA: California Academic Press (interpretation, argument analysis and evaluation, deduction, statistical inference).

6. Swartz, R., and Parks, S. (1994). Op. cit., p. 364.

7. See Swartz, R., & Parks, S. (1994). Op. cit., p. 350; Fisher, A. (2004). *Critical thinking: An introduction*. Cambridge, England: Cambridge University Press, p. 105.

8. Swartz, R. (1991). Developing writing prompts for assessing thinking and content learning in science classrooms. In S. Loucks-Horsley (Ed.), *New ways to assess learning in science*. Miami, FL: Miami Museum of Science (Ch. 1). Reprinted in Costa, A., & Kallick, B. (Eds.). (1995). *Assessment in the learning organization: Shifting the paradigm* (pp. 75–83). Alexandria, VA: Association for Supervision and Curriculum Development.

9. Swartz, R., & Parks, S. (1994). Op. cit., pp. 50–56.

10. Costa, A., & Kallick, B. (2001). *Assessing and reporting on habits of mind*. Alexandria, VA: Association for Supervision and Curriculum Development.

CHAPTER 7

Developing a
Thinking-Based Curriculum

The object of education is to prepare the young to educate themselves throughout their lives.

—Robert Maynard Hutchins, educator

L ISA WILLIAMS, the seventh-grade teacher we introduced you to in Chapter 3, has become quite proficient in teaching lessons that infuse instruction in skillful thinking into content instruction, but she is now in a quandary about this kind of teaching.

Lisa was originally part of a collaborative effort among teachers in her school to work on thinking skills and the development of important mental habits in order to improve student learning. The lessons were on parts–whole thinking, extended comparing and contrasting, determining the reliability of sources of information, predicting the likelihood of future events, determining the likely cause(s) of something that happens, extended brainstorming to develop creative ideas, decision making, and problem solving. The teachers supported these by emphasizing such mental habits as persisting in thinking tasks, managing the tendency to jump to conclusions, and listening to one another with an open mind. They, like Lisa, were aware that skillful versions of all these types of thinking could be taught to students from the earliest years of schooling. The lessons they developed and taught further confirmed this.

Restructuring the way they taught content to infuse instruction in these thinking skills was a lot of work even over the course of a year, but working together, sharing and critiquing ideas, and evaluating results, they all rose to the occasion. They realized that the lessons they developed during this period could be used again and again in subsequent years, and that working on and teaching these lessons during this first year was necessary for them to achieve mastery of the instructional techniques they needed to effectively teach these forms of skillful thinking to their students directly. Indeed, they all did achieve this mastery, coming to feel quite comfortable with the shifts in their classrooms from teacher-centered instruction to the more active student-centered instruction that this engendered. One of these teachers said, "I'll never ever go back to the kind of teaching I used to do before I learned how to teach this way!"

Lisa and the other teachers now face a new challenge. They want to make this kind of instruction the norm in their classrooms. The infusion lessons that they teach, however, must be integrated into appropriate units of study, and those units must be coordinated with others across grades, subject areas, and courses of study. To ensure that students continue to use, refine, and become more effective with the thinking skills, they must integrate thinking into the curriculum in a coherent, consistent, and systematic way.

For example, Lisa is especially interested in again teaching the lesson she developed on Europe and Asia in the 19th century. In this lesson students learned how to engage in an extended version of comparing and contrasting using the model for thinking skillfully about similarities and differences described at the beginning of Chapter 3.

This lesson had wonderful results in her classroom. It not only helped her students understand the meaning of *imperialism* and its mechanisms in the 19th century, it also helped them to start using this more skillful version of comparing and contrasting in other contexts. Lisa wants to do the same thing this year.

At the same time, Lisa knows that some of her students this year, and maybe all of them, are students that other members of her team taught last year, and so these students have already been introduced to some of the thinking skills and habits of mind that she wants to teach them, including skillful comparing and contrasting. She thus begins to question how to integrate teaching thinking directly, without creating repetition or overlooking students who need to be more focused in their progress. These are the same questions that are often asked about curricular content: What will be a repetition? What will constitute a spiraling of development? Where do we see gaps in our thinking skills curriculum? The kinds of lessons that these teachers have developed and taught on the thinking skills have all been highly structured and scaffolded, designed to introduce their students to a specific type of skillful thinking. Maybe these students don't need such highly structured lessons on these thinking skills anymore. Maybe they need to practice the skill and start to guide themselves in its use to follow up on what their pre–grade 7 teachers taught them, or perhaps they should be introduced to somewhat more sophisticated versions of the kinds of skillful thinking they have been already taught. Then again, maybe they aren't ready for this. What should she do?

Lisa is grappling with issues that she alone cannot resolve. These are broader curriculum issues than which classroom techniques of direct instruction she should use to infuse instruction in specific thinking skills and habits of mind into her own content instruction. These are issues about what thinking skills should be introduced at what grades and how follow-up instruction in thinking skills can be structured and coordinated from teacher to teacher so that it reinforces what has already been taught and further refines and develops it. What is needed is a map of thinking skills and habits of mind that determines how these will be implemented in the curriculum—across grades, subject areas, courses, and departments. These issues involve developing an approach to incorporating thinking-based learning into a schoolwide curriculum.

Typically, there is no one teacher who can make these decisions. Rather, they fall within the domain of a curriculum specialist and/or the collaborative group of instructors who deliver the curriculum to students. Furthermore, these issues are ripe for tackling by using the sophisticated electronic technologies that are now available in most schools and that can bridge classroom walls between teachers in an instant.

Curriculum

Educational programs—whether for K–12 students, medical school students, high school science students, or pilots—typically develop a curriculum that students must go through in order to be certified as having completed the program. This is not just a list of topics that have to be covered. Rather, there is an organization of topics and an indication of when, for how long, and in what sequence specific topics must be covered. The experience of learning based on such topic-oriented curricula is not unfamiliar to us. In fact, 99% of the readers of this book will have gone through a number of educational programs that were shaped by such specified curricula. This is how most K–12 educational programs are designed.

Traditionally, most curricula have two basic components. The first is a curriculum framework, which lists topics and expected learning outcomes in a specific sequence—what is to be covered at what grade level or at some other stage of the academic program. The second component specifies how this framework will be implemented—for example, the details of a high school introductory biology course syllabus or the plan for a grade 5 reading program. This usually includes readings, primarily from textbooks and/or other supplementary texts (e.g., novels), and detailed learning activities like writing, computer activities, laboratory work, and/or field trips.

In all this detail, the overall organizational pattern is typically a topic-by-topic approach to learning. So, for example, the topic for March in a mathematics program might be quadratic equations after the students have worked on factoring. The topic for the start of the school year for fifth-grade reading students might be components of a short story followed by character study and characterization. To facilitate this, the students in the math program might have to read the chapter in their text on factoring and do the exercises at the end of the chapter; the students in the fifth-grade reading program will have to read the chapter in their textbooks on the short story, Ray Bradbury's "The Flying Machine," and an O. Henry short story, and then sketch out the structure of these stories using a story map.

Many schools now develop plans for implementing a given curriculum framework by utilizing a process called *curriculum mapping*.[1] Curriculum maps require teachers to use a specific curriculum structure to map out the basis for what is taught in the classroom, derived from a broader and more general curriculum framework. This usually includes (a) essential questions that will serve as overarching conceptual questions that will drive the aspect of the curriculum being implemented, (b) content, which will be its focus, (c) skills, which will be developed and utilized to enhance a student's understanding of the content, (d) ways to assess learning progress, and (e) specific lessons. Such mapping has occurred in traditional content-oriented curricular settings. Table 7-1 shows an example of a secondary school curricular goal related to a concept that appears in the K–12 curriculum for every schoolchild in the United States: the balance of powers in the three branches of our government.

Even with curriculum mapping, such curricula leave out a very important array of skills and mental habits—those that relate to the demand that we teach students to be skillful thinkers and do it by infusing such instruction into content instruction. When this happens the enriched curriculum map that results looks like Table 7-2.

All this can be done using paper and pencil, but it has become a very powerful tool when implemented using an electronic database. Advanced technology can provide better ways to manage the information necessary to make a curriculum operational. This information can then be easily shared and cross-referenced to assessment data about student performance. Such databases maximize the benefits to the individual teacher by providing a "zoom lens" for classroom details and a "wide-angle lens" to capture how all of this fits into a particular curricular system. Coordination from teacher to teacher is easier, so teachers are able to plan what will precede and what will follow the course of study. The curricular system can be anything from a sixth-grade reading program to an anatomy program in a medical school.

As teachers engage in creating quality maps, professional conversations with other teachers usually result, and these eventually lead to some important agreements about what is to be addressed and how to craft the curriculum so that it is responsive to the needs of the particular students and is based on assessment results of student performance. These agreements are usually referred to as the core curriculum that, by agreement, will be addressed by every teacher who is teaching that course of study.

Such teaching agreements are now usually determined with a new "lens": seeing the curriculum through *standards* or *principles statements*. These statements might not be sufficiently explicit to define a curriculum

Table 7-1. Three Branches of Government I

Essential Questions	Content	Skills	Assessments	Lessons
What are the branches of the government of the United States and how do they operate?	The three branches of the U.S. government: the legislative, executive, and judiciary.	Reading a text for detail and organizing written and/or oral presentations.	Answering multiple-choice questions about the three branches of government.	Reading the textbook and answering questions in class about the three branches of the U.S. government.

Table 7-2. Three Branches of Government II

Essential Questions	Content	Skills	Assessments	Lessons
What is meant by "balance of powers" and how is this balance achieved by the government of the United States under the Constitution? <u>What kinds of thinking</u> do I need to engage in skillfully to answer this question most effectively?	The three branches of the U.S. government: the legislative, executive, and judiciary—how they operate, and their relationship to each other.	Reading a text for detail and organizing written and/or oral presentations <u>Skillful thinking</u>: Determining parts–whole relationships by attending to the function of the parts and how they work together. Using the mental habit of communicating ideas with accuracy and precision.	Writing a newspaper editorial about a specific case that involves the three branches of government, explaining how the balance of powers is demonstrated in this case.	Reading the Constitution and one case study, learning and using a strategy for skillful parts–whole thinking about the three branches and the U.S. government, and learning how to use appropriate vocabulary to describe this relationship accurately.

based on skillful thinking, but they can be. They provide a framework not only for what is to be taught but also for what the target expectations for performance will be.[2]

There are standards, and there are standards, however. Some may be pretty low. For example, a standard relating to the branches of government in the United States might be stated as: *The students will identify the three branches of government as organized in the Constitution.* Compare that to this standard about the same concept: *The students will explain how the three branches of government were designed, for what purpose, and how the functioning of the branches is central to maintaining a democracy in the United States.* Compare it yet again to this standard, into which skillful thinking is incorporated: *The students will explain with clarity and precision how the three branches of government were designed, for what purpose, and how the functioning of the branches is central to maintaining a democracy in the United States, and they will explain how this is an example of skillful parts–whole thinking.*

When the teachers engage in a professional conversation that identifies the significant concepts behind this standard, they are building core curriculum maps that are enhanced by the particularities of both content and skillful thinking. Thinking skills and habits of mind are addressed, with an emphasis on identifying the level of skillfulness that is expected.

As teachers work more with a standards-based or principle-based curriculum and develop curriculum maps, they develop and use a different mental model from the older objective or goal-oriented curricula. When a particular curriculum framework is cast in terms of standards or principles identified as central to the values of a school district, department of education, or education ministry, the alignment that takes place when teachers map instructional episodes must be with the standards or principles. Instead of being organized around standard recall activities or textbooks, the curriculum is organized around these standards or principles. When such standards integrate thinking-based standards and the instructional framework used is infusion, the model for shaping instruction that results is a very powerful one. Such standards can be identified and categorized in the following way:[3]

1. *Knowledge Standard*—The level of understanding of facts and concepts we want students to know.
2. *Reasoning Standard*—The complexity of thinking tasks that students will engage in to use what they know to reason and solve problems.
3. *Thinking Skill Standard*—The expected types of thinking that students will use skillfully, and how they will use these, when they reason and solve problems.
4. *Dispositions or Habits of Mind Standard*—The expected attitudes and mental dispositions that the students will manifest and engage in as they are learning

5. *Product Standard*—The quality of the concrete products that students will use their knowledge, reasoning, and skills to create.

In practice, the teaching agreements that result from this very sophisticated standards framework are interpreted by individual teachers through a process that is called *diary mapping*. This is what happens: Teachers map what they are actually teaching—perhaps some of the essential questions they have selected that match their population of students or perhaps some assessment that is based on the needs of the students—onto the curriculum map that has resulted from previous teacher interaction. When teachers do this kind of record keeping as they implement their individual curriculum, this reflects their thinking about their individual students and how they can best communicate the core curriculum to them in the classroom. This is where the art and craft of good teaching takes over.

Table 7-3 is an example of the "unpacked" standard mentioned above with an illustration of how thinking skills and habits of mind can be identified or embedded in the map. The diary map from an individual teacher is designated in italics.

The core is greatly enhanced by the thinking skills and habits of mind. Once the teacher considers what is in the core, she further enhances it to engage the interests of her students. The core and diary maps are saved in the electronic database to provide reports that help to identify repetitions, reinforce spiraling effects, and flag gaps. In any given school the teachers usually realize that curriculum mapping with an electronic database is a very powerful tool to find the best way to integrate a focus on skillful thinking. Table 7-3 illustrates this.

Note that in order to make certain that we are guiding an effective implementation of a thinking-based curriculum, it must be clear that it is skillful applications of types of thinking that we require. This can be done obliquely by using terms like *skillful* as prefixes, as in some of the maps above. It is more precise, however, to make explicit standards for skillful engagements with such types of thinking. So instead of saying that one learning standard is simply comparing and contrasting, a more precise statement of these objectives or learning standards is that students will learn to compare and contrast by identifying similarities and differences, determining which are significant, and drawing conclusions based on these (and, perhaps, making application of these conclusions beyond the classroom context). This makes clear what the thinking-skill expectation is and can provide valuable guidance to teachers whose teaching is designed to implement these standards.

As teachers dialogue about the standards, they recognize that some of the standards call for instruction that crafts such thinking as skillful comparing and contrasting or problem solving. Other standards, like the one above that explicates the content-based standards, require different but integrated mental activity. This is the power of using infusion as the model for interweaving the ingredients of a curriculum map

Table 7-3. Three Branches of Government III

Essential Questions	Content	Skills	Assess-ments	Lessons
What is meant by "balance of powers" and how is this balance achieved by the government of the United States under the Constitution? <u>What kinds of thinking</u> do I need to engage in skillfully to answer this question most effectively? *How might we read the signs or signals that would indicate that there will be a need for an issue to come before all three branches of government?*	The three branches of the U.S. government—the legislative, executive, and judiciary—how they operate, and their relationship to each other with regard to the functioning of democracy in America. *The role of the three branches in elections.*	Reading a text for detail and organizing written and/or oral presentations <u>Skillful Thinking</u>: Determining parts–whole relationships by attending to the function of the parts and how they work together. Exhibiting the mental habit of communi-cating ideas with accuracy and precision by using appropriate language. *Explicitly teach a strategy for skillful parts–whole thinking, together with a strategy for being flexible in our thinking and communicating with clarity and precision*	Writing a newspaper editorial about a specific case that involves the three branches of government, explaining how the balance of powers is demonstrated in this case, and incorporating skillful parts–whole thinking and/or problem-solving strategies in their explanations. *Critiquing the use of wiretaps in the war on terrorism and relating this to the balance of powers.*	Reading the Constitution and one case study, learning and using a strategy for skillful parts–whole thinking and/or problem solving about the three branches and the U.S. government, and learning how to use appropriate vocabulary to describe this relationship accurately. *Case study of the election of 2000. Skillful problem solving and review of parts–whole thinking. Applying these types of skillful thinking to the problems of the election of 2000 and developing a solution that they can defend.*

and will ensure that the students have an enduring understanding that meets the content standards of a curriculum framework. They develop their curriculum through this level of analysis of a variety of standards integrated into one map for power learning. The one-dimensional topic-based curriculum is now transformed into a thinking curriculum in which the topics are a vehicle for the thinking processes and the thinking processes are vehicles for a rich understanding of the topics.

We have looked in some depth at what should be taught in schools when we focus on thinking and how this can be taught in individual classrooms by infusing it into content instruction. We have also drawn out some of the implications of such a model for both content learning and thinking-skill development that impact on students' intellectual habits. Let's remember that we have articulated a three-part model for such instruction that revolves around the concept of skillful thinking. We need to help students learn the important focal questions or thinking demands that make a certain kind of thinking, like comparing and contrasting or decision making, skillful, and to develop the ability to answer these questions and satisfy these demands as they engage in that kind of thinking. We need to help students learn various strategic mental behaviors and attitudes that support and enhance the skillful engagement with this thinking, such as persisting in the thinking task until it is satisfactorily completed and listening with respect to the thinking of others on the same topic. We also need to teach students how to manage such enhanced thinking on their own, based on their conviction that the way they are engaging in this kind of thinking in a specific context is a viable, if not the best, way to do so.

Where in the K–12 curriculum should instruction directed at such thinking-oriented goals be placed?

Sequencing Instruction in Skillful Thinking by Degrees

In Chapter 3 we remarked how a first-grade teacher, Carol Chen, developed and taught her first-grade students a more skillful version of comparing and contrasting than simply listing similarities and differences, using two stories that she read to her students, "Goldilocks and the Three Bears," a classical folktale, and " Deep in the Forest," about a bear that got into the home of a family in Colorado. Instead of the more complex extension of comparing and contrasting that Lisa Williams taught her seventh-grade students, Ms. Chen simplified the strategy to be used by her students by adding only the question "What do these similarities and differences tell us about the things being compared?" She did this because she thought the additional prompting questions in the more sophisticated strategy that Ms. Williams used were well beyond what her students could easily grasp, and that as they moved up through the grades their teachers could elaborate the strategy they wanted their students to use to include questions about the importance of the similarities and differences and what patterns the similarities and differences displayed.

Carey Smythe, who taught in another first-grade classroom, did something similar to start her students thinking more skillfully about their decisions than just embracing the first idea that comes into their minds when they have to make a decision. Instead of teaching her students the sophisticated strategy for decision making that was taught in the fifth-grade lesson on *Shiloh* or the 12th-grade lesson on the bombing of Hiroshima, she employed a simpler three-question strategy for choosing (Figure 7-1). She introduced this to her students by discussing questions that they thought could be asked to make a good decision. She then read them the first part of the Dr. Seuss book *Horton Hatches the Egg*.[4]

This is a charming book in which a little elephant, Horton, agrees to sit on the egg of a bird while the bird goes off on a vacation. Horton faces many challenges: He is caught in a thunderstorm, the temperature falls and he is covered in ice, and his friends want him to come and play with them. Each time Horton is tempted, he reminds himself that he made a promise to Mayzie, the bird, that he would protect the egg, so he stays. He says that he means what he said—he will be 100% faithful. Figure 7-2 is a drawing one student made of Horton sitting on the egg.

Shortly thereafter, a new situation arises, and this one is much more challenging. Some hunters have come on the scene and spot Horton. What should he do? Ms. Smythe wants her students to "become Horton," at this juncture in the story, and use their version of skillful decision making to think about what is the best thing to do. She will guide them through this process in a careful and systematic way, not unlike the way Ms. Chen did with her students.

Figure 7-3 shows the responses from a group of students in Ms. Smythe's classroom. She has written their responses on a blown-up variation of a T-bar diagram for pros and cons in decision making.[5]

These two examples are typical of what primary-grade teachers have done to introduce their students to skillful thinking, including almost all the habits of mind we have discussed so far. This is one approach to integrating skillful thinking into content curriculum. It can include matching types of skillful thinking with curricular content by individual teachers, as well as aligning specific forms of skillful thinking and habits of mind with content contexts by a school, school district, state, or country. The model is

Figure 7-1. First-Grade Thinking Strategy Map for Skillful Decision Making

---

Choosing

1. What are some things I can do?
2. What will happen if I do these things?
3. Which are good things to do?

Figure 7-2. Student Drawing of Horton on the Egg

the same: Start with simplified strategies (like those above for comparing and contrasting and for decision making) and an emphasis on the basic language of the type of thinking or mental habit, which are introduced through introductory lessons and followed up with additional and varied practice, then move students to more developed strategies and more sophisticated language for the same types of thinking and intellectual habits. In a typical case, the simplified strategies would be introduced in grades K–2, and the more developed strategies in grades 3 and above. (In some cases these sequences may be delayed until more advanced grades, especially when new students who have not been exposed to thinking-based instruction transfer into grade 3 and above classrooms.)

Figure 7-4 shows what this progression looks like for comparing-and-contrasting and decision-making strategies.

Figure 7-3. Sample Student Responses

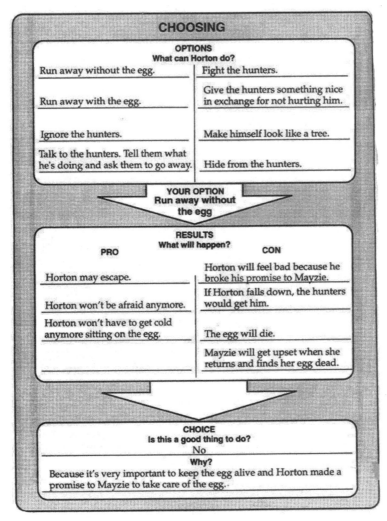

Similar progressions have been developed and implemented sequentially for a number of other types of skillful thinking and for the intellectual habits that enhance these.

After students gain proficiency and internalize the three-question strategy for decision making, teachers in grades 3, 4, or 5 can introduce them to the more developed five-question strategy through such lessons as that on *Shiloh*; deciding where to settle the New World for grade 4, which is about the exploration and settlement of the American colonies in the 16th and 17th centuries; and/or alternative energy sources for grade 7.

Figure 7-4. Strategy Progression

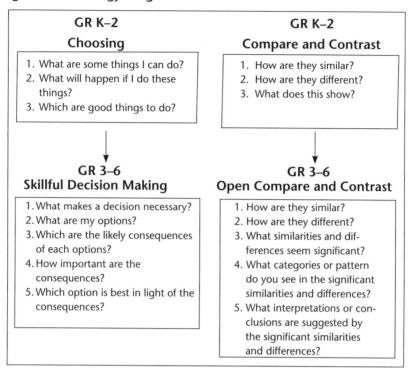

Similarly, such habits of mind as listening with understanding and empathy may be introduced through a simplified strategy that involves repeating what is heard (perhaps accompanied by the body language of a listener), in the primary grades, or becoming a more skillful and habitual listener, in later years, by more advanced behaviors. An increasingly wider range of situations and contexts is applied as students mature and progress through the grades.

Table 7-4 gives a description of increasing maturation toward more skillful and diverse applications of listening with understanding and empathy. This is not a rubric; rather, it provides a paradigm of the growth of a person's capacity for listening with understanding and empathy in increasingly wide and complex situations. It can be the basis for the development by a teacher of a sequenced instructional approach on how to manifest this intellectual behavior. It indicates how a "passive, beginning listener" who is just learning to listen grows into a "skillful, empathic listener." (Because this description may apply to adults as well as children, the absence of grade-level demarcations is intentional.)

Based on this sequence, a teacher might introduce students to listening skills directly by using this thinking strategy map (for good listening),

Table 7-4. Growth of Listening Skills

Passive Listening: *giving the appearance of listening.*

Understands that listening means sitting still, paying attention to others without interrupting.

When prompted, gives attention to the speaker. Can repeat what the speaker said in one's own words.

Follows minimum simple directions given by the speaker.

When empathizing, tells of own (autobiographical) stories rather than identifying the emotions of others.

Selective Listening: *listening for the parts of the conversation that are of interest.*

When asked, demonstrates skillful listening, including paraphrasing, summarizing, clarifying, acknowledging, and simple body posture (sitting up, facing listener, eye contact).

Summarizes and paraphrases others. Clarifies when meanings are unclear.

Follows complex directions (three or four steps) given by the speaker.

Identifies and describes in simple terms the emotional state of the speaker (happy, sad, angry).

Takes an empathetic stance and uses such terms as: "If I were John...," " If it were my choice...," "If I didn't have a bike...."

Attentive Listening: *attending to and focusing on what the speaker says and comparing that to one's own experiences.*

Infers emotional state from observing others' posture, facial expressions, and gestures.

Accurately paraphrases, clarifies, summarizes, builds upon, extends others' ideas.

Describes strategies for holding and/or synthesizing extensive information from the speaker.

Clarifies, probes others' ideas and points of view.

Empathic Listening: *listening and responding with both heart and mind to understand the speaker's words, intentions, feelings, and values.*

Listens with persistence and focused attention, abandoning extraneous self-talk.

Gathers data about the listener though many senses—observing body language, including posture and gesture; listening to pitch, volume, and intonation.

Monitors breathing and facial and muscle tension of the speaker and infers meaning, values, and emotional state.

Table 7-4. *continued*

> Mirrors body language, intonation, and pitch. Paces speech patterns and vocabulary.
>
> Pays attention to, is conscious of, and controls own inner thought processes: memories, emotions, inferences, assumptions, resistances, and biases.
>
> Suspends and holds in abeyance defenses, opinions, doubts, autobiographical messages, value judgments, or solutions to other's problems.
>
> Listens for content, emotions, and underlying values.
>
> Paraphrases accurately both verbally and nonverbally before inquiring and probing.
>
> Honestly and with candor voices own beliefs and uncertainties.
>
> Clarifies and strives to understand others' ideas and points of view.

derived from interaction with her students (Figure 7-5). After the students have made this a regular practice, the teacher can introduce the more complex thinking strategies of pause, paraphrase, and probe that we described in Chapter 1, Figure 1-6.

When unfolding strategies are introduced to students, it is natural to fine-tune them up through more advanced grades. For example, some secondary school lessons on skillful decision making elaborate question 3 in the grades 3–6 version (Fig. 7-4) with subquestions such as "What are the cons as well as the pros?" "What are the long-term as well as short-term consequences?" and "What are the consequences for others as well as yourself?"

Similar elaborations and fine-tuning can be used for behaviors related to important habits of mind, as appropriate, when students who have been introduced to these move into the higher grades. For example, teachers might add a third layer to the strategy for listening skillfully in which specific procedures for paraphrasing and clarifying questions are elaborated. Here's an example of this in an eighth-grade classroom in which the students are working with the "3P" strategy for skillful listening with understanding and respect:[6]

Figure 7-5. Good Listening

> ### Beginning Strategy for Good Listening
>
> 1. Wait till the speaker is finished.
> 2. Repeat what the speaker has said.

Let's start with the first "P"—pausing. There are three meanings of pausing:

Pausing your lips—there should be only one pair of lips moving in the classroom at any one time.

Pausing also means using wait time before responding to a person's answer or asking a question. Do not respond impulsively. Rather, consider options, alternatives, and other possibilities before answering. We want to compose our best, most thoughtful answer rather than giving an impulsive, off-the-top-of-our-head answer.

There is also "pausing the brain." It's like pushing the pause button on a VCR or DVD player. We set aside our thoughts that might be off the topic or that are about some personal experiences that we want to share but that won't necessarily contribute to the discussion.

Let's practice pausing in pairs. Each of you should read the second paragraph on page 45 about the projection of population trends in the United States and the world. When one partner has finished, tell your partner in your own words what that paragraph means to you. Before any of you say anything, however, count backwards from 3 to 1.

The students practice, and after a while the teacher invites reflection:

Teacher: How was that for you, when you had to pause?

Student 1: That was hard—not to say anything. I had a lot of ideas but I couldn't say them.

Student 2: It seemed weird. That's not the way we talk at home.

Student 3: I had to listen. While I had some ideas, Danielle had some different ideas. It was neat.

Teacher: So what did you have to do inside your head to remain silent?

Student 1: I had to tell myself not to say anything. I wanted to talk but couldn't while Maria was talking.

Student 4: Counting backward helped me remember to be quiet.

Student 5: Robbie forgot to pause and interrupted me. Can we try that again?

The teacher also works with the students to elaborate the next step in skillful listening.

Teacher: The second "P" is paraphrasing. Paraphrasing lets others know that you are listening, that you understand them or are trying to understand them, how you understand them, and that you care about their ideas. Paraphrasing implies that you are trying to understand another person before you give your ideas. It means summarizing or putting another person's idea into your own words. Here's an example. I'm going to ask Carlos to share his idea about controlling population. Pay attention to what I say. Carlos, say your idea again.

Carlos: I think we should pass a law limiting the number of children people can have. They do that in some other countries.

Teacher: So Carlos's suggestion is to control the population through legislation, making it against the law to have more than a certain number of children.

Teacher: What did you hear me do with Carlos's idea?

Student 2: You said it in your own words but you still used his idea.

Teacher: Yes, exactly. Now I want you to try it. Again, let's get into pairs and read the next paragraph on page 45.

The students practice. The teacher invites reflection on the experience:

Teacher: How was that for you, when you had to listen to and paraphrase your partner's idea?

Student 1: That was hard—Eric went on and on and I didn't get to share my idea.

Student 2: It seemed weird, too. That's not the way we talk at home, either.

Student 3: That was neat, too. Listening before prejudging someone's contribution makes sense. Being silent helps. I was surprised at the great ideas and how much Ellie added.

Teacher: *So what did you have to do inside your head to* paraphrase your partner's ideas?

Student 1: Eric talked a long time and I couldn't remember all he said. I had to remember his main idea.

Teacher: So what is the value of listening with understanding and empathy?

Student 5: If you don't listen to others' ideas and problems, you could miss a great idea or a giant problem that you had been unaware of before.

Teacher: Tonight at home, I'd like you to practice your paraphrasing with your parents or brothers or sisters. Let's also remember, when we practice, to use what we learned yesterday about pausing.

Student 2: They'll think I'm weird.

The elaboration continues.

> *Teacher:* The third "P" in our good listening skills is probing. This is appropriate when your partner says something or uses some words that you don't fully understand. You have to seek greater meaning and understanding of your partner's ideas, so you clarify the terms. Let me give you an example. Carlos, let's go back and reconstruct our conversation from yesterday. I'm going to demonstrate probing with Carlos, and the rest of you observe what I say.
>
> *Carlos:* I think we should pass a law limiting the number of children people can have. They do that in some other countries.
>
> *Teacher:* So Carlos's suggestion is to control the population through legislation, making it against the law to have more than a certain number of children. Carlos, how many children should be the limit?
>
> *Teacher:* What did you hear me do with Carlos's suggestion?
>
> *Student 2:* You asked him to be more specific.
>
> *Teacher:* Yes. Now, let me demonstrate some more. Carlos, when you said "other countries," which other countries do you know limit the number of children you can have? Again, what did you hear me do with Carlos's idea?
>
> *Student 5:* You made him be more specific. He had to give some exact names of countries; he couldn't just say "some countries."
>
> *Student 6:* Carlos had to make it clear to you what he knew and meant and then you could understand him better.
>
> *Teacher:* Yes, exactly. Now I want you to try it. Again, let's get into pairs and read the next paragraph you page 45. Let's also remember, when we practice, to use what we learned yesterday and the day before about pausing and paraphrasing.

The students then practice pausing, paraphrasing, and probing as they continue discussing the problem of population explosion. Set in a context in which the teacher also introduces students to the strategy for skillful problem solving, this becomes a tremendously powerful instructional strategy that is bound to lead to a deeper understanding of population explosion and its ramifications than reading the textbook alone would accomplish.

Toward the end of the period, the teacher asks the students to anticipate in what other situations it would be important to listen with understanding and empathy. Here are some examples of students' responses:

- I listened to the opinions of my Web page designer and I continued to get suggestions on how the pages looked and I continued to make them better.

- When I got my iPod I had to really listen to my sister, who knew how to download songs and videos onto it. It didn't make sense at first, and I was really confused but I kept probing her until I understood how to do it.
- When my mom gets mad at me for doing something she doesn't like, I wish she'd listen to my side so I'd know she really understands what's bugging me.
- In my dad's job, he has to listen all the time. He's a personnel manager, and almost every night he tells about some problem he's having between his employees and how he has to listen to the complaints and suggestions form each of them.
- I think I'll try this at home.

Sequencing Instruction in Skillful Thinking by Clustering Skills

Another important way to organize a thinking curriculum is to cluster skills in which one skill serves as a prerequisite for the next. For example, skillful classifying is based on, and incorporates, the ability to discern similarities and differences as well as identify significant similarities that form a basis for the classification system being used. This suggests that there might be a natural sequence in which to introduce students to types of skillful thinking. It could be that introducing students to skillful comparing and contrasting before introducing them to skillful classification will enhance their abilities at classification.

Let's examine this in some detail. One type of skillful classification involves discerning important attributes in common between two or more things and defining a category in which to group them in terms of these attributes. Thus, we might group things into the category of "Singapore-made items" because they all have the attribute of having been made in Singapore. We might want to do that because being made in Singapore is a mark of quality. It can be argued that all categorization and classification has its roots in similar processes, although some classificatory terms have taken on colloquial and generic forms of expression, like *river, country*, and *automobile*. Figure 7-6 shows a completed free-form graphic organizer developed by a group of sixth-grade students in which they classify animals by defining attributes related to the quality of self-protection.[7]

There is no doubt that these students have learned a tremendous amount about the protective systems of animals by skillfully classifying them in terms of these attributes. The strategy for skillful thinking in this lesson is what teachers have called "bottom-up classification," represented by the thinking strategy map in Figure 7-7.

This process of developing a classification system is richer and deeper than the types of classification activities we often give students. We typically start with already defined categories like "living things" and "non-

Figure 7-6. Classification of Animals by Self-Protection

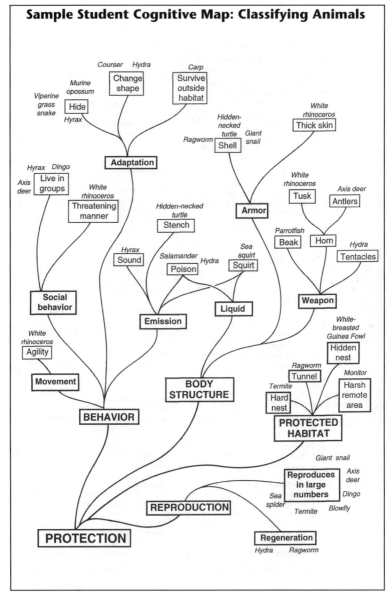

living things" or "narrative writing" and "persuasive writing," and then give students a group of samples and ask them to put the samples in the right category. Bottom-up classification promotes a considerable amount of creativity in developing categories, and it is based on our ability to

Figure 7-7. Thinking Strategy Map for Bottom-Up Classification[8]

Bottom-Up Classification
1. What characteristics do the given items have?
2. For any of these characteristics, what other items have the same characteristic?
3. How can you classify the group of all items that share this characteristic?
4. What subclassifications fall under this classification?
5. What purposes might be served by classifying these items according to this characteristic?

identify significant similarities in diverse items that can serve as a basis for grouping these items together. Hence, it is productive to introduce students to skillful comparing and contrasting before teaching them how to engage in skillful bottom-up classification.

At the same time, a case can be made for introducing more thinking skills early to students—in grades K–2. Four types of skillful thinking are especially important for early classroom instruction: comparing and contrasting, classifying, predicting, and sequencing. Researchers report that students who fail to develop a high degree of proficiency in these skills by the completion of the primary grades often fail to achieve grade-level performances thereafter in reading comprehension and independent learning.[9]

Other types of skillful thinking may be equally important for later instruction, but for different reasons. Some are complex combinations of a number of more discrete thinking episodes and thus particularly difficult for novices to master unaided. Skillful decision making, like problem solving, for example, consists of strategic and recursive use of specific episodes of thinking that should be done skillfully, such as developing criteria for the best choice, generating options, predicting likely consequences, judging the accuracy of information and the credibility of sources, and assessing options in light of their consequences. Figure 7-8 shows a diagram of the important episodes of skillful thinking in effective decision making. It provides a basis for sequencing the instruction in a curriculum. The key subskills of good decision making and problem solving are identified in the lower boxes.

Table 7-5 shows a plan that one department of education considered for an organized introduction to the skillful practice of different types of thinking in the curriculum.

The important job of curriculum-mapping a framework like this with the content curriculum has yet to be done. Articulating what the expecta-

Figure 7-8. Components of Skillful Decision Making[10]

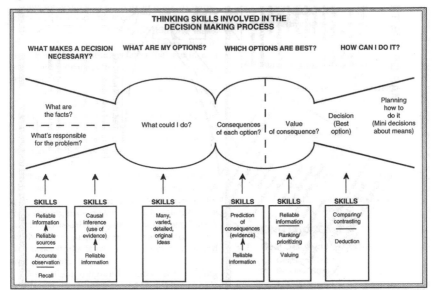

tion is for the skillful practice of these types of thinking and integrating them into the content curriculum will yield a rich version of a thinking curriculum organized on principles of progression from one type of thinking to another.

Problem-Based Learning

Hector Gonzales, a 12th-grade history teacher, has asked his students to "become" one of the historical figures they are studying as they actively engage in skillful problem solving in order to resolve an issue that this figure faces. They are involved in an extended instructional engagement with skillful thinking modeled on a lesson we touched on earlier in both Chapters 4 and 5, the lesson on the bombing of Hiroshima. Unlike what occurs in that lesson, Mr. Gonzales treats this material in a radically different way. To be sure, like the students mentioned earlier, these students have also been studying World War II. They know that the war with Germany has ended but that the fighting in the Pacific with Japan is still going on. They also know that the secret project that a number of American scientists have been engaged in has reached its successful culmination: An atomic bomb with the destructive force of 20,000 tons of TNT, enough destructive power to wipe out a moderate-size city, has been tested in the New Mexico desert. They know that atomic bombs were used by the United States to destroy the cities of Hiroshima and Nagasaki in Japan, thereby ending World War II. But this is all they have studied so far.

Table 7-5. Thinking Skill Sequence For Grades K–5

Basic Skills

Grades K–1:	Parts–Whole Compare and Contrast Sequencing
Grades 1–2:	Alternative Possibilities and Brainstorming Classification Predicting Decision Making and Problem Solving
Grades 3–5:	Causal Explanation Reliable Sources and Accuracy of Observation Reasons, Conclusions, and Arguments Uncovering Assumptions

Advanced Skills

Grades 5 & Above:	Analogy and Metaphor Generalization Reasoning by Analogy Conditional Reasoning and Deduction

Principles of Curriculum Design

1. In each case there should be an introductory lesson followed by additional practice in the thinking skill with new content.
2. In the lower grades the thinking skills should be introduced with a simplified strategy. Advanced strategies for the same skills should be introduced in the higher grades.
3. Teachers may choose to introduce skills designated for higher grades in the lower grades in appropriate contexts.

Mr. Gonzales now intends to facilitate their learning of further relevant historical details about this period in a radically different way from the way that such instruction is usually carried out.

Like the teachers who have taught the lesson on the bombing of Hiroshima, Mr. Gonzales sets the stage for his students' active engagement with skillful problem solving by saying, "Suppose you are President Truman. You, President Truman, want to bring the bloody war in the Pacific to an end and you now have the means to try to do so. But you want to think this through very carefully. You have a problem to solve and a decision to make." He then adds: "That is what I would like you to do in class over the next 4 weeks."

Thus begins a *problem-based curricular unit*—not just a lesson—in which the students will continue to learn about this crucial period in history, the beginning of the Atomic Age, but not by working through their textbooks. Rather, they accomplish this by thinking through this issue and gathering whatever relevant information they need themselves from a variety of sources, including the Internet, to make a wise choice that they can support and defend in detail. They have a full 4 weeks rather than one or two class periods to do this.

To help the students accomplish this thinking task, Mr. Gonzales will engage in some direct instruction in skillful problem solving and decision making, and in a number of the relevant subskills, such as predicting the likelihood of consequences and judging the reliability of sources of information. He will also work with the students to help them practice selected mental behaviors that will enhance this process, such as managing their impulsivity, communicating with clarity and precision, and listening to other points of view with empathy and understanding. Mr. Gonzales has developed a rich 4-week problem-based curricular unit in which the students learn an organized cluster of thinking skills that enhance their ability to find and understand relevant information about this period, World War II, and ultimately to make a wise choice. This is not just an extended version of the lesson we discussed earlier. It has a new twist. It is now a problem-based unit. This is the last model for organizing a thinking-based curriculum that we wish to explore in this chapter.

Problem-based learning is the most integrated approach to sequencing and organizing a thinking-based curriculum. The term, however, has come to mean a variety of things in connection with classroom instruction, only some of which refer to ways to organize a curriculum. In its pure form, problem-based learning takes place when the content material in a curriculum is delivered to students and learned by them through their engagement with solving one or more problems whose solutions require students to learn and understand the content material. It is not simply engaging students in problem-solving in the classroom, nor is it teaching the requisite content in standard ways followed by a culminating experience that involves using this information to work on projects like reorganizing a classroom or remodeling a needy person's house (sometimes called *project-based learning*). Contrary to these other activities, problem-based learning contrasts with the kind of standard topical approach we described earlier in this chapter. Figure 7-9 illustrates these two models.

It is important to recognize that direct instruction in skillful thinking, even in skillful problem solving, might not be integrated into a problem-based learning unit. The primary goal of such a unit is content understanding—understanding by doing—and that might not involve a commitment to infusing instruction in skillful thinking and important habits of mind into the unit. For this to happen requires a plan for such thinking-oriented instruction to be superimposed on the structure of a problem-based unit.

Figure 7-9. Problem-Based Versus Topic-Based Learning

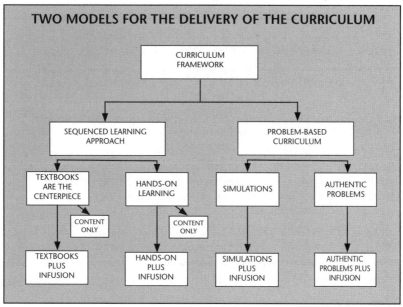

The examples we will describe have been selected because they show what can be done when problem-based learning is used as a vehicle for infusing instruction in problem solving and/or decision making as well as the subsidiary forms of skillful thinking and mental habits that perfect its practice.

Figure 7–10 is a 6-week curriculum structure that can be used to organize instruction provided in skillful thinking in a problem-based unit when this instruction is infused into the fabric of the unit. The seventh week is for an optional writing extension. The types of skillful thinking identified are in italics to indicate that they are taught directly.

What makes this thinking-based unit structure different from the sequences we described in the previous section of this chapter based on the relationships between types of thinking diagrammed in Figure 7–7 is that a sequence of lessons on different thinking skills structured to reflect 7–7 can involve lessons with quite different content focuses, spread out over a significant time interval. In these problem-based units the sequence of skillful thinking lessons may be the same, but they are woven into a sustained and deep exploration of a problem that keeps the content focus connected from lesson to lesson. This is what makes problem-based units extremely powerful learning structures into which instruction in these types of skillful thinking can be infused.

Problem-based learning was initially introduced as a radical way of organizing curricular units in medical school contexts. Various medical situa-

Figure 7-10. Infusing Instruction in Skillful Thinking into a Problem-Based Unit

FRAMEWORK FOR SIX-WEEK PROBLEM-BASED LEARNING UNIT PLUS WRITING EXTENSION	
WEEK 1	Introduction to situation that makes a decision necessary / generates a problem. Questions. *Skillful Problem-Identification*
WEEK 2	Problem solving: possible solutions. Gathering information about the problem. *Skillful Problem-Solving, Extended Brainstorming*
WEEK 3	Problem solving: gathering information to determine the likely pro and con consequences of the possible solutions *Skillfully Determining the Reliability of Sources of Information*
WEEK 4	Problem solving: determining the likely pro and con consequences of the possible solutions *Skillful Prediction*
WEEK 5	Problem solving: determining the importance of the consequences of the possible solutions *Skillful Sequencing by Rank*
WEEK 6	Problem solving: judging which of the possible solutions is best. Defending these choices. *Skillful Compare and Contrast*
WEEK 7	Writing a recommendation explaining why the chosen solution is best *Skillfully Writing Persuasive Prose*

tions, some very simple (e.g. a woman has come to your office complaining of chronic stiffness in her knees), are presented to new medical students. The students have to then diagnose the problem and prescribe a cure. In order to do this they must gather a wide variety of information, for example about knees. In curricular terms this takes the place of students learning this information as one of a number of topics covered in anatomy courses, using a standard anatomy textbook.

Recently this approach to curricular organization has been introduced into K-12 schooling, mainly in the secondary grades. Only some instances of problem-based learning in pre-college instruction, however, make direct instruction in skillful thinking part of their instructional mission *à la* Figure 7-10. One such 12th-grade physics unit doesn't just provide an in-depth exploration of a curricular topic, like we described in the example of the unit on the bombing of Hiroshima, it involves substituting a problem-based unit for a whole 6-week traditional unit on sound usually taught following the topics in the textbook. The problem-based unit began by the teacher announcing to the class that they will be acting like a team of sound engineers who have been called into their school because of all the complaints about the level of noise in the school cafeteria during the meal hours. The teacher selected this problem because he thought that in the course of trying to solve it the students would have to learn everything about sound that would have been taught if they used their textbooks, and perhaps more. As indicated in the model for such units in Figure 7-10 the students began by making a list of questions that they needed to answer in order to be able to solve the problem. They raised 72 questions; here are some of them:[11]

How big is the cafeteria?
How high is the ceiling?
How loud is the burger maker?
What type of floor?
Are the walls hollow?
Do they play music in the cafeteria?
What is the noise level?
Is there any structural damage?
Is the whole school there at one time?
Is there a specific seating arrangement?
What color is the interior of the cafeteria?
Do students have to eat to stay in the cafeteria?
How does noise travel?
Do students pop their drink cartoons?
Is the cafeteria air-conditioned?
Do students make animal noises?

The teacher then introduced them to the problem-solving strategy that we introduced in Chapter 1 (see Figure 1-3) and worked with the students to organize their questions around the different steps in the strategy. Indeed, some were questions about the cause of the noise, some were questions about the consequences of various solutions, and some were questions about sound, the answers to which would help the students assimilate this information once they acquired it. Figure 7-11 is a conceptual model for the process they would be going through.[12]

This is the same process represented by the week-by-week chart in Figure 7-10.

Notice how, true to Figure 7-10, this makes it clear that direct instruction in how to solve problems skillfully is an integral part of this unit.[13] Figure 7-12 shows one result.

Another high school physics teacher used the same approach as a vehicle to help his students learn about force and momentum. He posed the

Figure 7-11. Learning Model for Problem-Based Units

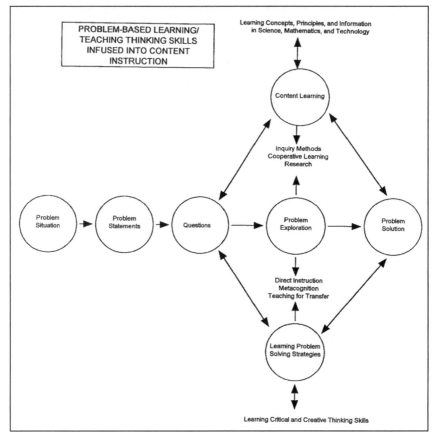

problem of redesigning a roller coaster, called "Desperado," to make it more exciting. They considered various alternatives and focused on putting one or more loops in the track. They drew sketches of these. They had to then determine how likely it would be for the passengers in the cars to fall out when the cars reached the top of the loop inverted, so they needed to consider alternative loops of different shapes and dimensions. As they moved along in the decision-making and problem-solving process, their teacher wanted to help them learn how to judge the likelihood of predictions skillfully and with accuracy and precision, so he worked with them on them subskill of effective decision making and problem solving. Figure 7-13 (overleaf) shows the thinking map he used to help the students predict the consequences of options.[14]

He also worked with them on ways of being accurate and precise by teaching them techniques for accurate calculations of the amount of force that would be exerted on an inverted body in one of the cars as it reached

Figure 7-12. Skillful Problem Solving

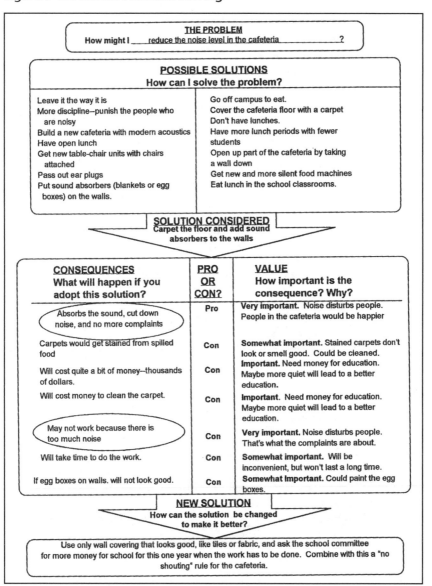

the inside top of the loop. For this they determined how to make exact calculations of the force factor. Figure 7-14 on the next page is a diagram of the roller coaster with the proposed site of the loop[15.]

Figure 7-15 on the next page is a graphic organizer for predicting the likelihood of options to determine whether a circular loop of specific dimensions would work.[16]

Figure 7-13. Thinking Strategy Map for Predicting Consequences

Predicting the Consequences of Options
1. What consequences might result from a specific option?
2. Does each consequence
a. count for or against the decision?
b. rank as important?
3. How likely are the consequences?
a. Is there evidence that counts for or against the likelihood of specific consequences?
b. Based on all the evidence, are the consequences likely, unlikely, or uncertain?
4. Is the decision advisable in light of the significance and likelihood of the consequences?

Figure 7-14. Roller Coaster Diagram

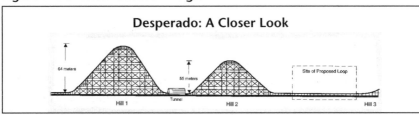

Figure 7-15. Graphic Organizer Predicting the Consequences of Options

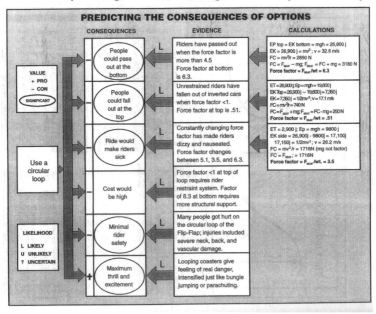

They rejected this option as not viable, given the calculations, that the teacher had them show in some additional boxes on the side of the graphic organizer.

The versatility of organizing curricular units according to a rich problem-based learning model into which instruction in skillful thinking is infused is revealed in one final and important example. This is a 6-week problem-based unit designed to get the students thinking about multicultural issues from different points of view. It is called "Filemoni's Dilemma" and is a unit, developed and taught in an intermediate school in New Zealand, that *makes problem-based learning its primary models for the delivery of curriculum.*[17] This particular unit was developed in part to speak to one of the important curriculum objectives of the national curriculum in New Zealand:

> Students will demonstrate knowledge and understandings of why and how individuals and groups sustain their culture and heritage. Students could demonstrate such knowledge and understandings when they give examples of ways in which people can retain their culture and heritage when they move to a new community.[18]

It is up to each school to interpret this in a context suitable for its students. Such content objectives are very important in an increasingly multicultural world. Meeting this type of objective through problem-based learning enriches what students learn in ways not often possible if this objective is treated as just another topic to be covered using a standard topical approach to curriculum organization. What is special about this example is that this enhanced problem-based curricular model is *integrated into the context of a whole school, not just one classroom.*

Samoa is an independent nation of islands in the Pacific. A large population of Samoans live and work in New Zealand. Unlike Cook Islanders, who can move freely in and out of New Zealand, Samoans have to apply to the New Zealand government for work and/or residency visas. This particular school in New Zealand has an immigrant Samoan population of around 6 percent, and another 12 percent from other Pacific nations. How could the nuances of the multicultural issues that such a situation gives rise to be fully appreciated by the students in the school—who are themselves mostly native New Zealanders and many of European background?

When Filemoni's Dilemma is taught, it is a major event at the school. It is not just taught in one classroom—it is the theme in every classroom. To develop a schoolwide interest in the problem, posters similar to movie posters are put up around the school 2 weeks before the unit begins. On the day the unit starts and during the next 5–6 weeks, flags with the name and logo of the unit are placed along the main entrance to the school (Figure 7-16).

Figure 7-16. Problem-Based Unit Banner

Instruction in the 20 classrooms in this seventh- to eighth-grade school then focuses on this unit. Thus, Tamsin Moller, one of the seventh-grade teachers, presents her students with the following scenario:

> Filemoni is a 13-year-old Samoan student. He is the eldest of five children. He lives in a village on the island of Upolu with his mother, father, and siblings. His parents are thinking about emigrating to New Zealand in the belief that the children will have a better life there.

They would be able to stay with extended family members in Auckland. However, Filemoni is very confused and has called upon his friend (you) in New Zealand to help him through this time. What advice would you give him, and why?

As in the other problem-based units, students can work on this challenge through the use of the strategy for skillful problem solving or for skillful decision making. In this case they work with skillful decision making, thinking about options and their consequences, as we have seen in other problem-based learning units. For this they use the graphic organizer for skillful decision making to guide and record their thoughts.[19] In having the students do this, Ms. Moller also emphasizes the importance of adopting the mental demeanor of flexibility in listening with an open mind to a variety of possible courses of action for Filemoni. In this school they call this whole process a "quest." Ms. Moller and her students are therefore challenged to provide a well-reasoned argument based on what they think is the best answer to the question "What should Filemoni do when faced with the possibility of coming to New Zealand?" This is the goal of the quest of this unit.

It is in this context that the students in this school are introduced for the first time to skillful comparing and contrasting, as one of the important subskills of good decision making.[20] They will use it as a thinking vehicle for comparing the two cultures and the different lifestyles that Filemoni will experience in each. This, of course, is based on the now-familiar thinking strategy in which the students are taken through a consideration not just of similarities and differences but also of which are important similarities between the two cultures, what patterns in the similarities and differences show up in this array, and what conclusions can be drawn that are suggested by these patterns and are based on the important similarities and differences. Once this strategy is introduced and the students get a taste of using it in this unit, Ms. Moller will follow this up with more practice for the students in skillful comparing and contrasting in other curricular contexts. In this unit, she guides them carefully through the process, focusing on Filemoni's dilemma. Because this is the first time they are being introduced to this form of extended comparing and contrasting, she uses some of the key instructional scaffolding we discussed earlier. Here is a sketch of how Ms. Moller integrates her instruction in skillful comparing and contrasting into the unit.

Ms. Moller starts by introducing the unit's scenario, which sets up the problem situation. She then asks the students to brainstorm questions they would like to try to answer, which they think will help them come to terms with this issue. Notice how this technique is like the one used in the lesson in high school physics on noise in the cafeteria. It represents a way to build up some thinking momentum in these units that many teachers have found very fruitful. Here are some of the questions that these students developed:

> Will they be able to continue their traditions?
>
> How do New Zealand and Samoa differ?
>
> What might Filemoni be giving up coming to New Zealand?
>
> What do we value about life in New Zealand?
>
> Will Filemoni face racism in New Zealand?
>
> What other problems might Filemoni face in New Zealand?
>
> What opportunities for a "better life" already exist in Samoa?
>
> What is life like in Samoa?
>
> Are the opportunities for a "better life" really going to be better in New Zealand?
>
> How well will Filemoni and his family adapt to a New Zealand lifestyle?

Think about the curiosity and potential for learning that this list of questions represents. How can the students find answers to these questions?

To support the teachers and students in their research, a group of teachers in the school developed a multimedia CD-ROM of resources to add to those from the school library and the Internet. The resources are embedded in a colorful on-screen illustration from the CD based on the theme of the quest. For Filemoni's Dilemma, the computer screen shows people sitting on mats in a traditional Samoan *fale* (thatched house with open-sided walls). When the students click on the people, they can listen to video interviews, read newspaper articles, and look at photographs of Samoan life. They will have to sort out which information contained on this CD provides them with answers to their questions about the benefits and problems faced by Filemoni when he considers emigrating to New Zealand. In every classroom, students can use a number of computer pods, so viewing the CD in class together is possible (Figure 7-17).

With the class full of library books on Samoa, suitable Internet sites bookmarked, and the CD-ROM loaded onto all their computers, Ms. Mollar's class is ready to investigate the questions they have constructed. They have already identified the steps for skillful comparing and contrasting as well as a graphic organizer that will keep the data they collect in an organized form and that will assist them when it is time to identify their new insights and understandings.

Figure 7-18 is a graphic organizer used by one group of students to sort out the similarities and differences between life and culture in Samoa and life in New Zealand, and to gain insight from this.

Figure 7-17. Students Viewing CD-ROM

As you can see, this compare-and-contrast activity now becomes one of the key contributors to the students' decisions about which option is best for Filemoni.

Ms. Moller decided that after the students have thought through this issue over a number of weeks, she would extend the unit to include their reporting on their results. The students can vary the way their new insights and understandings are shared. Some may choose to complete written reports, others to videotape role-plays that they engage in, and others may develop oral reports supported by a PowerPoint presentation. All will use their graphic organizers to help them structure their arguments. The quest will end with selected pairs of students sharing their new insights and understandings with the class in a concluding performance. This, she expects, will be a major event that will bring the quest that her class had undertaken to a dramatic close.

One of the many details from this event is especially worth mentioning. Ms. Moller asked the students to structure each performance as a reflective discussion in which the students in the audience, through careful listening and questioning, urge each other to define and clarify their terms, arguments, positions and ideas. They use questions like "What evidence do you have to back up your idea that he...?" "Could a consequence of your idea be...?" "How do you know your source is reliable when you said...?"

Figure 7-18. Graphic Organizer

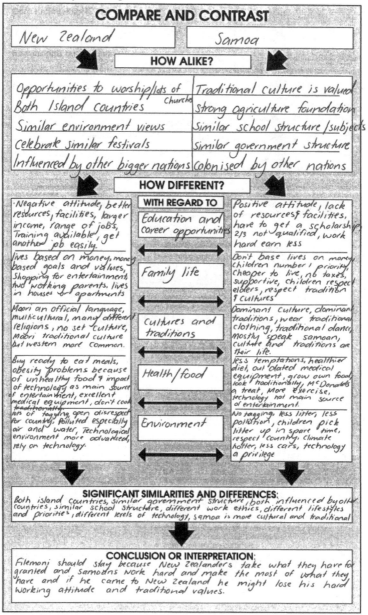

"What made you believe that...?" "Can you please explain a little more why you thought that...?" This is a variant on "Think-Pair-Share," but this time it is structured as an activity in which the students share their results with the whole class.

In this school of 19 other classrooms in which the same unit was undertaken, students from different classes share their results with each other. Active listening to each other with an open mind is explicitly flagged as one of the principles that students try to follow in these discussions. Following this whole-school interaction, each student is then given an opportunity to rethink what would be the best course of action for Filemoni, with the proviso that whether or not they change their minds, they should be prepared to explain why.

This, then, is a rich example of not just one teacher using a problem-based model to construct a curricular unit in an individual classroom but of a whole school using problem-based learning as the dominant model for its curriculum. If this school can do it, so can others.

These examples represent the kind of sequenced instruction that can occur when problem-based learning units are the vehicle for infusing instruction in skillful thinking into content instruction. They represent three ways of introducing problem-based units into a school:

- The teacher sets a problem that involves the students in a rich and deep exploration of a curricular topic
- The teacher sets a problem that involves the students in a rich and deep exploration of a curricular unit that is a substitute for a standard curricular unit
- The teacher sets a problem that involves the students in a rich and deep exploration of either a topic in the curriculum or a whole content unit in the curriculum, and coordinates this with other teachers in the school doing the same thing.

Of course in each case these problem-based units also involve the infusion of direct instruction in relevant and appropriate forms of skillful thinking together with the practice of appropriate habits of mind. We have illustrated how both the overarching form of skillful thinking—either problem solving or decision making—was treated by the teacher and students in these units, as well as how instruction in some of the subskills of decision making and problem solving flagged in Figures 7-7 and 7-10 were woven into such units.

To bring us full circle in this section, Figure 7-19 presents a plan for a 13-week high school or college course built on these principles of sequencing and progression but also structured to provide additional practice for students in the types of skillful thinking and mental habits that are introduced in the earlier weeks of the course. The decision-making lesson on the bombing of Hiroshima is once again the basis for the 6-week unit in the first half of the course. Instruction in the supporting skills and habits of mind for skillful decision making are sequenced into the course. The final assignment in the course is a metacognitive essay about the students'

Figure 7-19. 13-Week Problem-Based Learning Syllabus

Thinking Critically About Contemporary Issues

Course Structure

Week 1	*Skillful Decision Making: Student Reflection on Own Decisions/Introduction of Strategy for Skillful Decision Making*
Week 2	*The Bombing of Hiroshima: Generating Questions, Gathering Information/Application of Skillful Decision Making, I—Options, Consequences (pro & con)*
Week 3	*The Bombing of Hiroshima: Thinking Skills—Reliability of Sources (Japanese claims of their preparation for invasion) Gathering reliable information*
Week 4	*The Bombing of Hiroshima: Thinking Skills—Well-Founded Predictions (2,000,000 casualties in an invasion) Supporting judgments of consequences*
Week 5	*The Bombing of Hiroshima: Application of Skillful Decision Making II—Rating Consequences/Thinking Skill—Ranking (Civilian casualties/saving U.S. soldiers)*
Week 6	*The Bombing of Hiroshima: Application of Skillful Decision Making III—Comparing Options/Choosing the Best Option in Light of the Consequences*
Week 7	*The Bombing of Hiroshima: Writing assignment—Write a recommendation to Harry Truman about the best way to end World War II & support it.*
Week 8	*Transfer of Skillful Decision Making to Contemporary Moral/ Social Issue: Students generate & choose an issue/ Divide into decision-making groups*
Weeks 9–13	*Transfer of Skillful Decision Making to Contemporary Moral/Social Issue: Cooperative Learning Groups: Raising questions, gathering reliable information on issues related to (for example) racism, sexual harassment, euthanasia, capital punishment, gun control, etc./options, consequences, support of consequences, comparing options, choosing the best option/preparing report to class/report to class*

Final Paper: In this course we have explored using a basic strategy for decision making. Please put in your own words what you have learned about decision making that you think will be helpful in making your own decisions. Contrast this with the way you have made decisions in the past. Use examples from your thinking about the bombing of Hiroshima, your research topic, and at least two other presentations to support the ideas you present about decision making.

experiences with skillful decision making. But sequenced into the second half of this course is a repeat of the same type of skillful thinking challenge applied to a different, contemporary problem. This is now organized so that the students *guide themselves* in the forms of skillful thinking necessary to think these problems through carefully, and the instructor deliberately removes some of the scaffolding provided in the first half of the course to encourage this. This is indeed a most powerful curricular model for structuring a whole course into which all of the key ingredients in thinking-based learning are interwoven.

Conclusion

Highly scaffolded lessons in which students are introduced to a type of skillful thinking, like parts–whole analysis or comparing and contrasting, through direct instruction are very important to initiate the learning process for skillful thinking. When and where, in an overall curriculum, should such lessons be infused, and when and where should less scaffolded and more self-directed practice of these types of skillful thinking be prompted? These are questions that must be answered when a group of teachers is sufficiently familiar with these types of skillful thinking and productive mental habits, and when they have mastered the techniques of teaching these through direct instruction. Typically, no one teacher can decide how to answer these questions; they speak to the need for a coordinated across-the-curriculum and across-grade-level plan for thinking-based learning. Using the tool of curriculum mapping to develop an electronic curriculum database for a school is an exceptionally rich way to accomplish this.

To date there are three approaches to answering these questions. One is to introduce procedures for all the important types of skillful thinking and mental habits in the early years of schooling through simplified strategies, and then to fine-tune and elaborate these as students mature and move up through the grades. A second approach is to select types of thinking and habits of mind that are designated as "basic" and introduce these first, later sequencing in instruction in others that build on these. The third is to restructure the curriculum into problem-based units, work first with skillful problem solving and decision making and the accompanying mental habits, then provide direct instruction in the various subskills and additional mental habits that fine-tune these processes, and apply them all to problem-solving and decision-making organized units. We have provided examples of each of these curricular arrangements to illustrate their force.

These are obviously not exclusive alternatives, but they represent ways of answering an important set of questions about thinking-based learning that take us beyond issues of the methods and techniques of direct instruction in teaching skillful thinking. These are questions that any instructional community—be it a school, a school district, or even a national network of schools—needs to answer before it can claim to engage students fully in thinking-based learning. When they are answered and instruction takes place guided by these answers, the result will be the most powerful approach to learning we have experienced.

Notes

1. Jacobs, H. H. (1997). *Mapping the big picture.* Alexandria, VA: Association for Supervision and Curriculum Development.
2. Stiggins, R., Arter, J., Chappuis, J., & Chappuis, S. (2004). *Classroom assessment for student learning: Doing it well.* Portland, OR: Assessment Training Institute.
3. Ibid.
4. Seuss, Dr. (1941). *Horton hatches the egg.* New York: Random House.
5. Swartz, R., & Parks, S., (1994). Op. cit., p. 48. See pp. 44–49.
6. Adapted from Costa, A., & Garmston, R. (2002). *Cognitive coaching: A foundation for renaissance schools,* 2nd ed. Norwood, MA: Christopher-Gordon Publishers.
7. Swartz, R., Fischer, S., & Parks, S. (1999). Op. cit., p. 150.
8. Ibid., p. 132.
9. Jones, B. F., Amiran, M. R., & Katims, M. (1985). Teaching cognitive strategies and text structures within language arts programs. In J. W. Segal, S. F. Chipman, & R. Glaser (Eds.), *Thinking and learning skills, Vol. 1—Relating instruction to research* (pp. 259–290). Hillsdale, NJ: Erlbaum; Paris, S. G., Wilson, K. K., & Palincsar, A. S. (1986). Instructional approaches to reading comprehension. *Review of Educational Research 13,* 91–128; Siegler, R. (1998). *Children's thinking.* Englewood Cliffs, NJ: Prentice Hall.
10. Swartz, R., Fischer, S., & Parks, S. (1999). Op. cit., p. 8.
11. Swartz, R. (2003). Teaching science literacy through problem-based learning and critical thinking. In A. Costa & R. Liebermann (Eds.), *Supporting the spirit of learning.* Thousand Oaks, CA: Corwin. p. 135.
12. Swartz, R. (2003). Op. cit., p. 125.
13. Swartz, R. (2003). Op. cit., p. 135.
14. Swartz, R., Fischer, S., & Parks, S. (1999). Op. cit., p. 432.
15. Ibid., p. 460.
16. Ibid., p. 464.
17. For more information consult the website of the Birkdale Intermediate School in Auckland, New Zealand at *www.bis.school.nz.* Material from the school curriculum is reprinted with permission of the school.
18. The Ministry of Education, New Zealand (1997). *The New Zealand curriculum, social studies, Level 4, Achievement objectives and indicators,* p. 35. Wellington, New Zealand: Learning Media, Ltd.
19. See Figure 4.4.
20. See Figure 7.8.

CHAPTER 8

Leadership: Enhancing the Intellectual Ecology of the School

The most powerful form of learning, the most sophisticated form of staff de-velopment, comes not from listening to the good works of others but from sharing what we know with others. . . . By reflecting on what we do, by giv-ing it coherence, and by sharing and articulating our craft knowledge, we make meaning, we learn. Teachers in a learning community . . . are not "in-serviced." Instead they engage in continuous inquiry about teaching. They are researchers, students of teaching, who observe others teach, have others observe them talk about teaching, and help other teachers. In short, they are professionals.

—Roland Barth, *Improving Schools from Within* (1990)

D OUG ROSE, his assistant principal, and four of the teachers from his school have just returned from a 4-day International Conference on Thinking (ICOT), which takes place approximately every other year at different sites around the world. Their mission at this conference was to investigate the variety of presentations on how thinking instruc-tion has been implemented in K–12 contexts. They will report back to the rest of the faculty about which approach seems to be the most promising for implementation in their school.

The school did not have the necessary funds to send teachers to this conference. The trip was financed by the state department of education with a school improvement grant, for which Doug had applied after sur-veying the faculty on their ideas about how to boost their students' con-sistently below-average performance record. It is a public school, and the students come primarily from middle- to low-income families. Doug, a veteran principal, had assumed the principalship of the school in the pre-vious year. He had taken this job as a challenge. He recognized the prob-lems in the school before he decided to accept the position and made a commitment to do his best to help solve them.

The exploration of thinking-based education is part of the process Doug initiated to try to meet this challenge. Doug came to this school well aware of the positive results in performance, confidence, and moti-vation that thinking-based instruction can bring to a classroom. Some of the teachers in his previous school had brought instruction for thinking skills into their classrooms, and he had observed these results. He had also read articles in the educational journals that excited him about the learning potential of some of the thinking-oriented programs that were available. He was also aware that other educational innovations had positive impacts on learning, such as the introduction of advanced electronic technologies into the classroom. In his new school setting he considered these ideas ripe for serious implementation.

However, Doug did not want to impose these ideas on his staff. Rather, he saw these as ideas to which he might expose his staff, and he would try to help them think through what would be their priorities for implementation. He wanted to make changes undertaken as a group decision. In his initial survey, some teachers said they already taught students thinking skills, and Doug was happy to find that many teachers ranked this as their highest priority, with a special emphasis on critical and creative thinking. Overall, thinking-skill instruction was so well supported by the faculty that it stood out as their highest priority; hence this trip to ICOT. Doug wanted to find out more, and also help his staff to learn more about what others have done to implement this idea in their schools. Then his school could decide exactly how to bring an emphasis on thinking into teaching. In this chapter we will examine how Doug's leadership style impacted the way he moved his school toward making this emphasis fully operational.

Leadership Scope and Style

On the way back from the conference, Doug reflected on his long, tiring, challenging, yet exhilarating 4 days at the conference. How much easier it was during his beginning years as a principal! Taking the role of instructional leader had moved him from being a manager of his staff to a much stronger educational role. He was now much more vigilant about how all staff perform and how all students in the school learn, and much more involved in shaping the direction his school would take in maximizing its potential in both these arenas. He learned that he must master and juggle well the roles of coach, supervisor, evaluator, staff developer, and curriculum designer, as well as manager of the building. As an instructional leader, he must be able to direct many change efforts effectively. He wants to bring about significant instructional improvement in a short amount of time, defying the research on implementing change that suggests that it takes anywhere from 3 to 5 years to effect sustainable change. Doug must become a role model of higher-level thinking; he must be able to model the kind of thinking that we have been suggesting in this book.

Furthermore, he views his role as extending beyond the school itself. His conception of leadership in a school involves responding with constructive sensitivity to the extensive parental and community needs that surround providing an education. He wants to make the parents of his students an active part of the school community. He also feels an obligation to supervise before- and after-school child care programs, extended day kindergarten or child care, and after-school tutoring programs and study groups. These all require additional attention. The demands for a principal to be all things to all constituencies seem endless. A principal must be a good problem solver, an effective communicator, and an effective decision maker to meet these demands.

Technology adds to the burden. Although it serves as an opportunity to have more precise data and better communication with fewer phone calls, it also provides more opportunities for student learning. Along with this, it also presents a series of problems for him. For example, Doug faces at least 100 e-mails to answer every day. He is always seeking additional funds so that the technology for students is up to date, and he wants to invest in the latest technology for teachers so that they can have current and relevant data about student learning and their curriculum.

The years have taught him a lot. His advanced coursework at the university, the school district–sponsored workshops and seminars that he participated in and conducted, the professional conferences he has attended, the coaching he has received, and the amazing learning he has acquired by listening to staff, students, and parents have all contributed to the continual crafting of his skills as an educational leader. Perhaps most important, he has always respected others' ideas and believed that it is through dialogue and open responsiveness to others' ideas that communities function best and that what is best for those communities will more likely emerge this way than if only one individual decides these things. The combination of his experience, his knowledge of people and learning, and his attitude toward others defines his style as an educational leader.

Being well experienced as a principal, knowledgeable about educational policy and change processes, and aware of the research on leadership and school improvement, Doug considers the scope of his work. He draws upon his knowledge in the form of a mental checklist. "I know," he thinks to himself, "that I can't do it all. I also know that I am likely to leave this school sooner than most of the teachers are." Doug has therefore set specific goals for himself: "I must build a culture that is so strong that it can be sustained after I leave. Just as important, though, I must build leadership capacity in my staff." Doug is familiar with the habits of mind that help him to solve problems. He draws from prior knowledge, is flexible in his thinking, and remains open to continuous learning. He uses the thinking strategy map for problem solving and gathers information from all perspectives. He weighs what he is hearing carefully and seeks evidence to suggest that the issues that are being raised are significant and generalizable. These qualities must be transmitted to the teachers, for they are the ones who will operationalize the school's vision and sustain it as principals come and go.

It is in this milieu that Doug has brought his conviction that thinking-based learning is the mode of curriculum design and instructional skill that will lead to a more positive educational record that will make the teachers, parents, and students proud. His challenge has been how to use his leadership skills to make this the school's modus operandi through the active consensus of the school community. The trip to ICOT was a crucial component in the process of building that consensus.

Providing Support to Develop a Thinking Curriculum

There were three presentations at ICOT that impressed the group. One was on problem-based learning, another was on teaching students to develop important habits of mind, and the third was on infusing critical and creative thinking into content instruction. Doug had arranged the staff calendar at the school so that an upcoming early-release day, usually used for planning, could be used in its entirety for reports from the team about the conference and the development of an implementation plan. Prior to the meeting, the team distributed the literature from the conference about the three approaches. It was the team's conviction that these three approaches could be combined into a powerful classroom approach that their students could handle. In the end, the teachers accepted this and decided on a four-pronged approach.

- They would work first on introducing their students to the habits of mind that they thought were important based on the work already done in the field.
- They would then tackle ways of restructuring their teaching to introduce thinking skills to their students.
- At the same time a smaller team would experiment with developing problem-based units.
- While these approaches were being implemented, a parallel action research system would be established for monitoring the staff's progress and the effect it was having on the students.

The teachers asked Doug to use his familiarity with staff-development models to design a long-term staff development program that would enable them to follow this plan. Doug was delighted to do this.

Doug worked with his assistant principal to develop a plan for this project. He realized that this was a major commitment from his teachers, and he wanted to arrange a staff-development program that would be challenging but would not overly stress his teachers. He was well aware, from his own past experience, how crucial the pacing of such a program is. He had been involved in a project on inquiry learning when he was a teacher that had put such heavy demands on the teachers that in the end it was quite counterproductive. He wanted just the opposite to happen.

After discussions with his assistant and some teachers, Doug decided on a 3-year program. In the first year they would concentrate on the habits of mind. They would bring in a person with expertise in this area to conduct a staff-development program for everyone. The school would purchase a set of reference books on teaching and assessing habits of mind for each teacher.

In the second and third years they would work on infusing thinking skills, and as they went along they would integrate an emphasis on productive habits of mind into this work. Once again, they would bring in someone who had recognized expertise in this area to conduct a 2-year staff-development project on infusion, and the school would provide each teacher with relevant written and electronic resources to support this work.

Finally, Doug would put together a team of six teachers during the second year to work on learning about problem-based learning and developing three 6-week experimental problem-based units that included instruction in relevant thinking skills and prompted practice in the relevant intellectual habits. Table 8-1 outlines the essence of this plan.

Doug designed this plan so that teachers could be engaged with its operation beyond just being participants. Teachers could serve as an advisory group to watch over the process as the plan unfolded, they could serve in small action research groups, and they could also monitor selected student work. Doug knew that including as many teachers as possible in this work would make it more successful.

Doug added as a component the experimental use of advanced electronic technology, including the creation of a database with a library of units and lessons, the development and use of PowerPoint slides for the presentation of results to the community, and the active use of the Internet to search for information relevant to the problem-solving issues in the units.

Here are some basic details of the action research that Doug thought would be helpful as an ongoing formative process. For the first year, the teachers would focus on what was being accomplished in the restructuring of classroom instruction. During the second year, they would establish benchmarks to determine if the students were becoming aware of the attributes of skillful thinkers and if they were beginning to value the habits of mind and the thinking strategies they were learning. During the third year, the teachers would collect evidence of the students' spontaneous use of the skills and habits and see if the staff itself was beginning to internalize skillful thinking and the habits of mind.

Doug made provisions for sessions in which a group of teachers could be trained as trainers themselves so that the school would not have to continue to rely on outside consultants to continue this process, especially as new teachers entered the school. Peer coaching and peer training would be important in this project as the teachers gained more confidence

Table 8-1. 3-Year Plan

Year	Habits of Mind	Thinking Skills	Problem-Based Learning	Resources	Assessment
1	Whole school focuses on core group of habits of mind, others divided by grades. Teacher mastery by the end of the school year.	Study group gathers information about infusing skillful thinking.		Consultants with expertise on habits of mind. Books on habits of mind. Books on infusing thinking skills into content. Video technology to document work.	Study group gathers information about ways of assessing student thinking. Anecdotal records kept on ways that students exhibit habits of mind.
2	Further practice in teaching habits of mind.	Whole school focuses on core types of skillful thinking infused into content instruction. Infusion lessons developed, taught, and assessed.	Study group gathers information about problem-based learning.	Consultants with expertise on infusing instruction in skillful thinking into content instruction. Technology to establish a data base of infusion lesson plans.	Action-research team develops assessment instruments to assess skillful thinking. Database of indicators of skillful thinking by students.
2	Habits of mind identified for each thinking skill and integrated into the lessons taught on that thinking skill. Thinking skill instruction used as the primary context for the practice of the habits of mind.				
3	Whole school focuses on additional thinking skills infused into content instruction. Habits of minds identified for each thinking skill and integrated into lessons taught on that thinking skill. Mastery of the techniques of direct instruction of thinking skills infused into content instruction by all teachers. Parents brought in to learn about ways of supporting instruction in skillful thinking at home		Study group develops 3 problem-based learning units	Consultants with expertise in infusing thinking skills and in problem-based learning. Books on problem-based learning. Videos of classroom teaching from the school for study. Database of lessons and units that infuse skillful thinking.	Student performance is measured by thinking assessments as well as performance on standards-based tests.
3	Integration of direct instruction in skillful thinking into the three experimental problem-based learning units taught in three grades.				

in their abilities to provide viable thinking-based instruction. Here Doug saw a real potential for shifting the leadership of this project to his teaching staff.

Doug also wrote into his plan that he would try to send small teams of teachers to conferences on habits of mind, infusing thinking skills, and problem-based learning. To coordinate all of this, he appointed his assistant principal and one of the original investigating teachers.

The school had a very small staff-development budget, not enough to support such an extensive change project. Although the budget for books was relatively substantial, it, too, was insufficient to support the number of books, CDs, and other resources necessary for the project. Doug therefore applied for a grant from the state department of education for the staff-development modules and he applied to two computer industry foundations for money to support the action-research component of the plan.

Because the state department of education had funded the recent ICOT attendance, Doug thought that it would be disposed to continue funding, in order to bring what it had started to fruition. Doug had an idea. He offered to open his school to teachers and administrators from other schools as a model for the kinds of curricular changes that could take place to transform a school from a below-average performer to a high performer. That is, he thought he would make his school available as a public role model if this all worked, and was confident that it would.

Apparently, the state department of education had the same confidence: It fully funded these projects. Furthermore, one of the two computer industry foundations he applied to awarded the school a small grant to support the action research project. So they were off and running!

This enterprise is still in process, now in its third year. Already results are showing up. Every classroom has become a thinking classroom in which direct instruction on skillful thinking strategies and key intellectual habits takes place. Posters have been put up—some designed by the students—about these thinking strategies and habits of mind. There is a discernable shift in classrooms to a more student-centered approach, with more active learning taking place. The teachers' lounge is replete with anecdotes of great changes not only in learning but in interest to learn from some of the students who, just 2 years earlier, seemed to be destined to drop out of the process altogether. One teacher said that she was amazed that some students, originally deemed as "slow learners," were making rapid progress. Their insight, creativity, questioning, and thoughtfulness were causing the staff to reconsider what is meant by "intelligence."

Much more still needs to be done, but the school is ready to meet the challenges. After this initial reorientation to learning, Doug and the teaching staff are already aware that they need to institutionalize this kind of instruction. Right now it is somewhat haphazard. Thinking-oriented goals have to be written into the curriculum, phased in on a year-by-year basis, and matched to significant content to maximize the effect. For this project Doug has been reading up on curriculum mapping and on how to build a core curriculum electronic database that can integrate all the important components of the new school curriculum. Doug and his teaching staff are ready to meet this challenge!

Creating a Culture of Mindfulness

Doug is also aware that for a project like this to succeed, more than just these staff-development efforts have to take place. There also has to be an atmosphere in the school that supports the basic idea that skillful thinking is important and is a schoolwide goal. Doug realizes that many factors influence teachers' thinking as they make daily decisions about curriculum and instruction. These include their own culture, their knowledge of the content being taught, state and district standards of learning, the tests by which students will be assessed, their own cognitive and learning styles, knowledge of their students, and their professional values and beliefs about education. All of these influence their judgments about when to teach what to whom.

Less obvious but still vastly persuasive influences on teacher thought are the norms, policies, and culture of the school setting. Hidden but powerful cues emanate from the school environment. Doug's efforts to bring teaching for skillful thinking into the instructional programs will prove futile unless the school environment signals the staff, students, and community that the development of the intellect and cooperative decision making are the school's basic values. Efforts to enhance instructional competencies, develop curriculum, revise instructional materials, and improve test scores and assessment procedures are important components of the process of educational re-engineering, but it is also crucial that the climate in which parents, teachers, and students make their decisions is aligned with the goal of the development of intellectual potential. Teachers will more likely teach for thinking, creativity, and cooperation if they are in an intellectually stimulating, creative, and cooperative environment themselves.

Doug views himself as a role model and a mediator of staff and student intellectual capacities. He knows that the level of teachers' intellectual development has a direct relationship to student behavior and student performance. Higher-level intellectually functioning teachers produce higher-level intellectually functioning students.[1] Characteristic of these teachers is their ability to empathize, symbolize experience, and act in accordance with a disciplined commitment to skillful thinking to further important human values. In the classroom they should employ a greater range of instructional strategies, elicit more conceptual responses from students, and produce higher-achieving students who are more cooperative and involved in their work. Successful teachers are thoughtful teachers, and they stimulate their students to be thoughtful as well. Outside the classroom they should also model the kinds of skillful thinking and intellectual behaviors they are teaching students in the classroom. Doug considers creating such an environment in the school to be one of his major supporting responsibilities.

Doug's role is therefore to constantly monitor and enhance the conditions for continuous learning, the intellectual development of the staff, and the practice of skillful thinking in the overall life of the school as well as in the life of the classroom. He sees his role as analogous to that of the Environmental Protection Agency: monitoring and managing the environment to ensure that intellectual growth, creativity, cooperation, and skillful intellectual behavior are continually sustained and regenerated.

One of the ways that Doug facilitates this is to model these actions himself. He adopts the practice of using graphic organizers for decision making and problem solving when the matters faced are complex and require careful thought. He also comments aloud about his own thinking in order to model metacognitive reflection with his staff. He seeks their reflective suggestions about how to think through issues they face together. In short, he practices skillful thinking openly in designing strategies for achieving the vision of their school as a learning organization. Figure 8-1 shows a memo he wrote to the school staff that he posted on the school's Intranet.

Doug also knows that he needs to be thoughtful when he is supervising. He uses a "walk-through" strategy (visiting classrooms) to make certain that he stays in touch with instruction in the classroom. He knows what the teachers have been learning about teaching thinking, and he observes with these indicators in mind:

- How much of the talk in the classroom is teacher talk and how much is student talk?
- Is the teacher talk focused on thinking?
- Is the student talk focused on thinking?
- Is there evidence of the use of graphic organizers and thinking strategy maps?
- Are the students clear about the tasks in which they are engaged?
- Is there evidence on the walls to suggest that thinking is taking place?

The staff agreed that someone entering the classroom should be able to observe for indicators of thoughtful instruction. They also suggested that observers might want to talk with the students to check their understanding. Doug agreed to arrange for teachers to observe each other as well as for the mentor teachers and administrative team members to visit

Figure 8-1. Staff Memo

TO: All Staff Members, P.T.O. Board President, and District Area
       Coordinator
FROM: Doug Rose, Principal
RE: Agenda and Back-Up Materials for Staff Meeting, Wednesday,
       September 8

I am looking forward to our faculty meeting on Wednesday. We must make some important decisions together. I have met with and talked with several of our parents, board members, and district personnel to gather their ideas about these issues.

One of the several emerging and recurring themes deals with how we can all work together on behalf of our students using a process of decision making that is clearly understood and practical. As you recall, we agreed to employ a strategy map for skillful decision making in our own teaching. I'd like to suggest that we try this ourselves as we confront the decisions facing us in this school. We need to keep in mind the following questions:

1. What makes this decision necessary?
2. What are our options?
3. What are the likely consequences of each option?
4. How important are these consequences?
5. Which option is best in light of the consequences?

The decisions facing us, as I see them so far, are:

- Should we offer Chinese as a language?
- How do we best support our special education children?
- How do we best integrate technology into our curriculum and classrooms?
- What is the future of woodshop?
- Do we need a mental health curriculum?
- How do or should we use data to inform our practices?

I deeply believe that we must involve our teachers, staff, administrators, and board members working as a team toward mutual and well-articulated goals. So I want to set up teams from each group to think through these issues collaboratively. I'd like to discuss with all of you how we might do this, and I'd like to ask you to also think about whether there are any other school-issue oriented questions that we need to add to our list.

classrooms and have follow-up discussions with the teachers to hear about their questions, concerns, learning, modifications, and next steps.

He also agreed that at faculty meetings the teachers and he would have an opportunity to discuss the evidence that Doug collected related to thinking. The dialogue groups would be across grade levels and subject areas, and the focus would be on examples of practice in which thinking is taking place.

In the following section we will examine some basic studies of leadership in order to give you insight into some of the key characteristics found in Doug's leadership of his school. We believe that without the leadership qualities described in these studies, any changes would be outward manifestations only and would not represent the deeper results of a school as a thinking community that we witnessed being shaped by Doug's actions.

Leadership Qualities

Building Shared Norms and Values

> *If your vision statement sounds like motherhood and apple pie and is somewhat embarrassing, you're on the right track. You bet the farm.*
> —Peter Block (1987)[2]

Peter Senge[3] states that leadership in a learning organization starts with the principle of creative tension. He describes how creative tension emerges from seeing clearly where we want to be—the vision—and describing truthfully where we are now, our current reality. The gap between the two generates creative tension.

The principle of creative tension has long been recognized by leaders. Martin Luther King Jr. proclaimed the following in his "I have a dream" speech:

> Just as Socrates felt that it was necessary to create a tension in the mind, so that individuals could rise from the bondage of myths and half truths…so must we create the kind of tension in society that will help men rise from the dark depths of prejudice and racism.

This tension, according to Senge, can be resolved by raising current reality toward the vision. Effective leaders stimulate intellectual growth by causing creative organizational tension. Leaders create for themselves—and facilitate staff, students, and community—visions of what could be, images of desired states, valued aspirations, and scenarios of more appropriate futures.

Doug reflected on the progress his staff has made so far in pursuing their vision of a "mindful school"—a term borrowed from the Waikiki Elementary School in Honolulu—a thought-full learning community, a school that is a home for the mind. Doug thinks back on the many meetings with staff, students, and parents in which they struggled to hammer out such a vision for the school. After much dialogue, they all finally agreed that "Central School is a home for the active mind, always engaged in skillful thinking; a cooperative community that promotes knowledge, self-understanding, mutual respect, global understanding, adaptability to change, and a love for lifelong learning."

Doug knew the great value in the process of developing this mission statement. It provided an opportunity to problem-solve, listen, and empathize with each other's ideas, to explore the underlying assumptions, and to strive for clarity. He knew that this mission statement would be employed continually as a criterion for making decisions, developing policies, allocating resources, hiring staff, designing curriculum, disciplining students, and planning lessons. Doug knows that a school's mission statement is given substance and value when it is systematically assessed. When our values are clear, the day-to-day decisions we make are easy. We refer to our mission statement often because what gives an organization integrity is how the staff members perceive the congruence of its policies, vision, and mission with its daily practices. Furthermore, the mission statement that the groups developed is focused on long-term, enduring, and essential attributes that start to be developed in the school, but then expand outward into the community. It is as good for adults as it is for students.

Building and Maintaining Trust

> *Teamwork is the ability to work together toward a common vision, the ability to direct individual accomplishment toward organizational objectives. It is the fuel that allows common people to accomplish uncommon results.*
> —George Land and Beth Jarman[4]

In their study of school reform in Chicago, Bryk and Schneider found that student achievement was correlated with the level of relational trust in schools. They defined relational trust as occurring between the following groups:

- School professionals and parents
- Teachers and the principal
- Teachers and other teachers
- Teachers and students[5]

Furthermore, trust is a vital element in enhancing cognition. We know that higher-level, complex, and creative thinking closes down when trust is lacking in the environment or in relationships with others. Teachers are encouraged to inquire, speculate, construct meanings, experiment, self-evaluate, and self-prescribe when the leader manages a trusting environment. Building an atmosphere of trust is the leader's most important task. Doug knows, therefore, that trust cannot be built from rhetoric alone. It is a product of honest and caring interactions between people.

Humans, as social beings, mature intellectually in reciprocal relationships. Collaboratively, individuals generate and discuss ideas that elicit thinking that surpasses individual effort. Together and privately, they express different perspectives, agree and disagree, point out and resolve discrepancies, and weigh alternatives. Because people grow intellectually through this process, collegial interaction is a crucial factor in the intellectual ecology of the school.

The essence of building trust and collegiality is for people to work together to better understand how to work together. People are more likely to engage and grow in higher-level, creative, and experimental thought when they are in a trusting, risk-taking, and cooperative climate. Risk-taking requires a nonjudgmental atmosphere in which information can be shared without fear that it will be used for evaluative purposes.

Integro Canada, Inc. thinks of trust in two parts: personal and interpersonal. Personal trust is built through interpersonal behavior (e.g., Are you trustworthy? If I lend you $100, are you reliable enough that I can count on you to pay me back?). Interpersonal trust involves being relaxed, comfortable, unguarded, and open—you're willing to share (self-disclose) in a relationship with another person. When Integro analyzed comments about what trust is, it found four categories:[6]

- *Acceptance*—nonjudgmental behavior, listening to hear, and setting aside own opinions, suggestions and evaluative comments.
- *Reliability*—you can count on me; doing what you say you are going to do; accountability.
- *Openness*—sharing with you what I'm thinking; no hidden agenda; honesty; being clear about one's purpose and intention and being congruent in behavior.
- *Congruence*—emotionally honest; sincere; words, tone of voice and body language fit the situation.

The research on trust in schools offers insight into the development of trust among a school leader, the staff, the students, and the community. Tschannen-Moran[7] concludes that there are five facets that people rely on in making trust judgments:

- *Benevolence*—caring, extending good will, having positive intentions, supporting teachers, expressing appreciation for staff efforts, being fair, guarding confidential information.
- *Honesty*—having integrity, telling the truth, keeping promises, honoring agreements, having authenticity, accepting responsibility, avoiding manipulation, being real, being true to oneself.
- *Openness*—engaging in open communication, sharing important information, delegating, sharing decision making, sharing power.

- *Reliability*—being consistent, being dependable, demonstrating commitment, being dedicated, being diligent.
- *Competence*—setting an example, engaging in problem solving, fostering conflict resolution, working hard, pressing for results, setting standards, buffering teachers, handling difficult situations, being flexible.

Other research[8] indicates that staffs trust leaders who demonstrate competence, consistency, even-handedness in behavior, and integrity. Doug's role in his school could have been the prime example for these studies.

Facilitating Reflective Dialogue

Perkins[9] states, "Your organization functions and grows through conversations. The quality of those conversations determines how smart your organization is."

Baker, Costa, and Shalit[10] and Garmston and Wellman[11] identify eight norms that may serve as standards that are understood, agreed upon, adopted, monitored, and assessed by each participant when working as a facilitating and contributing member of a group. These are the glue that enables school and community groups to engage in productive and satisfying discourse:

1. *Pausing*. Taking turns is the ultimate in impulse control.[12] In a discourse, space is given for each person to talk. Time is taken before responding to or asking a question. Such silent time allows for more complex thinking, enhances all forms of discourse, and produces better decision making. Pausing is the tool that facilitative group members use to respectfully listen to each other.
2. *Paraphrasing*. Covey suggests that we seek to understand before being understood.[13] Paraphrasing lets others know that you are listening, that you understand, or are trying to understand and that you care.
3. *Probing and clarifying*. This is an effective inquiry skill when the speaker uses vocabulary, a vague concept, or terminology that is not fully understood by the listener. Probing and clarifying are intended to help the listener better understand the speaker. In groups, probing and clarifying increase the clarity and precision of the group's thinking by illuminating understandings, terminology, and interpretations.
4. *Putting your ideas on and pulling them off the table*. Groups are most productive when everyone shares their thoughts, dreams, mistakes, assumptions, and opinions. As they offer these, however, they should attempt to keep them relevant to the topic at hand. Be-

cause there are times when continuing to advocate a position might block the group's functioning, group members should sometimes volunteer to withdraw their ideas.

5. *Paying attention to oneself and others.* Meaningful dialogue is facilitated when each group member is sensitive to and conscious of the subtle cues expressed by oneself and others. Paying attention to learning styles, modalities, and beliefs when planning, facilitating, and participating in group meetings enhances group members' understanding of each other as they converse, discuss, deliberate, and make decisions.

6. *Presuming positive intentionality and positive presuppositions.* People operate from internal maps of their own reality, and we assume that they act with positive intentions. This assumption promotes and facilitates meaningful dialogue. Because our language contains overt and covert messages, deeper meanings can be misinterpreted. The subtle (and often unsubtle) way in which we embed presuppositions in our language can be hurtful or helpful to others. The deliberate use of positive presuppositions assumes and encourages positive actions

7. *Providing data.* Groups that exercise high levels of communicative competence act on information rather than hearsay, rumor, or speculation. Data serve as the energy source for group action and learning. Seeking, generating, and gathering data from group members as well as a variety of other primary and secondary sources enhances individual and group decision making.

8. *Pursuing a balance between advocacy and inquiry.* Advocating a position and inquiring into another's position assists the group to continue learning. Senge, Ross, Smith, Roberts, and Kleiner[14] suggest that balancing advocacy and inquiry is critical if an organization is to grow and learn.

Doug encourages individuals and groups to monitor and assess their own use of these eight norms of collaboration. During a faculty meeting, Doug invites the group to focus on one or several of these norms of collaboration. He might ask, "As we examine our agenda today and the problem we are focused on, which of the norms might be most important for us to employ?" The group generates several, and Doug asks them to pay attention to themselves to see which norm they are employing and what effects the norm has on group productivity.

Toward the end of the meeting, the teachers are invited to share their observations of themselves, to comment on what effects the use of the norms had on group productivity, and, as they consider future meetings, which ones might they want to focus on again. Individual faculty members are invited to make a "goal statement" for improvement of their own use of one or more of the goals.[15]

Supporting Coaching[16]

> *The current management culture, with its focus on controlling behavior,*
> *needs to be replaced by a management culture in which skillful coaching*
> *creates the climate, environment, and context that empowers employees and*
> *teams to generate results.*
>
> —R. Evered and J. Selman[17]

It is often said that teaching is one of the most lonely professions. In most schools, teachers go into the classroom and close the door, and no other adult sees them perform their most precious, creative, and professional craft. One way to stimulate intellectual growth is to "deprivatize" the craft of teaching so that teachers share their thought processes, planning, reflection, and instructional decisions.

One morning, soon after Doug arrives at school, Gina, a teacher with mentoring responsibilities, knocks on his office door. Their conversation goes something like this:

Doug: Hi, Gina. You're up bright and early. C'mon in; sit down.

Gina: I'm going to be coaching Mark today and I thought I might take a moment to share my plans with you.

Doug: So you're eager to take some next steps coaching our new teacher. What do you have in mind?

Gina: Well, Mark is really making great strides in his teaching. My goal for him is to develop even greater feelings of efficacy.

Doug: So you're seeing real growth in Mark. What indicators suggest Mark is making great strides?

Gina: Well, I've noticed his willingness to experiment with new ideas; he reads widely and his lessons clearly have a focus on skillful thinking. I've noticed a decline in his reliance on me to make suggestions for modifying his lessons—he's becoming more self-reliant.

Doug: You're pleased that he's becoming more autonomous. So what are your plans for coaching him today?

Gina: He wants to include more metacognitive questions in his interactions with his students—causing them to reflect on and to verbalize their thought processes.

Doug: Drawing upon what you know about student metacognition and classroom interaction, what are your plans for helping him include more metacognitive questions?

Gina: Well, that's where I'm uncertain. I think there might be several alternatives. One would be to share with him the ladder of metacognition so that he could see questions that are designed to invite each level of metacognition. Another option would be to have him describe what metacognitive processes he wants from his students and then to design questions to invite these thought processes. Yet another option would be for me to "walk him through" a lesson like one on skillful decision making that has a clear component that is designed to engage metacognition. I want him to feel secure, and I really appreciate his willingness to experiment like this.

Doug: Gina, as you recall, you said that you wanted him to gain greater feelings of efficacy. Of the three options you mentioned, which do you think would develop Mark's feeling of greater efficacy?

Gina: Hmm. Well I don't think walking him through the lesson would be good—that will just build greater dependency on me. I think a combination of the first two might work. I think I'll start by asking him to describe what it might look like and sound like if students are thinking metacognitively before, during, and after the lesson. I'll try to capture those on a list. Then I can invite him to design questions that might elicit each of those metacognitive processes. I think I'll leave him a copy of the ladder of metacognition as a take-away piece for him to put on "auto-ponder."

Doug: So your plan is to draw from him the desired descriptors of student metacognition, then have him design the questions to elicit those.

Gina: Exactly, but I think Mark is open to expanding his understanding of even greater complexity of metacognitive processes. Simply inviting students to think about their thinking does not necessarily help them get better at or to apply them in new settings. So I hope to "stretch" Mark's thinking a bit by providing a printed copy of the ladder of metacognition I think he will find it intriguing and that will give him some additional thoughts about how to take his students to even greater levels of complex thinking.

Doug: So, Gina, how did this brief conversation help?

Gina: Well, I'm much clearer now about what my coaching strategy will be. Your listening helped me think out loud about my plans. When you asked me which alternative would contribute to Mark's feelings of efficacy, that really caused me to evaluate my alternatives. Thanks!

Doug: I enjoyed our conversation. Let me know how it turns out and, if you wish, we can have another conversation as you reflect on your coaching with Mark.

Gina: Thanks. I'll get back to you.

Cognitive Coaching[SM] is one of the most powerful means to overcome the extreme isolation of teaching.[18] Coaching produces intellectual growth for a variety of reasons:

- *Coaching enhances instructional thought.* The act of teaching is itself an intellectual process. Jackson[19] found that teachers make more than 1,300 decisions a day. The behaviors observed in the classroom are artifacts of decisions that teachers make before, during, and after instruction. The purpose of coaching, therefore, is to enhance the teachers' capacity to plan, monitor, and reflect on their instructional decision making, perceptions, and intellectual functions. Costa and Garmston state that the intent of coaching is to modify teachers' capacity to modify themselves.[20]
- *Humans who desire to continually improve their craft will seek and profit from coaching.* Skillful artists, athletes, musicians, and dancers never lose their need for coaching. Likewise, in education, to continually perfect their craft, teachers profit from coaching.
- *To work effectively as a member of a team requires coaching.* Welding together the individual efforts of team members into a well-organized and efficient unit requires the persistence and stamina of an expert coach. This concerted effort, however, does not just happen. It takes someone—a conductor who "knows the score"—to provide the synergy. It takes time, persistence, practice, and coaching to develop a winning athletic team, a celebrated symphony orchestra, or a learning organization.
- *Few educational innovations achieve their full impact without a coaching component.* Joyce and Showers[21] found that efforts to bring about changes in classroom practice are fruitless unless the teacher is coached in the use of the innovation. Only when the component of coaching was added was the innovation internalized, valued, and transferred to classroom use.
- *Coaching enhances the intellectual capacities of teachers, which in turn produces greater intellectual achievements in students.*[22]

Lev Vygotsky has said the following:

> Every function in…cultural development appears twice: first, on the social level, and later on the individual level; first between people (inter-psychological), and then inside (intra-psychological). This applies equally to voluntary attention, to logical memory, and to the formation of concepts.
>
> All the higher functions originate as actual relationships between individuals.[23]

Vygotsky's statement provides a strong theoretical support for coaching as a means of intellectual growth. It is through social interaction that new concepts and intellectual behaviors are formed and grown, and, as was cited earlier, the teacher's level of intellectual development influences the student's level of intellectual development.

Encouraging Collaboration

> *Success depends above all, upon people. Build relationships, teams, partner-*
> *ships—and motivate people to contribute. Cultivate leadership, creativity,*
> *excellence. Listen; seek new ideas and advice.*
>
> —Ruth Scott

Human beings are made to be different. Diversity is the basis of biological survival. Each of us has a different genetic structure, unique facial features, a distinguishing thumbprint, and a distinctive signature. We
come from diverse backgrounds of knowledge, experience, and culture,
and each individualizes a preferred way of gathering, processing, and expressing information and knowledge. We even have a singular frequency
in which we vibrate.[24] Leaders are sensitive to and capitalize on these differences to enhance intellectual growth,

Intellectually effective people are comfortable in multiple areas of
functioning. They move flexibly from one style to another as the situation
demands. They have an uncanny ability to read contextual cues from the
situation or the environment about what is needed and then draw forth
from their vast repertoire the skills and capacities that are necessary to
function most effectively in any setting.

Organizational life might be easier if all members of the learning community thought and acted in a similar fashion and remained in their own
departments and grade levels. Limitations of time, isolation, and our obses-
sion with the archaic compartmentalization of the disciplines and grades
keep school staffs separated; thus, opportunity for teachers' intellectual
growth is limited. Leaders realize that humans grow intellectually through
resolving differences, achieving consensus, and stretching to accommodate
dissonance. They realize that there is a greater possibility for making connections, stimulating creativity, and increasing the capacity for complex
problem solving when such differences are bridged. (In some businesses,
this is referred to as "Skunkworks"—deliberately bringing together personnel from different departments, positions, and grade levels to make
connections and find new and divergent ways to solve problems.)

Interdependent learning communities are built not by obscuring diversity but by valuing the friction that differences bring and resolving
those differences in an atmosphere of trust and reciprocity.

We have already seen how Doug was committed to bringing his teaching staff together to function as a learning community to make changes
that would improve the functioning of the school, even though he himself
had very strong ideas on the subject. Whenever he can, Doug deliberately
brings together people of different political and religious persuasions, cultures, genders, cognitive styles, belief systems, modality preferences, and
intelligences to work on issues and problems. He structures groups com-
posed of representatives from different schools, departments, community

groups, and grade levels to envision and describe learning outcomes, to plan curriculum and staff development activities, and to allocate resources. This is one of the strongest leadership qualities that Doug displays in his school. It represents an attitude toward people and communities that is part of his very being.

Ensuring Opportunities for Cooperative Reflection on the Performance of Group Members

> *By three methods we may learn wisdom: first, by reflection, which is noblest; second, by imitation, which is the easiest; and third, by experience, which is the bitterest.*
>
> —Confucius

Practices that build a strong sense of professional community include (a) a close attention to process, and (b) a product with which teachers can walk away.[25] Doug sees the power of these practices as a means of improving instruction. Three practices that seem to have a great impact on teaching are lesson study, study of student work, and book study.

Lesson Study

Lesson study is a method that has been adapted from Japanese education.[26] A good example of lesson study is from an elementary school that follows this procedure:

1. Teachers identify a curricular area that students have difficulty understanding. In this example, fifth- and sixth-grade teachers chose "generating questions and managing impulsivity in problem solving."
2. Teachers meet together at the grade level and develop a lesson plan. They script the lesson and consider all the options. They consider the students, the need for differentiated instruction, and some of the variables they can anticipate. They make certain that the lesson will teach thinking, and they experiment with some of the strategies they are learning from their reading and research.
3. One of the teachers teaches the lesson, and as many teachers as possible observe the lesson. The observers take good notes of their observations. Since they all planned the lesson, they are able to focus more easily on students than on the teacher. They are expected to observe student learning.
4. The teachers come back to discuss their observations. Since they were all lesson designers, critique is easier. They talk about what worked and what did not work. They revise the lesson in light of what they observed.
5. Another teacher tries the lesson with an additional observation.

6. They reflect once again and enter the lesson in their database of lessons that have been tried, honed, and successfully taught.

This highly focused and shared responsibility for designing, teaching, and reflecting on student learning is a very powerful tool for building collaboration and professionalism.

Studying Student Work

Another way to encourage reflection on practice is to study student work. There are many protocols that are used for this purpose.[27] The essence of the practice is to bring examples of student work to the group. The person who brings the work will have the group consult with her about whether the work is reflective of the learning outcomes that have been identified. For example, the group might want to study whether students are showing evidence of skillful decision making or of metacognition in their work. They might study the responses of students in their writing or on a student-produced video to determine if the students are becoming more skillful in thinking about options and consequences or if they are thinking about how to do the kind of thinking with skill.

Here is an example of a student's writing about his own awareness of his decision-making processes. The questions for discussion are as follows: (a) How might we use this example as an adequate indicator of the student's awareness of how he conducts his own decision making? (b) How does this student's writing typify the class as a whole? (c) How does this student's observed behavior in everyday decision-making situations match what he has written? As you read this sample, consider how would you answer question (a).

> The way I go about making a decision is quite different from last year. Prior to learning about skilllful thinking, many of my decisions later brought regret. Many times I would just jump into a situation without thinking of the consequences until it was too late. Or a lot of times I would look at the consequences but almost bend the truth so that the consequences would end up in my favor. Never in the past did I go seek outside information to make a well-informed decision. Or many times I would seek advice from people who were just as knowledgeable or less knowledgeable than I am on the topic. Now that I have had proper instruction in the decision-making process, I am better off. When I attempt to make a decision now, no matter how important or minor it is, I write down every thought I have, unlike before, when I would just store the thoughts up in my head.

The key to the process of studying student work is the following:

1. Have a clearly defined purpose for the study with a set of guiding questions based on the relevant thinking strategy maps.

2. Establish a protocol for facilitating the discussion, such as who will present, how many minutes will there be for the presentation, how will people respond to the presentation, how many minutes will there be for response, and how many minutes will there be for a discussion and reflection on the work. If there is a clear facilitating protocol, it helps to move the group to focus on the work rather than on personalities.
3. Have ground rules for thoughtful work, using some of the habits of mind as the suggested dispositions and attitudes the group must maintain.
4. Reflect on group learning.

Part of the staff development project that Doug has designed is devoted to this. For each habit of mind or thinking skill that the teachers are learning how to teach, Doug has written in time for small groups of teachers to get together and discuss the effectiveness of their lessons by looking at student work before and after the lesson. Is there evidence of the thinking skill or intellectual habit that is being taught in this work? If not, perhaps the lesson should be modified. If so, the student might be ready to move to another level in his or her learning of skillful thinking.

Book Study

Doug not only encourages his teachers to study books that deal with teaching and other realms of education, he joins the groups on a regular basis. Much like the close study of text that they expect from their students, the teachers delve into their books chapter by chapter, seeking applications in their daily teaching.

Highly successful educators discuss student progress with their colleagues and share ideas with each other. They believe that collegial discussions centered on teaching and learning have more impact on their practices than formal administrative observations and evaluations.[28] Each of these practices helps to build a thoughtful—sensitive, caring, and "thought-full"—environment that supports the importance of skillful thinking.

Leaders Stimulate Continual Learning

> *Autopoesis: (Greek) Self-production. The characteristic of living systems to continuously renew themselves and to regulate this process in such a way that the integrity of their structure is maintained. It is a natural process which supports the quest for structure, process renewal, and integrity.*
> —Margaret Wheatley, educator and author

Senge[29] emphasizes that a characteristic of the learning organization is that it challenges existing mental models. The leader, in an atmosphere of trust, challenges existing practices, assumptions, policies, and traditional ways of delivering curriculum. Intellectual growth is found in disequilibrium, not balance. It is out of chaos that order is built, that learning takes place, that new understandings are forged, that new connections are bridged, and that organizations function more consistently with the mission, vision and goals.

Leaders search for problems where answers are not known. They encourage experimentation, action research, and data production. This implies that an atmosphere of choice, risk taking, and inquiry exists. Data are generated without fear that they will be used as a basis for evaluating success or failure. Creativity will more likely grow in a low-risk atmosphere.

Leaders empower teachers to develop an internalized locus of control. They appreciate the possibilities of continual growth efforts that marshal the motivations and unleash the talents of those who work directly with children day after day.

Leaders assist the teaching staff to design strategies for collecting data and to use the assessment data as feedback and a guide for informed and reflective practice.[30] Staff members will need help in learning how to design feedback spirals, including multiple ways of gathering such data, establishing criteria for judgment, and working together to develop their common understanding and reliability of observations and reporting of results.

Conclusion

Some people think that it is holding on that makes one strong. Sometimes it is letting go.

—Sylvia Robinson

After most of the students and teachers have gone home, Doug has a moment to reflect. Because thinking, cooperating, and respecting human uniqueness are best learned through imitation of significant others, Doug strives to model in his own behaviors the qualities and behaviors that he desires in his students and staff. He contemplates the quotations on his desk. His favorite reminder of a concern for human relationships is by Willi Unsoeld, the renowned Scandanavian mountain climber: "Take care of each other. Share your energies with the group. No one must feel alone, cut off, for that is when you do not make it."

Doug also reflects on the colorful posters on his wall that describe the qualities of leadership that display the kind of skillful thinking that the teachers in his school help students to develop. These are shown in Tables 8-2, 8-3, and 8-4.

The development of thinking, individuality, and collegiality as goals of education is not just kid stuff. Education will achieve an intellectual focus when the school becomes an intellectually stimulating environment—

a home for the mind for all who dwell there; when all the schools' inhabitants realize that freeing human intellectual potential is the goal of education; when staff members strive to get better at it themselves; and when they use their energies to enhance the intellectual skills and intelligent behaviors of others. Educational leaders serve as an "environmental protection agency," constantly monitoring the intellectual ecology of the school. Their chief purpose is to ensure that thinking, creativity, and collaboration will become neither endangered nor extinct by making them goals that are put into practice in the educational community.

Table 8-2. Skills That Leaders Display as They Engage in Skillful Thinking

1. Skillful decision making
Leaders consider options and consequences, both pro and con and for themselves and others, in making skillful decisions.
2. Skillful problem solving
Leaders identify problems and consider a variety of possible solutions, judging their consequences before determining which solution is best.
3. Skillful application of analysis where needed
Leaders strive to achieve a deep understanding of ideas by breaking them into components that are clearly understood. They use appropriate skills of comparison and contrast and of parts–whole analysis.
4. Skillful application of creative thinking where needed
Leaders strive to generate for consideration a variety of ideas of different types, including original ideas, suspending their judgment until a wide variety of ideas are "on the table." They use appropriate skills of extended brainstorming and synthesis.
5. Skillful application of critical thinking where needed
Leaders commit themselves to an open-minded search for available reasons or evidence before judging that an idea is worthy of acceptance or rejection, and they don't accept or reject an idea until there are good reasons for doing so. They use appropriate skills at judging credibility and inference.

Table 8-3. Metacognition

Metacognition
Leaders are aware of their own thoughts, strategies, feelings, actions, and effects on others. Leaders talk to themselves as they evaluate their plans, monitor their progress, and reflect on their actions.

Table 8-4. Habits That Leaders Hold in Mind as They Engage in Skillful Thinking

1. Persisting

Leaders remain focused. They have a commitment to task completion. They never lose sight of their own and their organization's mission, vision, and purposes.

2. Listening with understanding and empathy

Leaders strive to understand their followers. They devote enormous mental energy to comprehending and empathizing with others' thoughts and ideas.

3. Managing impulsivity

Leaders think before they act, remaining calm, thoughtful, and deliberative. Leaders often hold back before commenting, considering alternatives and exploring the consequences of their actions.

4. Thinking flexibly

Leaders are adaptable. They can change perspectives, generate alternatives, and consider options. They see the big picture and can analyze the parts. They are willing to acknowledge and respect others' points of view.

5. Striving for accuracy and precision

Leaders are truth seekers. They desire exactness, fidelity, and craftsmanship. Leaders do not accept mediocrity.

6. Questioning and problem posing

Leaders have intellectual curiosity, a need to discover, and a need to test ideas. They regard problems as opportunities to grow and learn.

7. Applying past knowledge to new situations

Leaders draw on their rich experiences, access prior knowledge, and transfer knowledge beyond the situation in which it is learned. They learn from their mistakes.

8. Gathering data through all the senses

Leaders have highly tuned observational skills. They continually collect information by listening, watching, moving, touching, tasting, and smelling.

9. Thinking and communicating with clarity and precision

Leaders articulate their ideas clearly in both written and oral form. They check for understanding and monitor their own clarity of terms and expressions.

10. Creating, imagining, and innovating

Leaders try to conceive problems differently by examining alternatives from many angles. They project themselves into diverse roles, use analogies, take risks, and push the boundaries of their own limits.

(continued overleaf)

Table 8-4. *continued*

---

11. Responding with wonderment and awe
Leaders find the world fascinating and mysterious. They are intrigued by discrepancies, compelled to mastery, and have the energy to enjoy the journey.

12. Taking responsible risks
Leaders are courageous adventurers as they live on the edge of their competence. They dare to take calculated risks.

13. Finding humor
Leaders have such high self-esteem that they do not take themselves too seriously. They are able to laugh at themselves and with others. They are capable of playfully interpreting everyday events.

14. Thinking interdependently
Leaders recognize the benefits of participation in collaborative efforts. They seek reciprocal relationships, both contributing to and learning from interaction with others.

15. Remaining open to continuous learning
Leaders resist complacency about their own knowledge. They have the humility to admit their weaknesses and display a sincere desire to continue to grow and learn.

Notes

1. Glickman, C. (1985). *Supervision of instruction: A developmental approach.* Newton, MA: Allyn & Bacon, p. 18.
2. Block, P. (1987). *The empowered manager.* San Francisco: Jossey-Bass, p. 122.
3. Senge, P. (1990). *The fifth discipline.* New York: Doubleday.
4. Land, G., & Jarman, B. (1992). *Break-point and beyond: Mastering the future today.* New York: Harper.
5. Bryk, A. S., & Schneider, B. (2002). *Trust in schools: A core resource for improvement.* New York: Russell Sage.
6. From Costa, A., & Garmston, R. (2004). *Cognitive coaching learning guide.* Norwood, MA: Christopher-Gordon.
7. Tschannen-Moran, M. (2004). *Trust matters.* San Francisco: Jossey-Bass, p. 34.
8. Bryk, A., & Schneider, B. (2002). Op. cit..
9. Perkins, D. (2002). *King Arthur's round table.* Hoboken, NJ: Wiley.
10. Baker, W., Costa, A., & Shalit, S. (1997). The norms of collaboration: Attaining communicative competence. In A. Costa & R. Liebmann (Eds.), *The process-centered school: Sustaining a renaissance community.* Thousand Oaks, CA: Corwin.
11. Garmston, R., & Wellman, B. (1999). *The adaptive school: A sourcebook for developing collaborative groups.* Norwood, MA: Christopher-Gordon.

12. Kotulak, R. (1997). *Inside the brain. Revolutionary discoveries of how the mind works.* Kansas City, MO: Andrews McMeel.
13. Covey, S. (1989). *The seven habits of highly effective people.* New York: Simon & Schuster.
14. Senge, P., Ross, R., Smith, B., Roberts, C., & Kleiner, A. (1994). *The fifth discipline fieldbook.* New York: Doubleday/Currency.
15. Costa, A., & Kallick, B. (1995). *Assessment in the learning organization: Shifting the paradigm.* Alexandria, VA: Association for Supervision and Curriculum Development.
16. Ellison, J., & Hayes, C. (2006). *Effective school leadership: Devloping principals though cognitive coaching.* Norwood, MA: Christopher-Gordon.
17. Evered, R., & Selman, J. (1989). Coaching and the art of management. *Organizational Dynamics, 18,* 16–32.
18. Costa, A., & Garmston, R. (2002). *Cognitive coaching: A foundation for renaissance schools,* 2nd ed. Norwood, MA: Christopher-Gordon.
19. Jackson, P. (1968). *Life in classrooms.* New York: Holt Rinehart Winston.
20. Costa, A., & Garmston, R. (2002). Op. cit.
21. Joyce, B., & Showers, B. (1988). *Student achievement through staff development.* New York: Longmans.
22. Edwards, J. (2002). Research on cognitive coaching (Chapter 14). In A. Costa and R. Garmston, *Cognitive coaching: A foundation for renaissance schools,* 2nd ed. (pp. 323–353). Norwood, MA: Christopher-Gordon.
23. Vygotsky, L. (1978). *Society of mind.* Cambridge, MA: Harvard University Press.
24. Leonard, G. (1978). *The silent pulse: A search for the perfect rhythm that exists in each of us.* New York: Bantam.
25. DuFour, R., & Eaker, R. (1998). *Professional learning communities at work: Best practices for enhancing student achievement.* Alexandria, VA: Association for Supervision and Curriculum Development.
26. Stigler, J., & Hiebert, J. (1999). *The teaching gap: Best ideas from the world's teachers for improving education in the classroom.* New York: Free Press.
27. McDonald, J., Mohr, N., Dichter, A., & McDonald, E. C. (2003). *The power of protocols.* New York: Teachers College Press.
28. Bello, N. (2004). *Reflective analysis of student work: Improving teaching through collaboration.* Thousand Oaks, CA: Corwin Press.
29. Senge, P. (1990). Op. cit.
30. Lipton, L., & Wellman, B. (2004). *Data-driven dialogue.* Sherman, CT: MiraVia.

References

Allen, R. (2003, Summer). Expanding writing's role in learning. *Curriculum Update*, 1–8.

Anderson, R. C., Spiro, R. J., & Montague, W. E. (Eds.). (1977). *Schooling and the acquisition of knowledge*. Hillside, NJ: Erlbaum.

Astington, J. W., & Olson, D. R. (1990). Metacognitive and metalinguistic language: Learning to talk about thought. *Applied Psychology: International Review, 39*, 77–87.

Baker, W., Costa, A., & Shalit, S. (1997). The norms of collaboration: Attaining communicative competence. In A. Costa & R. Liebmann (Eds.), *The process-centered school: Sustaining a renaissance community*. Thousand Oaks, CA: Corwin Press.

Bandura, A. (1997). *Self-efficacy: The exercise of control*. New York: Freeman.

Bello, N. (2004). *Reflective analysis of student work: Improving teaching through collaboration*. Thousand Oaks, CA: Corwin Press.

Bereiter, C. (1973). Elementary schools: Convenience or necessity? *Elementary School Journal, 73* (8), 435–445.

Beyer, B. K. (1987). *Practical strategies for the teaching of thinking*. Boston: Allyn & Bacon.

Beyer, B. K. (1988). *Developing a thinking skills program*. Boston: Allyn & Bacon.

Beyer, B. K. (1997). *Improving student thinking: A comprehensive approach*. Boston: Allyn & Bacon.

Beyer, B. (2001). What research says about teaching thinking skills. In A. Costa (Ed.), *Developing minds: A resource book for teaching thinking*. Alexandria, VA: Association for Supervision and Curriculum Development.

Beyer, B. K., Costa, A. L., & Presseisen, B. (2001). Glossary of thinking terms. In A. Costa (Ed.), *Developing minds: A resource book for teaching thinking*. Alexandria, VA: Association for Supervision and Curriculum Development.

Block, P. (1987). *The empowered manager*. San Francisco: Jossey-Bass.

Bloom, B. S., & Broder, L. J. (1950). *Problem-solving processes of college students*. Chicago: University of Chicago Press.

Brown, A. L. (1978). Knowing when, where, and how to remember: A problem of metacognition. In E. Glaser (Ed.), *Advances in instructional psychology*. Hillsdale, NJ: Erlbaum.

Brown, A., Campione, J., & Day, J. J. (1987). Learning to learn: On training students to learn from texts. *Educational Researcher, 10* (2), 14–21.

Brown, J. S., Collins, A., & Duiguid, P. (1989). Structured cognition in the culture of learning. *Educational Researcher, 18* (1), 32–42.

Bryk, A., & Schneider, B. (2002). *Trust in schools: A core resource for improvement*. New York: Russell Sage.

Burwell, B. (1995, December 6). Commentary. *USA Today*, p. 2C.

CBS "60 Minutes Wednesday" cancelled: Sitcoms will fill in. (2005, May 19). *USA Today*, p. 3D.

Clark, A. J., & Palm, H. (1990). Training in metacognition: An application to industry. In K. J. Kilhooy, M.T.G. Keane, R. H. Logies, & G. Erdos (Eds.), *Lines of thinking: Reflections on the psychology of thought* (Vol. 2). Chichester, UK: Wiley.

Cornbleth, C., & Korth, W. (1981). If remembering, understanding, and reasoning are important. *Social Education, 45* (4), 276, 278–279.

Costa, A. (2001). Mediating the metacognitive. In *Developing minds: A resource book for teaching thinking*. Alexandria, VA: Association for Supervision and Curriculum Development.

Costa, A., & Garmston, R. (2002). *Cognitive coaching: A foundation for renaissance schools,* 2nd ed. Norwood, MA: Christopher-Gordon.

Costa, A., & Kallick, B. (1995). *Assessment in the learning organization: Shifting the paradigm.* Alexandria, VA: Association for Supervision and Curriculum Development.

Costa, A., & Kallick, B. (2000). *Activating and engaging habits of mind.* Alexandria, VA: Association for Supervision and Curriculum Development.

Costa, A., & Kallick, B. (2001). *Assessing and reporting on habits of mind.* Alexandria, VA: Association for Supervision and Curriculum Development.

Costa, A., & Marzano, R. (2001). Teaching the language of thinking. In A. Costa (Ed.), *Developing minds: A resource book for teaching thinking*. Alexandria, VA: Association for Supervision and Curriculum Development.

Covey, S. (1989). *The seven habits of highly effective people*. New York: Simon and Schuster.

Dempster, F. N. (1993). Exposing our students to less should help them learn more. *Phi Delta Kappan, 74* (6), 433–437.

Dewey, J. (1933). *How we think*. Boston: Houghton Mifflin.

Doyle, W. (1983). Academic work. *Review of Educational Research, 53* (2), 159–199.

DuFour, R., & Eaker, R. (1998). *Professional learning communities at work: Best practices for enhancing student achievement.* Alexandria, VA: Association for Supervision and Curriculum Development.

Edwards, J. (1988). Measuring the effects of the direct teaching of thinking skills. *Human Intelligence Newsletter, 9* (3), 9–10.

Ellison, J., & Hayes, C. (2006). *Effective school leadership: Developing principals through cognitive coaching*. Norwood, MA: Christopher-Gordon.

Ennis, R. (1984). A taxonomy of critical thinking skills and dispositions. In R. Sternberg & J. Baron (Eds.), *Teaching thinking: Theory and practice*. New York: Freeman.

Ennis, R. (1985). *The Cornell test of critical thinking abilities,* 3d ed. Pacific Grove, CA: Critical Thinking.

Estes, T. H. (1972). Reading in the social studies: A review of research since 1950. In J. Laffery (Ed.), *Reading in the content areas*. Newark, DE: International Reading Association.

Evered, R., & Selman, J. (1989). Coaching and the art of management. *Organizational Dynamics, 18,* 16–32.

Feuerstein, R. (1980). *Instrumental enrichment*. Baltimore: University Park Press.

Flavell, J. H. (1976). Metacognitive aspects of problem solving. In L. B. Resnick (Ed.), *The nature of intelligence*. Hillsdale, NJ: Erlbaum.

Fletcher, R., & Portalupi, J. (1998). *Craft lessons: Teaching writing K–8*. Portland, ME: Stenhouse.

Flower, L. S., & Hayes, J. R. (1981). A cognitive process theory of writing. *College Composition and Communication, 32* (4), 365–387.

Fredericksen, N. (1984). Implications of cognitive theory for instruction in problem solving. *Review of Educational Research, 54,* 363–407.

Garmston, R., & Wellman, B. (1999). *The adaptive school: Developing collaborative groups.* Norwood, MA: Christopher-Gordon.

Gersten, R., & Carnine, D. (1986). Direct instruction in reading comprehension. *Educational Leadership, 41* (7), 70–78.

Glickman, C. (1985). *Supervision of instruction: A developmental approach.* Boston: Allyn & Bacon.

Goleman, D. (1995). *Emotional intelligence: Why it can matter more than IQ.* New York: Bantam.

Hayes, J. R., & Flower, L. S. (1981). Writing as problem solving. *Visible Language, 14,* 388–399.

Hong Kong Ministry of Education. (2002). *Personal, social, & humanities education.* Hong Kong, China: Curriculum Development Council.

Hurst, J. B., Kinney, M., & Weiss, S. J. (1983). The decision-making process. *Theory and Research in Social Education, 11* (3), 17–43.

Hurwitz, N., & Hurwitz, S. (2004). *Words on paper.* Available online at www.asbj.com.

Jackson, P. (1968). *Life in classrooms.* New York: Holt Rinehart Winston.

Jacobs, H. H. (1997). *Mapping the big picture.* Alexandria, VA: Association for Supervision and Curriculum Development.

Jones, B. F., Amiran, M. R., & Katims, M. (1985). Teaching cognitive strategies and text structures within language arts programs. In J. W. Segal, S. F. Chipman, & R. Glaser (Eds.), *Thinking and learning skills: Vol. 1. Relating instruction to research.* Hillsdale, NJ: Erlbaum.

Joyce, B. (1985). Models for teaching thinking. *Educational Leadership, 42,* 4–7.

Joyce, B., & Showers, B. (1983). *Power in staff development through research on training.* Alexandria, VA: Association for Supervision and Curriculum Development.

Joyce, B., & Showers, B. (1988*). Student achievement through staff development.* New York: Longman.

Kaufman, E. L., & Miller, N. E. (1958). Acquisition of a learning set by normal and mentally retarded children. *Journal of Comparative and Physiological Psychology, 5,* 614–621.

Kotulak, R. (1997). *Inside the brain: Revolutionary discoveries of how the mind works.* Kansas City, MO: Andrews McMeel.

Land, G., & Jarman, B. (1992). *Break-point and beyond: Mastering the future today.* New York: Harper.

Leonard, G. (1978). *The silent pulse: A search for the perfect rhythm that exists in each of us.* New York: Bantam Books.

Lipman, M. (1988, September). Critical thinking—what can it be? *Educational Leadership, 46* (1), 33–43.

Lipman, M. (1991). *Thinking in education.* Cambridge, UK: Cambridge University Press.

Lipton, L., & Wellman, B. (2004). *Data-driven dialogue.* Sherman, CT: MiraVia.

Lochhead, J. (2000). *Thinkback: A user's guide to minding the mind.* Hillsdale, NJ: Erlbaum.

Marzano, R. (1991). Fostering thinking across the curriculum through knowledge restructuring. *Journal of Reading, 34* (7), 18–24.

McDonald, J., Mohr, N., Dichter, A., & McDonald, E. C. (2003). *The power of protocols*. New York: Teachers College Press.

McGuinness, C. (2004). *Teaching thinking through infusion: ACTS in Northern Ireland*. London: Author.

McGuinness, C. (2005). Teaching thinking: Theory and practice. In *Pedagogy: Learning for Teaching*. London: British Psychological Association.

McTighe, J., & Lyman, F. T. (1988). Cueing thinking in the classroom: The promise of theory-embedded tools. *Educational Leadership, 45* (7), 18–24.

McTighe, J., & Lyman, F. T. (2001). Cueing thinking in the classroom: The promise of theory-embedded tools. In A. Costa (Ed.), *Developing minds: A resource book for teaching thinking*. Alexandria, VA: Association for Supervision and Curriculum Development.

Michigan State Board of Education. (1991). *Michigan goals and objectives for science education (K–12)*. Lansing, MI: Author.

National Center for History in the Schools. (1996). *National standards for United States history, grades 5–12*. Los Angeles: University of California Press.

New safeguards to avoid intelligence errors. (2005, July 29). *New York Times Digest*, p. 3.

Nickerson, R. (1989). On improving thinking through instruction. In E. Z. Rothkopf (Ed.), *Review of research in education* (Vol. 1). Washington, DC: American Educational Research Association.

Olson, D. R., & Astington, J. W. (1990). Talking about text: How literacy contributes to thought. *Journal of Pragmatics, 14*, 705–721.

Ong, A. C. (2006). Infusing instruction in thinking skills into content instruction. In A. C. Ong & G. Borich (Eds.), *Teaching strategies that promote thinking*. Singapore: McGraw-Hill.

Ong, A. C. (2006). Promoting social-emotional learning. In A. C. Ong & G. Borich (Eds.), *Teaching strategies that promote thinking*. Singapore: McGraw-Hill.

O'Reilly, K. (1990). *Evaluating viewpoints: Vol. 1. Colonies to constitution*. Pacific Grove, CA: Critical Thinking.

O'Sullivan, J. T., & Pressley, M. (1984). Completeness of instruction and strategy transfer. *Journal of Experimental Child Psychology, 38*, 275–288.

Papert, S. (1980). *Mindstorms: Children, computers, and powerful ideas*. New York: Basic Books.

Paris, S. G., Wilson, K. K., & Palincsar, A. S. (1986). Instructional approaches to reading comprehension. *Review of Educational Research, 13*, 91–128.

Parks, S., & Black, H. (1995). *Organizing thinking*. Pacific Grove, CA: Critical Thinking.

Pasnak, R., Brown, K., Kurkjian, M., Mattram, K., & Yamamoto, N. (1987). Cognitive gains through training on classification, seriation, and conservation. *Genetic, Social and General Psychology Monographs, 113* (3), 295–332.

Perkins, D. (1987). Myth and method in teaching thinking. *Teaching Thinking and Problem Solving, 9* (2), 1–2, 8–9.

Perkins, D. (1992). *Smart schools*. New York: Free Press.

Perkins, D. (2002). *King Arthur's round table*. New York: Wiley.

Perkins, D., Jay, E., & Tishman, S. (2000). Beyond abilities: A dispositional theory of thinking. *Merrill Palmer Quarterly, 39* (1), 1–21.

Perkins, D., & Salomon, G. (1987). Transfer and teaching thinking. In D. Perkins, J. Lochhead, & D. Bishop (Eds.), *Thinking: The second international conference*. Hillsdale, NJ: Erlbaum.

Perkins, D., & Salomon, G. (1988). Teaching for transfer. *Educational Leadership, 46* (1), 22–32.

Perkins, D. N., & Salomon, G. (1989, January/February). Are thinking skills context bound? *Educational Researcher, 18,* 16–25.

Perkins, D., & Swartz, R. (1989). The nine points about teaching thinking. In A. Costa, J. Bellanca, & R. Fogarty (Eds.), *If minds matter.* Pallatine, IL: Skylights.

Posner, M., & Keele, S. W. (1973). Skill learning. In R.M.W. Travers (Ed.), *Second handbook of research on teaching.* Chicago: Rand McNally.

Pressley, M., & Harris, K. (1990). What we really know about strategy instruction. *Educational Leadership, 48* (1), 31–34.

Reagan, R. (2001). Developing a lifetime of literacy. In A. Costa (Ed.), *Developing minds: A resource book for teaching thinking.* Alexandria, VA: Association for Supervision and Curriculum Development.

Rigney, J. W. (1980). Cognitive learning strategies and qualities in information processing. In R. Snow, P. Federico, & W. Montague (Eds.), *Aptitudes, learning, and instruction* (Vol. 1). Hillsdale, NJ: Erlbaum.

Rosenshine, B. (1979). Content, time, and direct instruction. In P. L. Peterson & H. Walberg (Eds.), *Research on teaching.* Berkeley, CA: McCutchen.

Rosenshine, B. (1983). Teaching functions in instructional programs. *Elementary School Journal, 83* (4), 335–351.

Rosenshine, B. (1986). Synthesis of research on explicit teaching. *Educational Leadership, 41* (7), 60–69.

Rosenshine, B. (1997). Advances in research on instruction. In J.T. Lloyd, E. J. Kameenui, & D. Chard (Eds.), *Issues in educating students with disabilities.* Mahwah, NJ: Erlbaum.

Rosenshine, B., & Meister, C. (1992). The use of scaffolds for teaching higher level cognitive strategies. *Educational Leadership, 49* (7), 26–33.

Scardamalia, M., & Bereiter, C. (1986). Research on written composition. In M. C. Wittrock (Ed.), *Handbook of research on teaching.* New York: Macmillan.

Schoenfeld, A. (1979). Can heuristics be taught? In J. Lochhead & J. Clement (Eds.), *Cognitive process instruction.* Philadelphia: Franklin Institute Press.

Senge, P. (1990). *The fifth discipline.* New York: Doubleday.

Senge, P., Ross, R., Smith, B., Roberts, C., & Kleiner, A. (1994). *The fifth discipline fieldbook.* New York: Doubleday.

Siegler, R. (1998). *Children's thinking.* Englewood Cliffs, NJ: Prentice-Hall.

Sinatra, R. (2000). Teaching learners to think, read, and write more effectively in content subjects. *The Clearing House, 73* (5), 266–276.

Speare, E. (1983). *The sign of the beaver.* Boston: Houghton Mifflin.

Sternberg, R., & Davidson, J. (1989). A four-prong model for intellectual development. *Journal of Research and Development in Education, 22* (3), 22–28.

Stiggins, R. J., Arter, J. A., Chappuis, J., & Chappuis, S. (2004). *Classroom assessment for student learning.* Portland, OR: Assessment Training Institute.

Stigler, J., & Hiebert, J. (1999). *The teaching gap: Best ideas from the world's teachers for improving education in the classroom.* New York: Free Press.

Swartz, R. (1987). Teaching for thinking: A developmental model for the infusion of thinking skills into mainstream instruction. In J. Baron & R. Sternberg (Eds.), *Teaching thinking skills: Theory and practice.* New York: Freeman.

Swartz, R. (2001). In the grip of emotion. In A. Costa (Ed.), *Developing minds: A resource book for teaching thinking.* Alexandria, VA: Association for Supervision and Curriculum Development.

Swartz, R. (2003). Teaching science literacy through problem-based learning and critical thinking. In A. Costa & R. Liebermann (Eds.), *Supporting the spirit of learning*. Thousand Oaks, CA: Corwin Press.

Swartz, R., Fischer, S., & Parks, S. (1999). *Infusing critical thinking into secondary science: A lesson design handbook*. Pacific Grove, CA: Critical Thinking.

Swartz, R., Kiser, M., & Larisey, J. (1999*). Teaching critical and creative thinking in language arts: Infusion lessons grades 1 & 2*. Pacific Grove, CA: Critical Thinking.

Swartz, R., Kiser, M. A., & Reagan, R. (1999). *Teaching critical and creative thinking in language arts: Lessons, grades 5 and 6*. Pacific Grove, CA: Critical Thinking.

Swartz, R., & Parks, S. (1994). *Infusing the teaching of critical and creative thinking into content instruction: A lesson design handbook for the elementary grades.* Pacific Grove, CA: Critical Thinking.

Swartz, R., & Perkins, D. (1990). *Teaching thinking: Issues and approaches*. Pacific Grove, CA: Critical Thinking.

Swartz, R., Whipple, T., Blasidell, G., & Kiser, M. A. (1999). *Teaching critical and creative thinking in language arts, grades 3 & 4.* Pacific grove, CA: Critical Thinking.

Tschannen-Moran, M. (2004). *Trust matters*. San Francisco: Jossey-Bass.

Unger, J., & Fleischman, S. (2004). Is process writing the "write stuff"? *Educational Leadership, 62* (2), 90–91.

Virginia Department of Public Instruction. (2001). *History and social science standards of learning for Virginia schools*. Richmond, VA: Author.

Vygotsky, L. S. (1962). *Thought and language*. Cambridge, MA: MIT Press.

Vygotsky, L. S. (1978). *Society of mind*. Cambridge, MA: Harvard University Press.

Whimbey, A., & Lochhead, J. (1999). *Problem solving and comprehension*. Mahwah, NJ: Erlbaum.

Whimbey, A., Lochhead, J., Linden, M., & Welsh, C. (2001). What is write for thinking? In A. Costa (Ed.), *Developing minds: A resource book for teaching thinking*. Alexandria, VA: Association for Supervision and Curriculum Development.

Wineburg, S. S. (1991). Historical problem solving: A study of the cognitive processes used in the evaluation of documentary and pictorial evidence. *Journal of Educational Psychology, 83* (1), 73–87.

Index

About The Authors

Barry K. Beyer, Ph.D., is professor emeritus in the Graduate School of Education of George Mason University in Fairfax, Virginia. He received his master's degree in history and education from Syracuse University (1954) and his doctorate in history from the University of Rochester (1962). His professional career has included 37 years of public school and university teaching, research, and administration.

Dr. Beyer has served as a consultant and staff developer in more than 120 school systems, colleges and universities, and state education agencies throughout the United States and Canada and has conducted numerous national clinics and institutes for ASCD, NCSS, NASSP, and other major professional and governmental organizations. As a specialist in the teaching of thinking skills and writing as well as in history and social studies teaching, Dr. Beyer has authored more than 100 articles and monographs in professional journals such as *Educational Leadership*, *Phi Delta Kappan*, and *Social Education*. He was a contributor to Arthur Costa's *Developing Minds* (2001). He was also a co-author of the nation's leading elementary school social studies programs, *The World Around Us* (Macmillan, 1989, 1995), and its successor, *Adventures in Time and Place* (Macmillan/McGraw-Hill, 1997, 1999, 2001).

Retired now, Dr. Beyer and his wife, reside in Pittsford, New York, where he continues—at a more relaxed pace—his writing, consulting, and staff development activities.

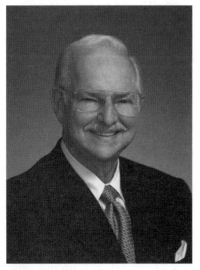

Arthur L. Costa, Ed.D., is an emeritus professor of education at California State University, Sacramento. He has served as a classroom teacher, a curriculum consultant, an assistant superintendent for instruction, and as the director of educational programs for the National Aeronautics and Space Administration (NASA). He has made presentations and conducted workshops in all 50 states of the United States as well on every continent.

Costa has written numerous books. His writings have been translated into Dutch, Chinese, Hebrew, Arabic, and Spanish.

Active in many professional organizations, Dr. Costa has served as president of the California Association for Supervision and Curriculum Development and was president of the National Association for Supervision and Curriculum Development from 1988 to 1989.

Bena Kallick, Ph.D., is a private consultant providing services to school districts, state departments of education, professional organizations, and public sector agencies throughout the United States. Dr. Kallick received her doctorate in educational evaluation from Union Graduate School. Her areas of focus include group dynamics, creative and critical thinking, and alternative assessment strategies in the classroom.

Formerly a Teachers' Center Director, Dr. Kallick also created a Children's Museum based on problem solving and invention. She was the coordinator of a high school alternative designed for at-risk students. She has produced audiotapes on "Creative and Critical Thinking: Teaching Alternatives" and "Collaborative Learning: Strategies to Encourage Thinking" with Marian Leibowitz. She is co-founder of Techpaths, a company designed to facilitate teachers' networks and communications about performance assessment. Dr. Kallick's teaching appointments have included Yale University School of Organization and Management, University of Massachusetts at Boston Center for Creative and Critical Thinking, and Union Graduate School. She is on the boards of Jobs for the Future and the Apple Foundation.

Rebecca Reagan, M.S. Ed., is a retired fifth-grade teacher in Lubbock, Texas, specializing in reading and writing. She received her B.A. and master's of science in education from Texas Tech University. She has done extensive staff-development work in the United States and abroad in the areas of critical and creative thinking and gifted education through the National Center for Teaching Thinking (P.O. Box 590607, Newton Center, MA 02459; tel: 617-965-4604; fax: 617-795-2606; e-mail: info@nctt.net; Web site: www.nctt.net). Readers may contact her at rebreagan@aol.com.

Robert Swartz, Ph.D., is an emeritus faculty member at the University of Massachusetts–Boston, where he was the founder of the graduate program on critical and creative thinking. He received his B.A. and Ph.D. in philosophy from Harvard University and studied under a Fulbright Scholarship at Oxford and Cambridge Universities in England. He is director of the

National Center for Teaching Thinking in Newton Center, Massachusetts. Through the Center he provides staff development to educators on restructuring curriculum by infusing critical and creative thinking into content instruction. His work has extended across the USA and into Venezuela, New Zealand, Australia, Hong Kong, Singapore, Malaysia, Israel, United Arab Emirates, Saudi Arabia, and Britain. He has also served as an educational consultant to various textbook publishers about infusing thinking skills into content-oriented textbooks, has worked with departments and ministries of education on projects related to working thinking instruction into a curriculum, and has consulted with various educational testing services on assessing skillful thinking.

Dr. Swartz is lead author of a series of lesson design handbooks. He has written articles on teaching and assessing skillful thinking, problem-based learning, the role of thinking in managing our emotions, and developing skills to help us think critically about arguments. He has been featured on public educational TV demonstrating how critical and creative thinking can be infused into content instruction.